Tantra & Erotic Trance

Volume Two

Tantra & Erotic Trance
Volume Two - Inner Work

by

John Ryan Haule

fisher king press

Tantra & Erotic Trance
Volume Two - Inner Work

Copyright © 2012 by John Ryan Haule
First Edition
ISBN 978-0-9776076-9-3 Paperback

Published simultaneously in Canada and the United States of America by Fisher King Press. For information on obtaining permission for use of material from this work, submit a written request to: **permissions@fisherkingpress.com**

Fisher King Press
PO Box 222321
Carmel, CA 93922
www.fisherkingpress.com
fisherking@fisherkingpress.com
+1-831-238-7799

Every effort has been made to trace all copyright holders; however, if any have been overlooked, the author will be pleased to make the necessary arrangements at the first opportunity.

Cover design by Ann Yoost Brecke © 2012.

For the Arrow Makers

Acknowledgements

The manuscript for this book has been out of circulation for a dozen years. I am therefore most grateful to Mel Mathews of Fisher King Press for recognizing its value and agreeing to publish it.

I am grateful, too, to Cornelia Dimmitt for her thorough review of the text of this book, based in her dual expertise in Sanskrit studies and Analytical Psychology. Thanks too to Jeffrey Timm for his encouragement and for suggesting important texts I had not discovered on my own. Thanks to Ann Yoost Brecke for sharing her library and acting as a sounding board for drafts, early and late, as well as for the art work on the covers. James M. Haule read and commented on late drafts, providing strong encouragement. I also could not have written this book without the help of colleagues, students and analysands who have shared their experiences and insights with me over the past three or four decades.

Contents

PREFACE

In Volume One of this study, "Outer Work," we described managing our orgasmic response so as to cultivate "erotic trance," the altered state of consciousness that is the foundation of all Tantric activity; and we used it to climb the "diamond ladder" of mystical ascent to a rung characterized by the management of overwhelming emotions.

Now in Volume Two, "Inner Work," we turn our attention away from "outer" goals having to do with our physiology and our relation to society at large and its prescriptions, to the much more subtle "interior" changes occurring in our consciousness. Continuing our climb up the rungs of the diamond ladder, we are introduced to the landscape of mysticism, a topography whose several regions are each characterized by the mastery of a different psychological capacity.

Yoga gives us an *interior* ladder in the form of the subtle body that is comprised of the chakras, each of which opens onto a distinctly different emotional realm. In this work our "feeling function" becomes highly differentiated. Tibetan mandala meditation disciplines our imaginative capacity, as we bring the heavenly palace of copulating gods and goddesses into being. By cultivating emptiness, we pare away our attachments to the memories that have been holding us back and the aspirations that narrow our future so that we can dwell in the present moment, without the props of doctrine and method.

Passing beyond our personal self, we are introduced to the divine oneness of the cosmos, pulsing between accomplished union and the vision of that with which we are united. We return from such ecstasy to live our temporal lives on two planes simultaneously as spiritual wayfarers.

Microcosm and Macrocosm

I

THE SUBTLE BODY

Kundalini was the theme of the last five chapters in Volume One of *Tantra and Erotic Trance*. In Volume One, Chapter Three, we saw that eros is able to mobilize emotion and imagination alongside physiology to overcome the stimulus-response loop of the orgasmic spasm reflex. In Volume One, Chapter Four, we expanded on the significance of eros, finding its fullest development in kundalini, for which we have physiological and historical evidence suggesting that kundalini (by whatever name) has been known and cultivated as a natural human capacity since at least the last Ice Age. In Volume One, Chapter Five, we saw how the mad saints use eros/kundalini unconsciously to overwhelm their ego and mobilize an unconscious process whereby the psyche as a whole is re-organized. Ego returns as an observer of processes that are understood to be of divine origin and that establish a larger center in the psyche which India has called atman or self. In Chapters Six and Seven, we considered the antinomian saints who strive to make the psychic re-organization conscious by deliberately entering the realm of the shadow—culturally defined areas of impurity and evil. The left-hand path of Tantra is a dangerous undertaking in which the antinomian saints court the dangers of powerful disturbance (sexual arousal, disgust, terror) in order to stimulate the integrating dragon of kundalini as a force which can meet those challenges by surging up from within. The heroic saints confront those terrible forces with kundalini, rendering them "non-terrible" worthy opponents.

For the antinomian saints, kundalini is merely the dragon of the soul's life energy: known only as a formidable and dangerous power which rises up from within, like a seed outgrowing its pod. It is enough for them to know that such a power exists. They familiarize themselves with it merely as an autonomous and potentially "friendly" force and never come to understand it in detail. In order to rise beyond the heroic rung of the diamond ladder to the next, it is necessary to learn the nature of kundalini in much finer detail. This task, as we have said, requires that the mystic redirect attention from the outside to the inside. As long as the disturbing force of disgust, compulsive sexuality, or terror is seen as coming from without, it is enough to know that kundalini is an inner dragon capable of neutralizing the exterior challenger. If we are to go beyond meeting exterior challenges, however, we have to familiarize ourselves with the details of what occurs within us as this inner dragon is mobilized.

Those who have turned their gaze inward and contemplated kundalini herself have found her to resemble a serpent that moves with the suddenness, brilliance, and zigzag course of a bolt of lightning and the indestructibility of a diamond. Traditionally, therefore, they have referred to kundalini with the term *vajra*, meaning thunderbolt, diamond, and adamantine. However, it is only the awakened kundalini that moves like this. For most individuals, she sleeps coiled up at the bottom of the body cavity or at the base of the spine, encircling an internal *linga* or phallus, drinking the vital energy[1] that is wasted by those men and women who have not learned the secret of her nature. Once aroused, she rises up through the body to the cranial vault; and along her serpentine path she draws attention to a subtle body comprised of several "centers," "chakras," or "wheels" that remained closed or "knotted" in those who have not familiarized themselves with kundalini.

In this chapter we shall begin discussion of the achievement required at the subtle-body rung of the diamond ladder by turning our attention inward to describe the nature of those chakras that comprise the subtle body. Afterwards, in Volume Two, Chapter Two, we shall see how familiarity with the subtle body enables the mystic to gain a certain mastery over the diamond body and convert it into an internal ladder of ascent.

THE SUBTLE BODY

To begin with it must be noted that the subtle body is an imaginal fact. It surely manifests itself with physiological and emotional accompaniments, but what we shall be describing in this chapter are not structures that can be laid bare through a careful dissection of the fleshly body. The chakras and the pathways that connect them—i.e., the subtle body itself—are perceptible only on the subtle plane. Discussion of the subtle body, therefore, implies familiarity with erotic trance. Indeed, anyone who recognizes some of the sensations and impression described below has to have entered an altered state of consciousness—whether acknowledged as such at the time or not. Although there are several traditional descriptions of the subtle body which disagree among themselves as to whether it is comprised of only four centers or more than twelve, and although we shall follow the most common tradition which identifies seven of them, we may say that at a minimum there is a center in the lower abdomen whose opening makes us aware of a monumental power at once frightening and promising, portending an uncommon adventure of some sort; another in the chest associated with transcendent

---

1 Although the texts generally describe this energy as "sperm" or one of its mythological equivalents, the fact that it is common to both men and women prompts my employment of this more general expression, "vital energy."

feelings of love and connectedness; a third in the brow whose opening reveals the subtle plane of the imaginal world; and one in the crown of the head which gives us access to the Absolute, God, or ultimate manifestation of the cosmos. In examining these centers and the ones in between, we shall be following Eliade, who says, "Careful reading of the texts suffices to show that the experiences in question are transphysiological and that all these 'centers' represent yogic states" (Eliade, 1969: 234). When Eliade calls the experiences "transphysiological," he seems to mean that although they are rooted in physiological changes and are described in physiological language, they transcend physiology in the sense that they are also changes in consciousness, manifestations of erotic trance.

At all four of the centers just mentioned, we encounter something that transcends the profane world of the ego and the persona field. In the lower abdomen a power is felt surging forth that manifests as incomparably greater than the ego and alerts us to the fact that the *I* we have believed ourselves to be is something like a pod about to be outgrown by its seed. At the heart center we become aware of a connectedness inconceivable to the subject/object dichotomy of everyday thinking and which dissolves the illusory barrier between ourselves and our partner and between ourselves and the world at large. In seeing the imaginal world through the "third eye" of the brow chakra, we become aware of essential realities hidden from our fleshly eyes which convince us of their greater, "cosmic" truth. At the crown chakra we become aware of the fullness of that larger reality and know our place in it—at once in-finitesimal and unlimited.

All these experiences reveal to our esoteric eyes the central fact of Tantrism, the fact that the subtle body itself is a sort of cosmos in miniature, filled with the power, connectedness, and vision—that is to say consciousness—that comprises the cosmos at large. "The essence of Tantric thought is that man is a microcosm. . . . In man is truth and through man it must be known (Dimock, 1989: 137). Evola says nearly the same thing, "The body in Tantrism is 'made cosmic' and is conceived of in terms of principles and powers that also act in the world" (Evola, 1983: 221). Because the same fundamental layers can be discovered in both the microcosm and the macrocosm, the various systems of yoga "map" the cosmos onto the body and the body onto the cosmos. They are, in the expression of Feuerstein (1989: 176), "psychocosmograms," that is, guides both to the microcosm of the psyche and the macrocosm of the universe.

> All things are unified through the microcosmic self. There are seeming dualities in the world, such as men and women, human and divine, self and not-self. But such dualities are only seeming, and the first step toward restoring the normal state of unity is the realization of this (Dimock, 1989: 138).

In the "transphysiological" language of Tantra, cosmic energy is said to flow into the microcosm through the chakras and thence to cycle through the subtle body and out again into the macrocosm. It is said that this happens in all of us, whether we know it or not and whether or not we cooperate in the process. Our degree of openness at the various chakras corresponds to our degree of consciousness; and our conscious participation in the macrocosm increases proportionately (Karagulla & Kunz, 1989: 36). More specifically, however, it can be said that each chakra, beginning at the base of the spine and proceeding upwards to the head, opens for us a separate and progressively higher "level of consciousness" (Sivananda Radha, 1990: 49). This means, for instance, that those who have awakened kundalini to the point of becoming aware of the center in the lower abdomen experience the world differently than those in whom kundalini is still asleep. Those who have opened their heart center have still another field of consciousness opened to them. Jung (1996: 13) summarizes this universal doctrine by pointing out that "each chakra is a whole world." He means that those in whom kundalini sleeps at the base of the spine live entirely in the empirical world and have no access to erotic trance. Those whose consciousness is centered in the lower abdomen have entered erotic trance, but the world they live in is impoverished compared to that available to those in whom the heart chakra has opened.

Prefacing his remarks by warning that the following is a very limited perspective on kundalini and the subtle body, Jung says we can get some idea of the "worlds" that are opened to us through the several chakras if we begin in the head and work downward. In this passage he avoids all reference to what we have called "erotic trance," and speaks only of how the various psychological possibilities symbolized by the chakras may be grasped in a preliminary manner by one who remains in ordinary consciousness:

> We begin in the head; we identify with our eyes and our consciousness: quite detached and objective, we survey the world. That is *ajna* [the brow chakra]. But we cannot linger forever in the pure spheres of detached observation, we must bring our thoughts into reality. We voice them and so trust them to the air. We clothe our knowledge in words, we are in the region of *vishuddha*, or the throat center. But as soon as we say something that is especially difficult, or that causes us positive or negative feelings, we have a throbbing of the heart, and then the *anahata* [heart] center begins to be activated. And still another step further, when for example a dispute with someone starts up, when we have become irritable and angry and get beside ourselves, then we are in *manipura* [the center located at the diaphragm or solar plexus].

> If we go lower still, the situation becomes impossible, because then the *body* begins to speak. For this reason, in England, everything below the diaphragm is taboo. Germans always go a little below it and hence easily become emotional. Russians live altogether below the diaphragm—they consist of emotions. French and Italians *behave* as though they were below it but they know perfectly well, and so does everyone else that they are not.

. . . *Svadhisthana* [the chakra in the lower abdomen] represents the level where psychic life may be said to begin. Only when this level became activated did mankind awaken from the sleep of the *muladhara* [at the base of the spine] and learn the first rules of bodily decency (Jung, 1996: 63).

Singling out sexuality as the central issue in kundalini, Ken Wilbur has taken a similar head-downward approach as Jung. Noting that Freud had it backwards, that "God-consciousness is not sublimated sexuality; sexuality is repressed God-consciousness" (Wilbur, 1990: 130), Wilbur says that we "tie knots" in our consciousness, beginning with how we see things, then how we conceptualize them, feel about them, and so on. At each chakra we "tie a knot" until what might have been God-consciousness is reduced to genital sexuality. What Freud sees as our maturation from the "polymorphous perversity" of the infant into adult genital sexuality, Wilbur sees as constriction:

The infant takes equal erotic and blissful delight in all the organs, surfaces, and activities of the body, and thus his entire cosmos is one of bliss, while the normal adult finds exuberance and bliss, if at all, in only one specific and narrow region of the body—the genitals. Genital bliss can thus be viewed in comparison with the body's natural possibilities, as a constriction, a restriction, a cramp, a knot. Note it is *not* so much genital sexuality that comprises the knot, but rather the *restriction of bliss to only one specific region* of the body, excluding all others (Wilbur, 122)

Kundalini yoga, therefore, wisely proceeds to reverse this tyranny of awareness and bliss step by careful step, untying the knots in what it sees as roughly the reverse of the order in which they were tied (Wilbur, 125).

Jung and Wilbur have taken a very Western and psychological approach to the subtle body of Tantrism. The reader who is familiar with traditional descriptions of the chakras as resembling open lotus flowers, each with a distinctive number of petals, each petal bearing a different letter of the Sanskrit alphabet, and so on, may be both relieved and puzzled. We are relieved to know that some sense can be made of the Hindu subtle body without entering the impenetrable world of Hindu iconography. On the other hand, we may wonder if something has been lost "in translation." No doubt something has been lost, but if we can begin to connect traditional descriptions of the subtle body with bodily and imaginal experiences we ourselves have actually had, we will have gained a great deal.

My intention is to sketch a phenomenology of sexual/mystical experiences with the metaphor of the diamond ladder serving as an organizing image. Now as we approach the subtle-body rung and our attention is directed within, it will be useful to begin with common physio-imaginal and emotional experiences that are readily available to anyone who has noticed bodily reactions and imagery in ordinary life. For the mystics differ from the rest of us primarily in the fact that they have taken their erotic trances seriously, investigated them, and learned to obtain some mastery of them—at least in the sense that their imaginal life has attained some stability. Imaginal experiences are so much denigrated by our persona field that most of us in the West discard our experiences as merely imagin*ary*—therefore private, idiosyncratic, and undependable. In doing so, we fail to notice that we may already be familiar with experiences that the mystics have taken so much for granted and so ubiquitous as not to merit comment.

In discussing the interior diamond ladder that is comprised of the chakras, therefore, I shall emphasize bodily/imaginal experiences that are readily available to all of us and employ as much as possible of Jung's 1932 lectures on kundalini yoga (Jung, 1996). Jung's account is not only psychologically sound and easy to understand but also validated by several writers far more immersed in Indian thought than was Jung (e.g., Mookerjee, 1989; Svoboda, 1994; van Lysebeth, 1995; Sinha, 1993; Dimock, 1989; McDaniel, 1989; and the close approximation of Eliade's thought to Jung's). Evola (1992, 1995) attacks Jung's writings on yoga and alchemy for having missed the point of mysticism through his therapeutic interests, and Wilbur (1982) seems to agree. But this, in fact, is the advantage of Jung's writings. He roots his observations in experiences that are available to us all—precisely the thing we need to bring mystical claims down out of the stratosphere to a grounded place where we can connect them with our own experience and begin to appreciate that the mystics are people very much like ourselves—people who differ from us primarily in the fact that they have attended to experiences that we habitually discard.

Proceeding upwards from the base of the spine to the head, as is traditional, I shall try to draw out the psychological and mystical significance of the seven chakras by describing how I have experienced them, filled out sometimes with reports I have gathered from others. I do not mean to suggest that everyone has to experience what I have, only that the concreteness of one individual's experience may give the reader a handle by which to grasp what the mystics have claimed. Such quasi-bodily experiences by no means exhaust the significance of the various chakras but are intended only as a starting point. What I hope to provide is surely a "low level" appreciation of the subtle body. But if successful this account should help readers to identify similar experiences in their own lives and provide a concrete foundation for the chapters that follow. My fundamental assumption, here, is that we all have a far wider acquaintance with erotic trance than we are inclined to believe. I find this verified again and again as I listen to the experiences of my patients, who often describe with some embarrassment sensations and images that seem irrational and crazy to them only because they are unfamiliar with the literature of mystical states.

FIRST CHAKRA, MULADHARA, AT THE BASE OF THE SPINE

The muladhara is the place where kundalini sleeps. Apparently for this reason it is ignored in some systems. Because kundalini is asleep, the experience of the world from this "root chakra" is familiar to us all. It is the ordinary world devoid of erotic trance. Jung observes: "We are in our roots right here in this world—when you buy your ticket from the streetcar conductor, for instance, or for the theater, or pay the waiter—that is reality as you touch it. And then the self is asleep, which means that all things concerning the gods are asleep" (Jung, 1996: 14). Mookerjee calls it "the root center of physical experience" (Mookerjee, 1989: 39); and Evola says it is characterized by ordinary sexual desire (Evola, 1992: 173).

Ordinary individuals live their entire lives in the root chakra. Therefore it is not characterized merely by physicality but above all by our unconscious participation in the persona field, the social consensus that discards all imaginal experiences as invalid and that might well be called "group-think" or "mass-mindedness." Evola enumerates qualities typical of the root chakra: "greed, false knowledge, credulity, delusions, indulgence in coarse pleasures, and the force that induces sleep" (Evola, 1992: 151). Following Jung, Arnold Mindell associates the muladhara with toilet training and says that all of our "cramping" comes from our inability to let go in public life because the knot we have tied in the root chakra restricts "the inner animal or child who defecates and urinates at will" (Mindell, 1982: 40). Such "cramping" results from our determination not to embarrass ourselves by falling afoul of the expectations of the persona field.

Vimalananda refers to the traditional Hindu association of the muladhara with the primal element of earth. For the Greeks there were four elements: earth, water, air, and fire, in ascending order of subtlety. The Hindus have five, adding ether as the element more subtle than fire. In both systems, earth is the principle of inertia, weight, and dullness. Vimalananda says, "Once the Kundalini Shakti enters the Muladhara Chakra the entire Earth Element must be transformed before She can move to the Svadhisthana Chakra" (Svoboda, 1994: 77). He seems to imply that the muladhara is not merely the center of ignorance, where the subtle plane never appears. Indeed, to experience it *as a chakra* requires that our esoteric eyes be opened—even while we remain within its sphere of influence.

Svoboda's guru suggests that there is a moment when kundalini is awake in the root chakra, and then the boring constancy of the empirical world will be seen as changing, in the process of transformation. I take this to mean that the first beginnings of erotic trance must be found in the root chakra, in the interval between kundalini's awakening and her ascent. Logically, this makes sense. But he gives us little to go on in identifying this moment. I am inclined to think that it corresponds to what we will consider in Volume Two, Chapter Four. There is a moment between every pair of identifiable experiences when our mind is empty. The yogin learns to recognize these moments and expands upon them. They constitute our opportunity to enter a very high state of yogic trance. Normally the first moment of kundalini's awakening escapes our notice because we fail to catch sight of that empty moment that occurs between our blindness to anything but the empirical world, and that fall into confusion that characterizes the opening of the second chakra.

Theoretically, all of the chakras lie outside of our awareness as long as they are "closed" or "knotted." But when they "open" they are experienced as whirling vortices. When I learned this detail, it opened my eyes to sensations I had long had regarding the second chakra, the svadhisthana, and helped me to become aware of less obvious impressions in other parts of my body. Despite that, it was some time before I recognized the experience of the muladhara opening. Indeed, to this day I have rarely noticed the muladhara as the first chakra to open. It is usually only while practicing carezza that I experience a great whirling aperture in the space between my anus and scrotum (the perineum), pointing downward toward my feet. We might guess that no chakra's opening can be recognized before we enter erotic trance and that it is therefore easy to miss the opening of the root chakra which above all characterizes our state of ignorance regarding the subtle plane.

SECOND CHAKRA, SVADHISTHANA, IN THE LOWER ABDOMEN

Long before I had heard of the chakras or kundalini, I was very much aware—indeed uncomfortably conscious—of the sensation that must be the most elementary experience of the opening of the second chakra. From my teens until well into my twenties, I found that whenever I met a girl or a woman who appeared to me as a potential "earthly Venus," a yawning hole seemed to open in my lower abdomen. I described it to myself as "opening like the eye of a camera." The sensation was so vivid that I thought I could almost "see" in my mind's eye the "iris" of a camera's aperture spinning open below my navel. Unlike a camera's eye, however, it never reached a pre-determined diameter where it could mercifully stop but kept on whirling, almost painfully, opening wider and wider, causing unbearable tension. This was accompanied by an overwhelming feeling of vulnerability. I felt I had lost all protection, the barrier that gives us anonymity and comfortable mystery in the eyes of others. My "boundaries" were dissolving. I thought it must surely be apparent to everyone in my vicinity, especially to the young woman who had occasioned it. It never dawned on me that she might be having somewhat the same sensation. For that I seemed to need conversation, which of course was difficult to conduct under the circumstances.

The primal element that the Hindus associate with svadhisthana is water. Evola has tied that together with my familiar experience quite economically, in saying the emotions generated by the chakra in the lower abdomen are: "terrifying unleashed power, sexual drive, aversion, shame, and languor, the force that causes thirst" (Evola, 1992: 151-2). Jung likens the water of svadhisthana to what he calls the Night Sea Journey. This is the central image in his *Symbols of Transformation* (*CW 5*), based on the ancient mythological theme whereby the sun sinks into the Western Sea at night, whence it passes underneath us all night long, fighting the forces of darkness to arise renewed out of the Eastern Sea at dawn. All psychological transformation, Jung tells us, happens in exactly this way. An old ego-attitude requires renewal, and this can only take place through a terrifying confrontation with the forces of the unconscious. To be swallowed up by the unconscious means madness, but to struggle consciously with the demons of the unconscious leads to a transformation of the ego-attitude whence we arise renewed. He observes that the elephant traditionally painted in the center of the Hindu icon for the muladhara becomes in the svidhisthana the leviathan, the undersea monster.

> Now, the second center has all the attributes that characterize the unconscious. Therefore we may assume that the way out of our *muladhara* existence leads into the water. A man I know who is not in analysis has had interesting dreams representing this quite frequently, and they were all identical. He found himself moving along a certain road . . . the dream always began with such a movement—and then, to his great amazement, all these roads inevitably led into water, the second cakra.
>
> Therefore, the first demand of a mystery cult always has been to go into water, into the baptismal fount. The way into any higher development leads through water, with the danger of being swallowed by the monster. . . . Baptism is a symbolical drowning. . . . It is a symbolic death out of which new life comes, a newborn babe (1996: 16).

The second chakra, as it opens in the lower abdomen, brings to our awareness all the promise and terror of eros. We are in an erotic trance. Eros appeared between me and those women before whom I felt closeness, sexual desire, shame, terror, and the loss of all protection. I knew—although I lacked the words to express it—that a harrowing adventure lay before me. I was in danger of losing everything I had known about myself. Perhaps I would violate all the rules I took for immutable. I no longer stood with the elephant, stolid as the earth and possessing an impeccable memory—recalling all the experiences that made me "me." Now I was looking into the watery abyss of my destruction, highly unlikely to survive any so-called transformative process. When the svadhisthana inspires such fright, it is because we cling to our ego, ahamkara, the memory of me and mine. After experiences like this, I know Vimalananda is not exaggerating when he says, "Whenever trouble increases during your *sadhana*, you can be sure that you are getting closer to your deity" (Svoboda, 1994: 126).

I was resisting my deity. I had no idea what she wanted of me, but I was sure I was unprepared and inadequate to the challenge. Implicitly, I had already learned some of Vimalananda's wisdom: "Those who ride Kundalini without knowing their destination risk losing their way" (Svoboda, 1994: 20). Jung is more specific:

> The gods . . . are germs in us, germs in the *muladhara*, and when they begin to move they have the effect of an earthquake which naturally shakes us, and even shakes our houses down. . . . To fly is one's own activity, and one can safely come down again, but when one is carried upward [by a great wind or by kundalini], it is not under one's control, and one will be put down after a while in a most disagreeable way—then it means catastrophe. So you see, it is wise not to identify with these experiences, but to handle them as if they were outside the human realm. That is the safest thing to do—and really absolutely necessary. Otherwise you get an inflation, and inflation is just a minor form of lunacy, a mitigated term for it. And if you get so absolutely inflated that you burst, it is schizophrenia (Jung, 1996: 27).

If the yawning of the abdominal chakra causes us this much discomfort, we are surely not ready for our Night Sea Journey. But if we should ever have the strength to enter some distance into the fray—like a vira, not a mad saint—and come out of it in one piece, the opening of the svadhisthana can become a source of information. We risk the life of our sanity, but it is not we ourselves, our limited egos, that face down the enemy. It is the dragon of our soul's energy that takes on the leviathan. We come out of the experience knowing something of the nature of kundalini. She has opened our eyes for the first time to the subtle plane; and although it scared the life out of us when it first occupied the field of our vision, we have now claimed a parcel—marked some boundaries and familiarized ourselves with the flora. It is therefore with delight that I have found the svadhisthana opening sometimes when I am in session with a patient. It gives evidence of a powerful bond between us, at a nearly instinctual level; and while open, it gives our communication added significance. There is nothing shameful, sexual, or greedy about the experience. It is informative. Its disturbing power has been neutralized, turned from a worthy opponent into an ally.

An additional detail may be worth mentioning. Sometimes when my svadhisthana has opened with a patient, I have also "seen" a tube connecting our bodies at the level of the abdomen. I have never seen this reported in the literature, but find it a useful experience insofar as the tube is distinctly different with each individual. Sometimes it seems made of flesh of different colors and textures, once it appeared to be made of glass, and on another occasion it was comprised of countless threadlike tubes, braided, in white and red. Each time it has given me a useful impression regarding the sort of relationship shared with the patient. I had believed this experience was unique to me, and therefore hardly worth mentioning, until I heard an interview with the world religions expert, Huston Smith, on National Public Radio's program, "Fresh Air."[2] Terri Gross asked Smith if he had ever experienced "satori."[3] In reply he told a story about his seemingly fruitless struggles with the koan[4] assigned to him ("Does a dog have Buddha nature?"). He had many frustrating meetings with his Zen master (Roshi), until one day something inexplicable but momentous occurred and Smith saw that his Roshi and he were connected to one another, abdomen-to-abdomen, by a tube. This "tubed" experience was his "satori."

THIRD CHAKRA, MANIPURA, AT THE SOLAR PLEXUS

Would-be heroes who enter the abysmal waters of the svadhisthana, aware of their fright but moved by the greater force of kundalini, emerge renewed like the rising sun in manipura, whose element is fire and location the solar plexus. The one who trembled before an adventure that clearly appeared too formidable steps out of the abyss with new self-knowledge. In retrospect it is clear to us that before our plunge—when we still lived in the ordinary world of the root chakra—we had little idea what we stood for, we were unaware of the essential and nearly impersonal principles on which our life is founded. But having been put to the test, we find our existence has simplified itself. We have jettisoned the illusory ideals of our "false self," that persona we subliminally formed so that we could hold our head up in the hectic and ephemeral world of social consensus. In the process we have been whittled down to our essentials—the real principles that ought to have been guiding our life but which we had hidden from ourselves in shame, false modesty, and cowardice. In manipura we find our essential being.

Such at any rate is the promise and potential of manipura, the solar plexus of our being. Jung's description of this chakra, whose Sanskrit name means "fullness of jewels," is somewhat more ambivalent. He articulates two aspects of manipura.

> [*Manipura*] is the fire center, really the place where the sun rises. The sun now appears; the first light comes after baptism. This is like the initiation rites in the Isis mysteries, according to Apuleius, where the initiate at the end of the ceremony was put upon a pedestal and worshipped as the [sun-]god Helios, the deification that always follows the baptismal rite. You

---

2 First aired in 1966. I heard it repeated on April 2, 1999, while revising this manuscript.

3 Satori: the experience of "awakening" or "enlightenment" in Zen.

4 Koan: A saying, phrase, or story given to a student of Zen to be meditated upon with the idea of finding an "answer." Koans always take the form of conundrums designed to frustrate the student's reasoning and everyday thinking powers so as to bring about a break-through, i.e., satori.

are born into a new existence; you are a very different being and have a different name (Jung, 1996: 30-1).

As long as you are in the *manipura* you are in the terrible heat of the center of the earth, as it were. There is only the fire of passions, of wishes, of illusions. It is the fire of which the Buddha speaks in his sermon in Benares where he says, The whole world is in flames, your ears, your eyes, everywhere you pour out the fire of desire, and that is the fire of illusion because you desire things which are futile. Yet there is the great treasure of the released emotional energy.

So when people become acquainted with the unconscious they often get into an extraordinary state—they flare up, they explode, old buried emotions come up, they begin to weep about things which happened forty years ago. That simply means that they were prematurely detached from that state of life; they have forgotten that there are buried fires still burning. Then they were unconscious, but when they touch the lower centers [i.e., the first three chakras], they get back into that world and become aware that it is still hot, like a fire that has been left forgotten under the ashes. But take away the ashes and there are still the glowing embers underneath, as it is said of pilgrims going to Mecca: they leave their fires buried under the ashes, and when they return the following year the embers are still glowing (Jung, 35-6).

Jung reveals that the manipura is as much a dual experience as are the first two chakras we have considered. In the first kundalini sleeps, but she may also be awakened. In the second we are confronted with destruction; but if we allow kundalini under the aspect of virya to confront those dangers, we can be transformed. In the third we have access to our essential being, but the smallness of our remembered ego-identity may seize upon resentments and unresolved issues from the distant past. The passion that might proceed directly from our essential being may be distorted by our neurotic defenses. Still the passion is an important achievement; for, "A man who is not on fire is nothing: he is ridiculous, he is two-dimensional" (Jung, 1996: 34).

The person who trembled before the abyss of svadhisthana had no real passion—at least nothing that burned from within. That former being of ours was unacquainted with the inner fire and too apt to become a shuttle-cock between fear and pretension. In manipura we are introduced to our essential being, but an important task remains for us. We have to learn to face up to its truth and stop protecting ourselves with illusions about who we wish we were, who we are afraid we might be, and our resentments concerning the obstacles that prevented us from realizing these things years ago.

In its best sense—that is to say, when it is "open"—manipura presents us with a sobering realization of the identity that lurks beneath all the lies we have constructed about ourselves; and this is the source of the real fire of our being. It is the "center of the life force" (Mookerjee, 1986: 40). At its worst, when the manipura is still knotted and closed, we immerse ourselves in illusory fantasies about our essential identity and manifest a passion that betrays its neurotic nature by consistently missing the mark. Evola says that the combustion of the manipura is desire in the form of "a burning, shining substance," characterized by emotions such as: "anger, fear, astonishment, violence, pride, and hunger" (Evola, 1992: 152). Mindell describes it in terms of: "gut knowledge . . . where many assertive reactions are repressed and turned into aggressions and anger. Stomach cramps, ulcers, 'heart burn,' diabetes, and cancer . . ." (Mindell, 1982: 41). But when stripped of its neurotic illusions, this third chakra "confers knowledge of character and the dispositions of human beings" (Evola, 1992: 158).

This means that when it is "open" the manipura dissolves the barriers between us and opens our eyes to imaginal realities. In the erotic trance of the solar-plexus chakra, we apprehend the subtle reality of our own essential being and that of our partner. The amazing thing about all the chakras, when they open, is that the rigid boundary of the rational and empirical world that divides the subject resolutely off from the object is dissolved in an imaginal trance. The "object," especially our partner, is no longer a mysterious "other," closed off from us, living a private existence that we can apprehend only from the outside. The erotic trance made possible by the rise of kundalini and her opening of the chakras reveals greater realities that are available only on the subtle plane. When the manipura chakra opens, we have an immediate intuition, self-evidently true, of our own essential being and that of our partner.

By my mid-twenties I had already begun to appreciate this aspect of erotic encounters. The thorough confusion brought on by the opening of the abdominal chakra which had characterized my adolescence had cleared somewhat, and I could see that, however intimidating the challenge might be, it also revealed something essential about both me and the individual I had newly met. It appears that greater familiarity with erotic openings had tempered my panic. The watery abyss of the svadhisthana no longer blurred my vision so completely. I pursued some of those visions made possible by the opening of the solar-plexus chakra—the glimpses of what seemed to be the other person's "essential being," the personality that underlay all the confusing details of everyday life. I felt I had become acquainted with a reliable core of information. I found that retaining this vision in my memory and comparing it with the details I learned later only confirmed the truth of realities seen on the subtle plane.

We may surely be mistaken about such things. For when the manipura is activated but still knotted, our vision of our own being as well as that of our partner will be distorted with our own defensive illusions. We may be led into an erotic involvement filled with delusions, misunderstandings, and emotional disasters. Patients have told me, for example, that they were so convinced by an initial erotic trance that they and their future partner were "made for one another" that they naturally assumed all the everyday details of living together would be worked out miraculously. When things became more complicated and intractable, they were

15

inclined to believe that they could never again trust such visions. They want to retreat from all experiences of the subtle plane out of fear of being misled again. But they are missing a crucial distinction. The vision of their partner's essential being may well have been accurate enough. What failed was their assessment of the defenses which distort the way we live that essential being. Information about subtle realities such as the essential being of ourselves and our partner does not absolve us from the necessity of struggling with our illusions and defenses in everyday life. It is the potential for an "inflation" ("I know everything I need to know") and self-delusion ("therefore everything will take care of itself") that has prompted Jung to insist that the "gods" activated in the various chakras must be viewed as impersonal third parties. The vision of my essential being is not "me," it is the greater personality I might become; and the same is true of my partner.

I have never felt the manipura opening like a whirling lotus flower or camera eye. Its most powerful quasi-bodily manifestation, however, did reflect its theoretical nature as the locus of my essential being. Some years ago, when my son had just earned his driver's license, he had an accident while driving to high school. I hurried to the hospital; and as I passed through the inner doorway of the emergency room to the cubicles where patients were awaiting examination, my straight-ahead gaze locked onto the eyes of my son, his upper body elevated on an examination table. The moment our eyes met, I felt a powerful blow to the solar plexus. The depth of our connectedness was immediately apparent, almost as though our joint life of sixteen years passed before my eyes. The essential nature of our bond was unmistakable. He had suffered no injuries. The ambulance ride to the hospital had merely been a precaution. But the immanent possibility of disaster had stripped away all illusion, and we met one another in the essential being of manipura.

We allude to this reality of holding our essential being in the region of our solar plexus when we speak of being punched or kicked "in the gut" by events that seem to challenge the ground of our conscious existence. The metaphors of everyday life often reveal their origins in the ancient and timeless discoveries of the kundalini tradition. An analogous experience was reported to me by a female colleague who had undergone treatment by an urban shaman. I asked her what she had experienced, and she jabbed me as hard as she could with the extended fingers of her right hand in my solar plexus. "It was like this," she said, and jabbed me repeatedly. "I felt my solar plexus being pushed inward by a force I could not control." Months later, when I met her at another conference, the experience was still with her, and she jabbed me again.

A more vivid description of the power and fire of kundalini as she manifests in the manipura chakra can be found in Jung's autobiography (Jung, 1961), when he describes his meeting with Freud, in 1909, in the elder man's study in Vienna.[5] Jung had come prepared with a series of questions on parapsychology, which Freud rejected as utter nonsense:

> in terms of so shallow a positivism that I had difficulty in checking the sharp retort on the tip of my tongue. . . .
>
> While Freud was going on this way, I had a curious sensation. It was as if my diaphragm were made of iron and were becoming red-hot—a glowing vault. And at that moment there was such a loud report in the bookcase, which stood right next to us, that we both started up in alarm, fearing the thing was going to topple over on us. I said to Freud: "There, that is an example of a so-called catalytic exteriorization phenomenon."
>
> "Oh come," he exclaimed. "That is sheer bosh."
>
> "It is not," I replied. "You are mistaken, Herr Professor. And to prove my point I now predict that in a moment there will be another such loud report!" Sure enough, no sooner had I said the words than the same detonation went off in the bookcase.
>
> To this day I do not know what gave me this certainty. But I knew beyond all doubt that the report would come again. Freud only stared at me. I do not know what was in his mind, or what his look meant. In any case, this incident aroused his mistrust of me, and I had the feeling that I done something against him. I never afterward discussed the incident with him (Jung, 1961: 155-6).

Clearly Jung sees this meeting as having marked the beginning of the end of his relationship with Freud. Both men felt the essential ground of their existence challenged in this encounter. Freud had placed his reputation and all his efforts into constructing a rational and "scientific" psychology that would stand up to the empirical criticisms of the nineteenth century, while Jung had been vitally concerned with parapsychology from childhood, had delivered papers on the subject before his college debating society, had written his doctoral dissertation on mediumship, and eventually coined the term "synchronicity" to describe the "non-causal but meaningful connections" with which parapsychology concerns itself. Parapsychology's reality was as essential for Jung as its rejection was for Freud. Both men were involved at the level of the manipura chakra.

When Jung bit his tongue and suppressed a spontaneous "retort," he immediately became aware of an impersonal force—a blazing fire at the solar plexus that heated his diaphragm until it was a glowing vault. A "knot" in his manipura flamed up in suppressed rage—a powerful defense against Freud's withering remarks. When the bookcase popped, he knew in the erotic trance of his aroused state that the sound was connected with the unbearable pressure and heat below his diaphragm. The energy of his kundalini was out of control, and it would

---

5 Of course Jung never connects this incident with the language of kundalini yoga.

happen again. Under the circumstances, we might wonder if Freud was less frightened of parapsychology than of Jung's manipura demonstration. It must surely have sufficed to convince him Jung was determined to "kill the father." Indeed, at their next meeting the drama continued: Freud fainted as Jung went on and on about some peat-bog corpses that had been recently discovered. At a third meeting in 1912, Freud fainted as Jung became enthusiastic over the Egyptian monotheist, Amenophis IV (Ikhnaton) who had removed his father's name from the monuments he had built (Jung 1961: 156-7).

All three incidents suggest a conflict at the level of the solar plexus; but the one with the bookcase gives us the most information. It appears that the rage of a knotted manipura combined with the opening of the subtle plane whereby Jung had precognitive abilities. The bounds of ordinary reality were dissolved as an inner experience of fire was accompanied by an outer physical event. The "essential being" of the two men seemed to be at stake. Both of them had knots in their manipura. Even Freud's fright suggests that—deny it as he might—he was convinced of Jung's "killing the father" so thoroughly that he was unable to doubt it. He, too, was in a sort of trance, and in retrospect no one doubts that he was right.

Much later in his life, it appears that Jung had learned to use the opening of his manipura in his conduct of analysis. His patients report sessions in which the ordinary world dissolved into "whirling molecules" and they could no longer say what distinguished them from the furniture in the room. On such occasions Jung spoke to them of dreams they had had but not reported. He seemed to speak, as they said, to their "essential condition." Jung himself described this situation as "thinking unconsciously" and attending to a third party to whom he referred as "the Three-Million-Year-Old Man" (cf. Haule, 1999a). It appears Jung was employing a vision of the essential being of his patient as well as his own that became available through a mutual opening of the manipura chakra. To avoid becoming "inflated" with this knowledge, he ascribed it to the agency of a third party of superhuman intelligence and wisdom—very much as an Indian would refer to Shiva or Shakti, even kundalini, as the divinity responsible for an erotic vision.

FOURTH CHAKRA, ANAHATA, THE HEART CENTER

A great transition occurs when we traverse the diaphragm from the solar plexus to the heart center. We leave "the lower chakras" with their close connection to the physical body and enter "the higher chakras." In the lower three we move between ego and its essential core, what Evola calls "the principle of individuality,"[6] the me beneath my pretensions. My essen-

───────────────

6 He uses the Latin expression, *principium individuationis*.

tial being and the fierce desires, defenses, and illusions that distort it have a personal quality. However, in the anahata:

> One no longer identifies with one's desires. . . . It is hard to talk of these things because most people are still identified with *manipura*. . . . The diaphragm would correspond to the surface of the earth, and apparently in getting into the *anahata* we reach the condition where we are lifted up from the earth. . . . You rise above the horizon . . . if you're identical with the sun (Jung, 1996: 36-7).

Jung sticks close to the imagery of the Night Sea Journey in his articulation of the chakras. In the second, the sun sets in the Western Sea and begins its struggle with the darkness of the unconscious. In the third, light dawns in the East, but the sun has not yet detached itself from the earth, which Jung emphasizes by speaking of the blaze of manipura as the fire at the center of the earth. Only in anahata does the sun of our being break free of the earth and rise into the air. Anahata is traditionally identified with the primal element of air: "because the heart is closely associated with the lungs. One must be naïve to understand these things. In primitive experience, it is the same thing. In fact it is a psychological truth" (Jung, 1996: 36). It is also a physiological truth, for our breathing and heart rate are very closely related. The heartbeat that speeds up in the face of sexual arousal, terror, and the like, can be controlled by the breathing exercises of yoga.

In the earth of muladhara where kundalini sleeps, we are stolid and unmoving in our identification with rationality, empirical facts, and the assumptions of our social consensus. In the water of svadhisthana we plunge into the chaotic emotional turbulence of the unconscious. In the fire of manipura we can become caught in passions of a very personal nature. But when we rise into the air of anahata, we detach ourselves from our personal identity. In the solar center, for example, I am convinced that in seeing my essential being I am seeing "the real me"; and as I direct my manipura-inspired gaze upon you, I perceive "the real you." But in the heart center a real "detachment" takes place.

For example, when we experience one another sexually through any of the lower chakras, we cannot avoid the impression of viscerality. Negatively, we may feel "invaded" through the abdomen or "punched in the gut" of the solar plexus; positively, we may feel "entered" or "joined." The bodily foundation of these experiences and the sense that they are "mine" is never lost. But when my heart chakra has spun open, I have had the most airy feeling of transcendent bliss. "Bliss" is not an appropriate word to describe what happens in the lower chakras. We may talk of pleasure, pain, intimations of truth, and the like; but we are never moved to speak of bliss. We thus feel a crucial distinction between the lower and the upper chakras. Furthermore, we are moved to call it *transcendent* bliss. It is neither mine nor yours.

It transcends us both and "comes to us," as though bestowed from on high. When our heart chakras spin open, there is no doubt in our minds that they are spinning in unison and that the oneness we experience is supremely light. In my experience, it can take place while we are fully clothed and without the physical activities of love-making. Toomer seems to have alluded to the heart chakra when he said that he had dropped the weight of "that me."

Although there is a sensation in our chest, it is as though our entire body has been "sublimed"[7] and turned into air, flowing through the vortex of my anahata into yours and back again. "I" and "you" persist, but a discarnate "we" predominates. Jung alludes to this experiential fact when he says that "individuation" begins in the heart chakra. In his language *individuation* does not mean "individuality," but rather one's connection with what is transpersonal, impersonal, or collective. Our personhood is rooted in what we share with all humankind, and indeed with the universe. The process of individuation for Jung establishes a living relationship with the impersonal ground of existence that he calls "the collective unconscious" or "the self." When we realize the centrality of the self, we discover that the ego we thought exhausted the reality of who we are has become merely an "appendix" of the larger reality the Hindus call atman.

> In *anahata* individuation begins. . . . Individuation is becoming that thing which is not the ego, and that is very strange. . . . The ego discovers itself as being a mere appendix of the self in a sort of loose connection. For the ego is always far down in the *muladhara* and suddenly becomes aware of something up above on the fourth story, in *anahata*, and that is the self (Jung, 1996: 39-40).

> In *anahata* . . . [one] gets the first inkling of the power and substantiality, or the real existence, of psychical things. . . . One cannot catch them with a butterfly net, nor can one find them under microscopes. They become visible only in the *anahata* (Jung, 1996: 45).

In the texts of Tantrism, the heart center is often described as a "void" that is "free of duality" and characterized by the state of bliss (Silburn, 1988: 7). "When Kundalini touches the heart center, [the yogin] breaks the attachment that ties him to the body" (Silburn, 1988: 73). Traditionally this condition of being beyond the body and the empirical world is symbolized by the "unstruck sound" which is the literal meaning of anahata (Evola, 1992: 153). Everything written about the anahata chakra emphasizes sublimity. It is not only we who are "sublimed," but the field of our consciousness as well. It is the immaterial world, the subtle plane as a realm in itself and not merely the esoteric significance of empirical realities. This

---

7 In chemistry, to "sublime" is to pass directly from the solid state to the gaseous state without becoming a liquid in between. You can see this on a warm, humid day in winter when the snow turns directly into steam and may even produce a fog.

is what Jung means when he says we get our "first inkling of the power and substantiality, or the real existence, of psychical things." Erotic trance becomes spiritual to a degree unknown at the lower chakras.

Whenever a chakra opens for us, the boundaries of everyday life are obliterated. When the svadhisthana opens in the lower abdomen, we have the sense that the two of us are dissolving into an erotic and dangerous *we*. At the manipura this dissolution manifests itself in our intuition of the essential being of the other. At the anahata it gives us the ability to "detect the *feelings* of other people" (Evola, 1992: 158; italics added). This is also why it is the primary center of love. But we can only read the feelings of others accurately when the anahata chakra is open. It may be activated but remain knotted. Then it can be characterized by a narcissistic self-love that includes, "hope, anxiety, apprehension, doubt, remorse, and hesitation" (Evola, 1992: 153). Mindell attributes to a knotted heart center, "hypochondria, skipping heart beats, cramping, stopping, over-excitement, and naïve sentimentality" (Mindell, 1982: 42). To be moved by the feelings that predominate in anahata without being detached from our ego-centered concerns distorts them as surely as our intuitions of essential being may be at the third chakra. If the open anahata is characterized above all by detachment from the body, from the personal realm, and from the outer world, a knotted anahata reveals persisting attachments, personal desires, and possessiveness.

When the anahata is knotted, its activation may be extremely painful. Typically this condition arises when we fall deeply in love with an individual who pretends not to reciprocate our feelings. Unable to conceal his feelings entirely, our would-be partner inadvertently gives us ample evidence that he loves us in return but cannot submit, perhaps, to the tumult of his own svadhisthana. Pulling back in fear, he frustrates our hopes and maintains distance. When our anahata chakra is knotted, we can feel this ambivalent rejection as a tearing or cutting right down the center of our chest. Such a torment results from our own knotted heart center. We have not yet risen above the surface of the inner earth of our diaphragm, and are still filled with personal attachments. We want to possess this beloved who rejects us. Unable to love in the pure, airy letting-be of an open anahata, our chest is clenched shut; and every attempt by the heart center to open seems to tear our flesh. Our pain is evidence that our "deity" is approaching and demanding that we let go of our attachments.

Intermediate between the bliss of a whirling anahata and the torment of a torn anahata lies the nearly sublime sensation that our heart center opens ecstatically like a groove in our chest that may sometimes expand to involve the lower chakras in an openness extending from pubis to clavicle. We may feel that our partner nestles in that tender and sensitive trough or that we nestle inside our partner. Often it is difficult to determine which of us contains the other. The knottedness of the anahata is no longer experienced as painful. It is, indeed, delightful; but its rootedness in the physical body, now transformed through our erotic trance, reveals that we are perhaps lying on the surface of the inner earth and have not yet risen into the air. The subtle plane predominates over sensual realities. In *Divine Madness* (Haule, 2010: 154-6) I recounted an example of a couple who had reached a state like this and then were astonished to see that their coupling was but a footnote to the "real event": gigantic spirit beings were uniting in the air surrounding them. Although innocent of the whirling sensation so frequently described, their eyes were opened to "the real existence of psychical things": the full spirituality and independence of a divine subtle plane. Consistent with Jung's expression of the ego finding itself an "appendix" to a self which manifests "up above on the fourth story," those lovers felt personally "left out" of the main event, a pair of egos who were only permitted to observe.

Ioan Couliano says that this experience is cross-cultural and invariably associated with the space of the heart as it exists in the subtle body:

> . . . "cleansing one's pneuma" or hegemonikon, or "cleansing one's heart." These are the theoretical givens that make it possible to understand a number of mystico-magic Oriental techniques that place much importance on the transparency, purity, and brilliance of the "seat of the heart," such as Taoism, Yoga, Sufism, and Hesychasm.[8] Whether or not it is designated by the vocables *hsin, akasa, hrdaya, qalb,* or *kardia,* this "cardiac space" always represents the phantasmic synthesizer whose cleanliness is the condition essential to all manifestation of divinity (1986: 114).

A "clean" heart-space is uncontaminated with personal attachments, assumptions, and desires. In the literature of Sufism and Buddhism, this heart-center requirement is often expressed as "polishing the mirror of the heart"; for only a mirror devoid of all dust fragments and fingerprints can reflect the realities of the subtle plane without distortion. What Couliano calls "phantasmic synthesizer" is precisely the imagination, what Corbin calls, employing the capital letter *I,* "active Imagination." This is our imaginal capacity, our faculty for transcending the merely personal and gaining access to the *mundus imaginalis,* the imaginal world—an objective and impersonal reality which is substantially the same for all who enter. Whatever differences may be found from one individual to another are attributed solely to personal predispositions, to smudges on the mirror of the heart.

---

8 Hesychasm: the mystical practice of the Orthodox Church, discovered by the monks of the monastery at Mt. Athos in the fourteenth century. By repeating the mantra, "Lord Jesus Christ, Son of God, have mercy on me," they sought a vision of "the Divine Light, the Energy, not the essence of the godhead," through yoga-like practices (Ferguson, 1977).

The examples of mysticism described in Volume One of this work have had relatively little to do with the heart chakra. The mad saints enter into the turbulence of svadhisthana's watery abyss and lose their ego-orientation. Kundalini obliterates the world of their ego; and if they survive the ordeal psychologically, kundalini has brought them through the abyss to their essential being in manipura. The antinomian saints struggle with the same transit, but do so in a far more conscious manner. If any of them rose to the level of the anahata, we have paid little attention to this development. In the chapters that follow, however, the vast majority of the examples will be centered in the heart chakra. Despite the doctrine that kundalini sleeps and wakes in the root chakra, it is commonly said that "Kundalini usually chooses to stir from the heart" (Silburn, 1988: 28), or that the heart chakra is "where we always are"—a reference to the self or atman rather than the ego.

The great Bengali poet, Ramprasad Sen, says that he wants to dwell only in the heart chakra because (a) one cannot remain long in the crown chakra where complete union is attained, (b) in the lower levels one cannot "enjoy" the experience, and (c) in the heart center one is intoxicated but remains aware of one's surroundings (McLean, 1998: 75-6). In the verse that follows, the "cage of green bamboo" refers to the rib cage. "Lalan" is one of Ramprasad's names.

> Mind, your only hope is to stay in the cage,
>
> The cage you have made of green bamboo.
>
> One day the cage will fall down,
>
> Lalan says, When the cage is opened
>
> That bird will fly away somewhere.
>
> (McLean, 1998: 82).

FIFTH CHAKRA, VISHUDDHA, THE THROAT CENTER

The primal element of vishuddha, the throat chakra, is ether, which is itself a highly abstract notion. In the West *ether* has come to mean a certain sort of aromatic compound. This is not at all the primal element ether. Indeed, ether no longer plays a role in modern physics and chemistry.[9] In late antiquity, the Middle Ages, the Renaissance, the Enlightenment, and even to the nineteenth century, ether still had a role to play as the rarefied medium through

---

9 Unless one sees it smuggled back in the form of the "fields" through which the energy-packets of quantum theory propagate themselves; or in the "no-place" where Bohm's "implicate order" lies

which the stars and planets move. India's ether plays a role something like that of our own discarded notion, but it also and more importantly refers to a level of psychological and mystical experience. In Sanskrit, ether is *akasha*:

> [*Akasha*] means literally "radiance." Early on, it acquired the meaning of "space" or "ether," and served as a frequent comparison for the transcendent Self, which is described as being brighter than a myriad of suns. . . . In later times, *akasha* came to be regarded as the finest of the five material elements (*bhuta*) of the manifest cosmos. In this sense, the concept is similar to Aristotle's "quintessence" and the "luminiferous ether" of nineteenth century physics—a notion that was abandoned at the beginning of our century (Feuerstein, 1990).

In Jung's words, ether is: "Matter that is not matter, and such a thing must necessarily be a concept. . . . One reaches a sphere of abstraction. There one steps beyond the empirical world, as it were, and lands in a world of concepts" (Jung, 1996: 42). In being "beyond the empirical world," vishuddha has much in common with the heart chakra as well as the upper two centers. But the heart chakra is characterized primarily by feeling, while the throat chakra brings conceptual realities to our awareness. In an open anahata we can feel the feelings of others; in an open vishuddha we can detect their *thoughts* (Evola, 1992: 158). If in anahata we rise into the air, in vishuddha we rise into a much more abstract space comprised of ether:

> [In *vishuddha*] one should admit that all one's psychical facts have nothing to do with material facts. For instance, the anger which you feel for somebody or something, no matter how justified it is, is not caused by those external things. It is a phenomenon all by itself. . . . In other words, our worst enemy is perhaps within ourselves.

> If you reach that stage, you begin to leave the *anahata* (Jung, 1996: 49).

The clarity with which Jung spoke of the first four chakras appears to desert him as he gets to the fifth. Appearing to recognize this, he throws up his hands before the task of describing the chakras remaining, "It doesn't help to speculate about the *ajna* and *sahasrara* and God knows what" (Jung, 47). It is not only Jung, however, who begins to speak obscurely when he reaches the fifth chakra. I have found no accounts of what it feels like to have the throat center open like a whirling lotus, and have not experienced it myself. Possibly my throat chakra is particularly knotted. I am well known, in fact, as one who has frequently to clear my throat—a factor that is certainly related to my constant post-nasal drip, but may well have psychological and spiritual dimensions as well. Evola says that an open throat center makes it possible for, "Atma [to] see itself in everything and dominate past present and future." Meanwhile a

---

"folded up." As we shall see in Volume Two, Chapter Four, there is ample reason for considering this mythological interpretation of certain obscure notions in modern physics.

knotted vishuddha is characterized by emotions of "affection, sadness, respect, devotion, happiness, regret, and relationship" (Evola, 1992: 154).

Clear distinctions between anahata, vishuddha, and ajna (the brow chakra), are hard to find. But if vishuddha is associated, as tradition holds, with a facility in the use of words and concepts, it would seem that my writing employs the throat chakra. The reader will perhaps be the best judge as to whether this book testifies to an open or a closed vishuddha, but I think my experience in writing is not unique to me. I find that some other power, entirely impersonal and "not me," proposes images and words which in the first instance I simply observe. Often a whole scene unfolds for me, and I simply write down the words that come by way of articulating it. Sometimes words and phrases come of their own and the images follow.

If this is a description of kundalini proposing and my ego disposing, then perhaps Muhammad is the best historical example of a man who worked entirely from the vishuddha. For by his own account he merely repeated word-for-word what the Angel Gabriel spoke to his inner ear when he was reciting the texts that eventually were assembled as the Qu'ran. So respectful was he of the divine origin of those words, that he eschewed all ego participation in the process. Every one of his inspired pronouncements began with the word, "Recite." Kundalini, in the person of Gabriel, began every entry into the oral record that became the Qu'ran with the command to Muhammad that he was to "recite" what followed, and Muhammad was so worshipful in his regard for the impersonal source of what he was to say that he did not omit even the initial word of command.

In my case, ego plays a much larger role. I argue with kundalini, telling her that this is not yet the time for this particular idea, image, or set of words. I wait for her to speak to the issue at hand, reminding her that she got me into this or that difficulty and that it is her responsibility to get me out of it. I also do not hesitate to shape her material with an eye to my imagined reader. Sometimes I become depressed at the way things are going and block my access to the impersonal source of inspiration. I also have to submit myself to a great deal of ego-centered research, studying what others have said and accumulating a supply of material which kundalini shapes by turning up my interest. But it is generally she who finds the conceptual connections between the various ideas I have found in my academic sources. While the dialogue is going on between me and kundalini, I often lose track of time and my commitments in the empirical world. In a few instances this has led to embarrassment, but I find that generally kundalini or some other watchman keeps track of these things—not unlike the internal clock-keeper who wakes me in the morning or at the end of an occasional afternoon nap at precisely the right moment, eliminating the need for an alarm clock.

According to the Hindus, ether is the element that transmits vibrations—particularly those of sound. Thus the pronouncing of mantras is said to be associated with the vishuddha, not only because mantras are phrases, words, or isolated syllables, but also because mantras are said to change our consciousness through the etheric vibrations produced when we speak them aloud. Music—especially the music of the spheres—belongs to the vishuddha. A musician once told me that the throat chakra is his most dependable access to the subtle body and the subtle plane. He can open it at will by pronouncing the mantra given him by a guru. But it also opens of its own and enables him to perceive that the *world* is ethereal and comprised of vibrations.

SIXTH CHAKRA, AJNA, CENTERED ABOVE THE EYEBROWS

A great deal of nonsense has been written about the brow chakra, often called the "third eye," especially in Western literature. New-age accounts credit the third eye with every sort of imagery, making little or no attempt to distinguish the imaginal from the imaginary. Ajna is different from the other "higher chakras" in that it has more to do with imagery than the others. The heart chakra is responsible primarily for feelings, the throat center for concepts and words, and the crown chakra for cosmic vision. What distinguishes the brow chakra is imagery of a mythological and impersonal character. It is our eye into "Indra's Heaven," to use the metaphor from our earlier story about Nanda, the Buddha's half-brother.

The myth that we live without knowing it *as* a myth—and perhaps without knowing that we are living a myth at all—represents the unacknowledged ground of our personal existence. When our ajna is open, this impersonal ground expresses itself in imagery and narrative. It has a thoroughly impersonal character. The extent to which we live our life centered in the ego's concerns obscures the mythological foundation and enables us to depart from our psychological roots in various neurotic ways. When the mythological foundation of our life is acknowledged, however, it does indeed form the basis of our existence; and ajna, as our imaginal access to our foundation, envisions the ruling myth of our life. In this sense it is the "command center." Beyond that: "It is the receiver for the guru's telepathic communications to the student. Hence it is also called the *guru-chakra*. . . . Its activation is said to lead to all kinds of psychic powers (*siddhi*), notably clairvoyance and the ability to communicate telepathically" (Feuerstein, 1990).

Mookerjee says the ajna "controls" the various states of consciousness that one gains through meditation (Mookerjee, 1986: 42). It gives us "simultaneous knowledge of things as they really are"; and is the perceiver of cosmic consciousness (Mookerjee, 12). Silburn says that these visions occur while the body, will, and intellect are "benumbed," although the "heart keeps watch" (Silburn, 1988: 74). This seems to mean that genuine ajna experience requires a real detachment from the body, as is true of all the higher chakras. Karagulla, a medical doctor who reports her educated observations, notes that while a clairvoyant is "seeing" invisible or imaginal realities, the eyes appear "slightly dilated and fixed," and the pupils do not react in the normal way to light (Karagulla & Kunz, 1989: 84).

A dramatic story about the opening of the ajna chakra constitutes a turning point in the biography of Ramakrishna. A naked, wandering guru named Tota attempted to initiate Ramakrishna into his own fairly orthodox practice of Vedanta. Meanwhile, Ramakrishna reports being delighted with Tota's nakedness and used the opportunity to play with the elder man's "little penis," apparently as though it were the member of a boy—thus expressing Ramakrishna's unconscious identification with homosexuality and Tantra.[10] Tota became frustrated by this sexual play and by Ramakrishna's devotion to the goddess, believing that it kept Ramakrishna's eyes closed to Vedanta's formless vision of brahman:

> The graceful form of his Mother kept appearing to him, floating in his psychic sky to challenge the command of the monk who had smirked at Ramakrishna's devotion. Finally, Tota took a piece of sharp glass and embedded it in Ramakrishna's forehead: "Concentrate here," he said. Once again the goddess appeared, but this time the saint imagined that his newfound knowledge was a sword and cut the goddess in two. At once his mind ascended past name and form and merged into the formless *brahman*. Within a mere three days, he had attained what it took Tota forty years to accomplish (Kripal, 1995: 152).

The ultimate victor in this story was Ramakrishna, who brought Tota to such despair that he wandered into the river to commit suicide, where he had a vision of the goddess, the Mother of the Universe, and realized that, "*Brahman* and the *sakti* of *brahman* are nondifferent!" (Kripal, 1995: 153). But the detail about embedding the piece of sharp glass in Ramakrishna's forehead appears to be an authentic reference to what it feels like to have the brow chakra open. Bhattacharya's introduction to the ajna chakra was very similar. His "instructor," a little Vaishnavite yogin named Narada, removed a brown bead from his hair and pressed it into Bhattacharya's forehead. Bhattacharya gives a lengthy series of incidents in which reality and illusion are so interwoven with one another that it is impossible to distinguish one from the other. The ajna brings us visions, but no little discernment is required before we can utilize them. Bhattachaya says, "To this day I feel much embrarrased for this brow-reaction [the seeing of visions]; and I always stand in fear of it" (Bhattacharya, 1988: 287). His confusion and embarrassment betray a certain "knottedness" in his ajna.

---

10 Not only does this playful sexuality suggest that Ramakrishna was infantilizing the elder guru, it also implies that Ramakrishna was initiating Tota into his own unconscious Tantric practice at the same time that Tota was endeavoring to initiate Ramakrishna into Vedanta.

I have never felt my own brow chakra open, but several people have reported to me that they have experienced it as a vertical split in the forehead, suggestive of the Indian icons in which a third eye is positioned vertically between the two horizontal fleshly eyes.[11] One woman told me she experienced it as an unusually sharp and persisting headache in the center of her forehead that was "so immobilizing that I couldn't get out of bed to get an aspirin" and that when she closed her eyes she had an image of a "gridlocked woven pattern in multiple colors." Apparently her knotted ajna was trying to open. Further evidence of the knottedness of her ajna is suggested by the fact that she was assailed by visions she found extremely disturbing. For example, a vision or dream of a car crash convinced her that one of her grown children was in danger of dying in an automobile accident. She entered a psychotic-like state that lasted a couple of weeks, and restored her sanity by returning to the yogic practices she had been neglecting. On her return to sanity, she said that the lesson she had learned from all that had happened was that such visions were "true but not literal." In short, she had learned that the visions belong to the subtle plane and not to the empirical world.

Muktananda's experience confirms that the sensation accompanying an opening ajna chakra may be a powerful pain in the forehead:

> I started to feel a pain between the eyebrows, which was so strong I could not sleep at night. Then a light came in meditation, like a candle flame without a wick, and stood motionless in the *ajna chakra*, the two-petaled lotus between the eyebrows (Muktananda, 1978: 128).

SEVENTH CHAKRA, SAHASRARA, AT THE CROWN OF THE HEAD

Sahasrara, meaning "thousand," refers to the "thousand-petaled lotus" or "thousand-spoked wheel" that represents the crown chakra, sometimes located at the crown of the skull, where the energy of kundalini may be felt to exit, and sometimes located some four inches above the crown of the head. "The Sahasrara is the centre of quintessential consciousness, where integration of all polarities is experienced, and the paradoxical act of transcendence is accomplished in passing beyond ever-changing *samsara*[12] and 'emerging from time and space'"

---

11 This vertical placement of the "third eye" seems to represent a minority position among Indian iconographers, as the eye in the center of the brow is more frequently represented in the horizontal position. It is tempting to think that those who place it vertically may be more fully initiated.

12 Samsara: the eternal round of death and rebirth, also the empirical or profane world, the source of all illusion. We are fated to be reborn into the empirical world after every death until we attain the transcending consciousness which sees through it. Once this is achieved, our death ends the struggle and we enter forever into the full reality of what is.

(Mookerjee, 1986: 44). It is the point at which semen rising through the central channel (sushumna) is said to be transformed into nectar and the point where Sadashiva, as the union of Shiva and Shakti, occurs. Silburn says that to pass beyond the brow chakra, it is necessary to have mastered meditation's goal of samadhi, the state of non-dual consciousness (Silburn, 1988: 29). What is attained in the sahasrara is the "splendor of consciousness"; and it does not come about through self-effort. In Christian terms, it is a matter of "grace," i.e., supernatural agency, a gift of God. What is seen in the high attainment of samadhi in the crown chakra is a vision of "the very nature of things" (Silburn, 1988: 31).

"The very nature of things" may be called Sadashiva, Shakti, consciousness, brahman, or given a large number of names; but the essence of the vision involves seeing the underlying nature of reality. The empirical world is revealed as a limited and illusory vision of ultimate reality, which may be described as the energy that lies behind what we see with our fleshly eyes.[13] It is the fundamental experience of "Thou art That." Gopi Krishna's meditation on the thousand-petaled lotus of his sahasrara gives us a distorted hint of what the experience may be. To approach the experience more clearly, we will have to consider the nature of samadhi and the Buddhist doctrine of nothingness (*shunyata*) or "co-dependent origination" in Volume Two, Chapters Four and Five. For now it will be enough to know that it transcends all earlier experiences and is the goal of mysticism. "Indra's Heaven" and its analogues that become available to our imaginal vision in the brow chakra are also revealed to be a limited and illusory perspective on the ultimate when the yogin's sahasrara opens.

* * *

This survey of the seven centers that comprise the subtle body represents a very limited account. We have striven to remain close to everyday consciousness so as to reveal aspects of the subtle-body experience that many readers may have had and in the hope that experiences that have not been had can at least be vividly imagined. Surely more complete and officially "correct" versions are available. I have tried to keep this account simple by not going beyond my own experience. The point is that we encounter a whole world of experience at each chakra, for each one brings a unique perspective to bear, with its own physiology, emotion, and imaginal structure. The chakras are the gateways to the several dimensions of the subtle plane, where what is "out there" and what is "in here" are not different. We all experience the subtle

---

13 This doctrine that the empirical world is a limited aspect of ultimate reality is common to the various schools of Tantra. It contrasts with the Vedanta doctrine of Shankara, whereby the empirical world has no reality at all, is merely an illusion. For Tantra, the empirical world is a real but limited perspective on "the very nature of things." It is illusory insofar as it poses as the way things really are; but it is real insofar as it constitutes a limited aspect of ultimate reality.

body in fragmentary ways. Most of us discard these glimpses because we have no way of naming and categorizing them. They have no place within our Western consensus. I am convinced that the best way to proceed is to begin taking note of the experiences we are already having, and not to try to force ourselves to have the experiences we find described in books. Thus the descriptions above are not meant to be taken as a blueprint so much as a set of clues.

2

INTERNAL LADDER

Erotic trance is about changing the world. In the examples we have considered, erotic trance supervenes as a result of our physiological and emotional arousal and presents us with an imaginal vision supremely convincing in its self-evident truth and compelling reality. The empirical world is altered or even replaced by another world whose overwhelming significance we are incapable of doubting. Because the vision appears on its own and may even surprise us with its unexpected character, it may seem to those who only read about such occurrences that it must be arbitrary. Only the subjective conviction of a trance state that leaves us no option to doubt can lend the vision a quality of just-so-ness, so that the practitioner can say, "Although I'd never have guessed it, this clearly is the way things really are."

Not every erotic trance has this character of being wholly unexpected. Indeed, it is well known that in some traditions, particularly Tibetan Buddhism, the meditative vision is carefully predetermined in minute detail. Consider, for example, the highly elaborate mandalas that are designed to resemble the floorplan of a temple with a god and goddess coupled in the center. Arranged about this central pair in concentric circles are other divine couples. At the four "gates" of the temple other gods are to be found; and in a wider circle outside the sanctuary, still others—each distinctively attired and in a characteristic pose. Border designs are vividly painted in a variety of colors, providing us enough detail for hours of study before we can hope to have an even approximate sense for the intricacy of the design.

Such mandalas may also be painstakingly painted over the course of several days by one or several monks using colored sand. If so, the mandala is used for a single ritual purpose and then destroyed by stirring the colored sand grains into chaos. The mandala represents the ordered divine world of mythology, perceptible through the third eye of the ajna chakra. That heavenly world is created and brought to earth by means of ritual trance and then destroyed when the communal altered state of consciousness ends and the monks return to ordinary consciousness. The fact that it can be painted in advance of the ritual indicates clearly enough that the monks are not surprised by the view that occupies their consciousness when they enter trance. They know exactly what to expect.

More important than the sand painting, however, is the visualization that takes place in the minds of the monks who perform the ritual.

> We must remember—and this point should be emphasized—that the visualization is per-
> formed during a ritual; that is, the practitioner is reciting a text . . . , and the visualization
> takes place in time with the rhythmically chanted textual description of the evocation. . . .
> The reading of the ritual text in the assembly hall often goes at break-neck speed, and the vast
> majority of monks are unable to visualize that quickly, if indeed they are able to visualize at
> all. Practice in speed and accuracy came in a monk's periods of solitary contemplation, where
> the pace might be slowed sufficiently to allow concentration on the process of forming the
> deity, but there was never a break in the ritual process itself, for the solitary yogin so timed
> his contemplative periods that they fitted the structure of the ritual as a whole (Beyer, 1973:
> 71).

The simplest way to think about this sort of ritual is to take note of three gross stages in an ideal performance of the work: (1) Before the ritual begins, the monks are in an ordinary state of consciousness. (2) By means of the ritual, they enter an erotic trance wherein the ordinary world is vividly replaced by the subtle world of the mandala, a palace of gods and goddesses. (3) At the end of the ritual, they deliberately destroy it and re-enter the world of everyday. When the visualization works like this, the stolidity of ordinary consciousness, its rootedness in the empirical world, is seriously undermined. The monk realizes the arbitrariness of *any* world construction. The sacred world gains a stability and reliability that clearly rivals the givenness of the profane world.

In an "ideal performance" of the ritual, all the monks would be capable of visualizing the mandala at the "break-neck speed" of their chanting. As it stands, however, few can do so. Those with some facility have, in their private practice, been able to make parts of it vividly present; and they strive to use what they have accomplished in private to add to the communal ritual. Factoring in the well-established principle that people can accomplish more in group practice than they can in solitude, we can well imagine that, difficult as it must be, the mandalic world of the divine palace becomes at least vaguely present for the community as a whole. The result, although surely less than ideal, must nevertheless be a powerful evocation of the world of the gods, whose invocation and banishment certainly serves to loosen the absolute character of the profane world.

Stephen Beyer, whose book *The Cult of Tara* (1973) not only describes the process in detail but builds upon his own practice in a Tibetan monastery, tells us that the novice monk works first at producing a clear and vivid mental picture of the mandala, beginning with the image of the principal deity and allowing the rest to remain vague. If the central figure has several faces and hands, the novice is to begin with the principal face and pair of arms. When these become clear and vivid, additional details are added.

> Once the deity's body has appeared in this rough way, the practitioner must practice in the same way the formation of all the subtle parts, the other faces and hands, the ornaments, and so on. After that he must contemplate the deity's consort in the same way; then he adds on the other deities of the retinue; and finally he should be able to settle his mind one-pointedly on a complete and vivid formation of all the rough and subtle parts simultaneously, the entire retinue of the residential palace and all the deities who are its residents (Beyer, 1973: 70).

What we see taking place in this process is a form of discipline we have not yet considered. We have determined that erotic trance involves at least three distinct but mutually contributing elements: physiology, emotion, and imagination. Those who practice carezza seek to master physiology. Those who follow the heroic and antinomian path strive to master the emotions which disturb the uninitiated but which can be turned into strength through gaining familiarity with the upsurge of kundalini. Beyer's Tibetan monks are working to master their imagination, so that what appears fortuitously and in an unpredictable fashion for mystics on the lower rungs of the diamond ladder attains for them a real stability and predictability. The difficulty of this achievement can easily be experienced by any reader who will take the time to pause and try to hold before the mind's eye for perhaps ten seconds the image of a red, capital letter *A*. Possibly that red *A* will appear immediately. But if it does, it is likely to change colors, becoming yellow, blue, or black. It may stand on its head, lie on its side. Its straight lines may become rubbery. Inevitably it will begin to disintegrate. It takes on a life of its own and frustrates our attempts to hold it steady.[14]

Overcoming what is for us a nearly insuperable difficulty will constitute "the first qualification" for the novice monk. After what would doubtless be years of practice, the monk will be able to hold the whole mandala steady in his erotic trance. At this point, a richness of imaginal experience becomes possible—something that is wholly beyond the power of those who have not submitted to the discipline of the imaginal path. For instance, as we gain control of the imagination, we create opportunities to witness subtle but important changes in the mandala. Consider for example that god in the upper right quadrant, a few inches from the central pair of divine consorts. He should be sitting on a red lotus petal; but the day he insists upon sitting on a blue petal, kundalini appears to be sending us some very specific information. The stability of the mandala as a whole enables us to appreciate the finest of nuances. There is no

---

14 This sample exercise was proposed by Beyer in a lecture he gave in Philadelphia in 1972, during a pre-publication speaking tour on behalf of his book. What happened to the capital letter *A* describes my experience as I sat in the audience.

telling how we will interpret this alteration. Perhaps it indicates some resistance in ourselves, possibly a passionate defense in the region of our solar plexus. Or it may give evidence relating to our intention in performing the ritual, a statement related to the goal we are trying to achieve. Perhaps it is a particularly auspicious or inauspicious moment for performing the ritual. We will need to know what that god in the upper right quadrant stands for, what role he plays in the mythic narratives underlying the mandala itself. Such subtlety in apprehension is impossible for those who have not mastered imagination.

THE MESOCOSM

Surely it is possible to begin one's mystic path with the way of imagination. There are all sorts of mystical schools, and the earnest student will likely "shop the metaphysical mall" until she finds an approach that best suits her own nature and speaks most directly to her experience. But in the end none of them fail to address the three principal elements of erotic trance: physiology, emotion, and imagination. Indeed, Beyer's monks do not at all neglect the body. They identify every aspect of the mandala with a specific body-part as this quotation from the Tantric College at Trashilhunpo illustrates:

> Before and behind my body, to the right and the left, are the four sides of the mandala; my mouth and nose, anus and penis, are the four gates; the five-colored winds of my five knowledges—the steeds of my constructs—are the five-tiered walls; my tongue-perception is the jeweled border, my intestines the net, my sinews the half net, my portion of semen the half-moons, my eye perception the mirrors, my nose perception the flower garlands, my tongue the bells, my body the yak tails, my ear and body perceptions the flags and silken streamers on the balconies; my calves, thighs, upper and lower arms are the eight pillars, my stomach the flask within the mandala, my ears the vajra-marked half-moons in the intermediate directions; my five aggregates, purified, are the five colors of the mandala; my secret place,[15] navel, heart, and tip of my nose are the four gateways, my eyes the wheels, my mind perception the deer and my nose the flags that decorate the gateways; my mind is the lotus in the middle—and in this way all the parts of my body become the various parts of the divine mansion (Beyer, 1973: 72).

Between the microcosm of the subtle body and the macrocosm of the universe at large, resides what D. G. White (1996) calls the "mesocosm" of the mandala.[16] The mandala is a

---

15 Secret place: the root chakra, located in the perineum, between the anus and the sex organs.

16 D. G. White is not concerned with Tibetan mandalas, but with the mandalic fire-altars of ancient Hinduism and the alchemical vessels of the medieval Siddha tradition. Nevertheless, his term *meso-*

"psycho-cosmo-gram," an entity in itself which maps both the body and the greater cosmos. By means of the mesocosmic image, the body is brought into line with the cosmos; and the energy that surges through the universe, carrying the stars and planets on their courses, is the same kundalini that rises through the body, opening our eyes in a graded series of erotic trance states, as she activates the several chakras, each with its own physiology and psychology.

Only the emotional and physiological components of erotic trance that we have considered extensively in the first eight chapters of this book can account for the fact that the mandala of the divine palace becomes "real" enough for the monk that it can replace the empirical world during the course of the ritual. It is not merely the way we "see" things that must be rearranged. For the empirical world is truly compelling, and only a world that is equally compelling can convince us that the empirical world is not absolute. In the empirical world, for example, our life is at stake every time we cross a busy street or traverse a narrow mountain ridge. We cannot afford to let our minds wander and neglect the on-coming cars or the loose stones. Similarly, our sanity is at stake when the svadhisthana chakra opens in the lower abdomen. Our personal identity is at stake in the solar plexus, our feeling-connectedness in the heart center, our conceptualization of the world and ourselves at the throat chakra, and so on. Thus the mandala works as a mesocosm only when it is informed with the physiology and emotion that are rooted in the subtle body. According to the *Anguttara-nikaya* (II, 48), the Buddha himself preached this doctrine: "It is in this fathom-long carcass, friend, with its impressions and its ideas, that, I declare, lies the world, and the cause of the world, and the cessation of the world, and the course of action that leads to the cessation of the world" (Eliade, 1969: 179).

In this body lies the world and the cause of the world: It is, for example, the body's potential as seated spectator that gives rise to chairs and amphitheaters and the dramas that take place on stage. In this way the body as incarnate observer causes the empirical world to appear as object, set over against the subjective ego as other. In this body lies the cessation of the world and the course of action that leads to the cessation of the world: the subtle body which opens in distinctive ways in response to the rise of kundalini stops the world of subject/object empiricism. The subtle body reveals itself as participant in an energic process far greater than the world, where subject and object evaporate as the illusion they always were, when the spectator's chair is abandoned for the meditation mat. Then the body becomes the instrument whereby the energy of the macrocosm and that of the microcosm are recognized as one and indivisible.

---

cosm describes any such intermediate symbolic structure that maps the cosmos to the body and the body to the cosmos.

The mandala meditators seek to stop the world through a disciplined imagination that painstakingly creates a cosmic palace of the gods. It rivals the reality of the empirical world by calling on the physiological and emotional energy of kundalini rising through the body—a force as overwhelming and death-dealing to the ego as a car crash or an avalanche. In doing so, it reveals that what has been "stopped" is nothing but a conventional illusion, and what surges forth in its place is a power of far greater ultimacy; for it is the origin of the possibility of every world. It is the brahman or Shakti that can take any form and therefore is the ground of everything that *can* appear.

SUBTLE BODY AS MESOCOSM

Whether we start with the imaginal construct of a detailed mandala or with the physiological arousal of carezza, the body is the instrument by which the world is stopped. Some mystical schools, having recognized this fact, have dispensed with the mesocosmic palace of the gods and directed their attention to the subtle body itself. For them the subtle body—as the object of meditation—is itself the mesocosm. In fact the subtle body is a collection of mandalas. Every one of the chakras in Indian and Tibetan culture can be represented as a mandala, a lotus flower with a specific number of petals, each one bearing a Sanskrit letter or a seated divinity with a certain number of faces, arms, and ornaments. It is therefore possible to master the imagination by carefully constructing these four, seven, or twelve mandalas in our erotic trance. But it is also possible to pay attention to the "plumbing" through which kundalini rises: the sushumna nadi that describes the course of her ascent and the "spoked wheels" of the chakras where she spreads out in opening those bodily centers, and where she becomes indistinguishable from the kundalini of the cosmos as she flows out and in—a single energy, the stuff of consciousness that animates "my" subtle body and the universe at large.

In our efforts to familiarize ourselves with kundalini more intimately and in greater detail than the antinomian saints who are aware only of the life energy of the soul as it surges forth to face down the sexually disturbing figure of an enchanted or divine challenger so as to convert that challenge into worthy opposition—to transform the energy of sexual disturbance into worshipful consortship—we can find no better guide than one who has taken the subtle body's "plumbing" as the object of meditation. To this end we shall consider some of the details in Geshe Kelsang Gyatso's *Clear Light of Bliss* (1992). But before doing so we require some orientation; for I have found that several individuals to whom I have recommended Gyatso's book have seen only dry technical details. One angry woman pointed out to me that if this is a book about sexual mysticism, it is sadly lacking in that it fails to provide any reference to women. Even the icons on the cover and between each pair of chapters give us only the figure of an isolated man in meditation.

Again we require the guidance of a shameless and uninhibited teacher like Vimalananda. In effect, he tells us to hook up with a Bhairavi (or Bhairava) and behave with her like a vira so as to learn that kundalini will surge forth and "absorb her power." Although he does not remind us of this context on every page, Gyatso's position is not so different as it might seem. He says, in effect: Let's look at that instrument, the subtle body, that "hooks up" and "absorbs." If we allow ourselves to get lost in the details of Gyatso's book, it is possible to forget that his subtle body is hooking up with a Bhairavi.

The doctrine of the body as the instrument of liberation is universal in Tantra. For example, members of the Nath sect:

"advocate neither outer religious practices not scriptural knowledge. Their only emphasis is on a direct path, as short as possible, a way which the mystic discovers within himself, right in his own body—the privileged place for the experience of the Godhead, the energy, or the universe" (Silburn, 1988: 122).

The Pine Forest Myth of Shiva makes the same point:

"[Siva] sports with the daughters and the wives of the sages, with erect hair, a great penis, naked, with an excited look. He laughs, sings, dances charmingly, speaks like a madman, speaks sweetly, laughs horribly." A later text is more blunt: Siva violated a thousand sages' wives (O'Flaherty, 1973: 173).

The tragedy for the sages is that they need their wives as assistants in performing religious sacrifice. They have been blinded by their rituals and have not seen that it is in their bodies, which are their means of becoming "second Shivas," that realization takes place. Shiva says: "Those ascetics who lust for their wives' lotus mouths [vaginas] will worship my linga and do honor to me with their wives, and they will regain their sight" (O'Flaherty, 1973: 201).

THE SEXUAL INITIATION OF YESHE TSOGYEL

In one of the sacred texts of Tibetan Buddhism, which certainly informs Gyatso's meditation on the subtle body's "plumbing," the great female sexual mystic Yeshe Tsogyel describes her initiatory sexual union with her guru Pema Heruka. In this passage, lotus and vajra refer to vagina and penis, as well as to the mandala and the diamond body:

Then with three fingers stirring the pollen dust of the lotus, I offered my *mandala* to the *mandala* of the Guru's Body with an intense snake-like dance. The *mandala* of dynamic space having gathered into itself the nature of the Great Pema Heruka himself by means of the hook of the lower member's focal point, the Absolute Heruka, his magnificent flaming *vajra* in a state of rapacity and violent abuse, his wrinkles uncreased, projecting his full emanation, took command of the lotus throne with a roar of scornful laughter that flooded appearances with glory, transmuting them into pure pleasure. Thus he revealed to me the Mandala of the Blazing Sun of Radiant Inner Space, conferring his power upon me (Dowman, 1984: 40).

This is a fairly explicit passage. She stirs the "pollen dust" of her "lotus" with three fingers, and offers the mandala of her subtle body to his with a "snake-like dance" that personifies kundalini. She uses the physiology of sexual arousal to waken her kundalini through masturbation. She identifies with the kundalini that opens her abdominal chakra, thereby using the energy that terrifies those of us who feel victimized by an animal-like power we cannot control. In her erotic trance she allows the impersonal instinctuality of the svadhisthana chakra to enact the serpentine goddess's overwhelming intentions. Her ego is "out of the way." Kundalini is the life energy of her soul, and the Lady Yeshe has become the instrument of that power—not only for awakening herself but also her guru. The svadhisthana's opening dissolves the ego-erected barriers between them, so that it is no longer her "I" and his "you," but their "we" which opens as a "mandala of dynamic space."[17]

That "mandala" that opens up between them is the subtle plane, which becomes filled with "the nature of the Great Pema Heruka," presumably his essential being which is ageless and innocent of the wrinkles that bespeak the long biography of Pema's ego. All of this happens "by means of the hook of . . . his magnificent *vajra*," that is by the arousal of kundalini that not only makes his penis spring erect (its "wrinkles uncreased") but also wakens kundalini herself who "stops" the empirical world in favor of "the Blazing Sun of Radiant Inner Space." This is the mandala of the ultimate vision, that seen in the crown chakra—the universe as the macrocosmic orgasm that reflects their microcosmic bliss.

The lotus throne is Yeshe's vulva within which sits Heruka's vajra penis, unmoving as any of the lotus-sitting gods of a mandala palace. It is always the "Shiva" that is unmoving, while Shakti's nature is to move constantly with utter freedom. For her vibrations constitute the underlying energy which assumes all the forms that comprise the empirical world as well as all the forms that populate the subtle plane.

---

17 In a minor way, the various schools of psychoanalysis have recognized this phenomenon as "transitional space," the "interactive field," the intermediate realm where transference and countertransference are two aspects of the same unity.

The Lady Yeshe goes on to describe how each of her chakras were opened, her attachments destroyed, and a different mandalic palace of the gods opened before each one (Dowman, 40-1). Everything changes through that "roar of scornful laughter," that is, laugher at the puny illusions of the empirical world, revealing the "glory" that fills them when our subtle eyes are opened by the uprush of kundalini.[18] Simultaneously she sees all the mandalas that constitute her subtle body, each differentiated from the others by its unique vision of the subtle plane. Above all is the Blazing Sun of Radiant Inner Space, the view from her crown chakra. But her awareness of her subtle body is so refined that she misses none of the nuances. Every level of erotic trance—every lotus on the interior diamond ladder—is simultaneously present; and she sees it all in a glance as the monks who have become experts in mandala meditation see the entire palace of the gods in complete detail.

This sounds like an impossible achievement for any human being, regardless of the degree of her familiarity with erotic trance and her mastery of imagination. The reader may suspect we have fallen under the influence of another "Sun among exaggerators." In fact the life of Yeshe—although she was an historical individual, the favorite consort of Padma Sambhava, also known as Pema, the legendary/historical founder of Tibetan Buddhism in the eighth century—is a "revealed text," a *terma*. The Tantric yogin Taksham Nuden discovered it on the subtle plane a thousand years after Yeshe's death and employed all the literary devices of Tibetan hagiography in writing it down[19] (Dowman, 1984: xii-xvii). It has less "historical accuracy" than the New Testament. But is it an exaggeration worthy of Vimalananda? Does it possess an "emotional accuracy" that renders its historical exaggeration irrelevant? Again we have to look to the community that reveres the text to see that it has become a classic precisely because it articulates the goal of sexual yoga. Just as only a few mandala meditators can imaginally construct the palace of the gods at break-neck speed, so few if any mystical consort

---

18 A fuller description of "glory" occurs later in the book. Dowman translates the text as follows: "The one naked mind arising from within, the absolute Awareness of primal purity (which is the sameness of all phenomena) is all-pervasive, and dammed like a lake the golden-eyed fishes of heightened perception multiply. Sustaining the consummation of visionary experience and pleasure, on the wings of perfect creativity, running and jumping in the meadows of visionary appearances, you fly into the sky-matrix and vanish. In the immense space of absolute Awareness, the seed-essence of pure pleasure stands thick as a lake, Pure Being and Seed-Essence glisten and pulsate, and seed-syllables and light garlands sparkle and shimmer, the vision of reality manifest expands, intensive visionary experience increases and the castle of optimal Knowledge is finally seized." Dowman comments: "This is not only a poetical expression of the four visions; it is a metaphysical statement, and also precise instruction on the practice. Unfortunately the precision of the terminology is lost in translation . . ." (Dowman, 142).

19 Dowman finds evidence of several authors in the text he translated.

pairs can see the various levels of the subtle plane in a single glance. Nevertheless, it remains the goal and expresses what is theoretically possible for any human being who has mastered the imaginal dimension of erotic trance.

THE SUBTLE BODY AS LADDER

It is beyond my powers to analyze a single palace of the gods, much less a condominium tower of stacked residences. But even if I were to attempt such a thing, my analysis would surely exceed the patience of my readers. To understand the achievement of the subtle-body rung of the diamond ladder, we require a description much simpler than a series of mandala palaces, some way to see the subtle body as fitted out with rungs that can be recognized and distinguished from one another. For ladders are a universal metaphor for us. It is not only the mystics who speak in terms of ladders: for example, Jacob's vision in Genesis of a ladder between heaven and earth with angels ascending and descending; Muhammad's ascension through seven heavens to the presence of God; the *merkabah* ("throne" or "chariot") mystics of Judaism, who speak of the same graded ascent to the divine throne; the "states," and "stations" of the Sufi path; the levels of yogic trance states. We also see our everyday lives in terms of ladders: the steps of maturation; the stages of life; the rise of our careers; the hierarchy of a business or law firm; the "glass ceiling" that limits the rise of women and minorities. In all these cases a ladder tells us what to expect of ourselves and of our world and is useful to the extent we can recognize the rungs.

Thus, when it comes to the internal ladder of the subtle body, we need some relatively simple index for recognizing the stages of kundalini's arousal. For it is not enough to know that kundalini rises and changes our consciousness, we need to recognize the course of these changes in some detail. "Even more important than awakening Kundalini is learning how to direct it so that it remains at chosen centers of consciousness" (Ajaya, 1990: 100). In *The Clear Light of Bliss* (1992) Gyatso has recognized this. Indeed, he defines the subtle body as comprised of two elements. The first is the movement of an impersonal, spiritual force, the energy of kundalini, which he calls "a very subtle wind." This "wind" blows through the cosmos to animate it and blows as well through our bodies, where it activates the chakras. But the wind does not become a subtle *body* until it is recognized as such. We must appropriate that impersonal movement as stirring and flowing through *us*. We have to learn to recognize it, know where it is within us, and which direction it is moving. We have to have a "mentality" that is attuned to the movement of kundalini. This he calls our "very subtle mind": "Our subtle body is the very subtle wind upon which our very subtle mind is mounted" (Gyatso, 1992: 38). By "gathering" those subtle winds and "riding" them with our consciousness, we familiarize ourselves with the passageways and chakra-stations that comprise our subtle body—what I have called the "plumbing" of the subtle body.

> Mounted winds and the minds that mount them are inseparable, just like the body and its shadow, and so if the mind gathers within a vacuole inside the central channel the winds must also gather there. Strong and consistent practice of this meditation will cause the central channel gradually to open (Gyatso, 1992: 31).

Kundalini moves through the channels of our subtle body only when she is aroused. Her arousal generates "bliss," but in Gyatso's language mere bliss implies attachment. We become attached to the being who generates bliss in us, as anyone who has ever fallen in love knows very well. It requires no skill at all. Skillful practice—our familiarizing ourselves with our subtle body in all its details—is the means for transforming bliss into the spiritual path. Only the bliss-filled mind can ride the wind of kundalini. In this way our attachment reveals the movement of kundalini and enables us to "mount" it. Then comes the crucial transition: we detach ourselves from the blissful movement by making it the object of our meditation. By changing the standpoint of the observer from the saddled rider of the wind to a place outside, where the rider's movements can be followed as though presented on a movie screen, we turn the microcosm into a mesocosm. We dis-identify with the process and become its observer. This, too, is the goal expressed in the autobiography of Yeshe Tsogyel: "Desireless, blissful wisdom is the essence of all desirable goals, undistractedly going and coming in endless space" (Dowman, 1982: ix). As long as we remain attached to our bliss and distracted by its movements, we cannot go or come in endless space. We are stuck where we remain attached. Vimalananda puts the same idea into a challenge: "Try to enjoy sex without self-identification and you will see how hard it is" (Svoboda, 1997: 148).

HOOKING UP WITH A BHAIRAVI

Gyatso's book can be misunderstood if we forget how that bliss-attachment is actually achieved. He reveals the background of the practice in the introduction to the book and rarely refers to it again before the end. His entire effort is devoted to the exercises which enable the meditator to transform attached bliss into detached wisdom. Therefore, as I describe some of those exercises, I shall amplify them by recalling the context, to which Gyatso devotes only three sentences:

> In Action Tantra the meditator generates bliss by looking at a visualized goddess, and then transforms that bliss into the path. In Performance Tantra, the meditator generates bliss by

exchanging smiles with the goddess, and in Yoga Tantra by holding hands with her and so forth. In Highest Yoga Tantra the meditator generates bliss by imagining sexual embrace with a consort and, at advanced stages, by engaging in actual embrace; and then transforms that bliss into the spiritual path (Gyatso, 1992: 4).

Obviously the female practitioner will visualize a god, and the homosexual practitioner a divinity of the same sex. The gender of the imagined divinity is incidental. Nevertheless, for simplicity I shall continue to speak of goddesses.

Although Gyatso's language is highly restrained, he is clearly talking about sexual bliss and sexual attachment. Therefore the visualized goddess will have to resemble the one Vimalananda alludes to when he gives Svoboda instructions on how to attract a visualized "enchanted woman" and then resist her advances so as to attract the attentions of a goddess. Evidently goddesses are attracted only to the strongest of viras, only to those who have some chance of engaging with them as worthy opponents. For the goddess Vimalananda and Gyatso have in mind is clearly a sexual enchantress of formidable power. Very likely she is going to be naked with flying hair and dripping genitals. Engaging with her is a dangerous business. We need only recall how disorienting Muktananda's enchanted woman was for him—and he never referred to her as a goddess but only as a "girl."

Imagining a wanton goddess vividly enough that she stirs our kundalini and makes our penis burrow into our navel, as the girl in the red aura did for Muktananda, is already an exceptional achievement. We have to be well-established in the employment of erotic trance even to consider Gyatso's exercises. But if we are capable of invoking such an imaginal consort, Gyatso tells us how to conduct ourselves—something that Vimalananda leaves entirely to our undisciplined imagination. Vimalananda says that if we do not dare take that sexual goddess for our consort we must treat her as a mother. Gyatso never gives us that option. But at the same time he knows she is too much for us and gives us a graded series of steps in dealing with her.

When we first see her, the mere sight of her beauty and sexual excitement is enough to generate bliss in us; and that bliss implies attachment. Thus we begin Gyatso's meditation exercises with the intention of transforming that initial bliss at the sight of the goddess into detached wisdom. Only then are we able to exchange smiles with her. Exchanged smiles, as we know from our everyday experience, amounts to flirting and generates far more excitement than the mere sight of a potential partner. Thus, at the level of smiles we have to begin our work of detachment all over again. The kundalini generated within us has to be as potent as the disturbing energy generated by the flirtatious goddess if we are to neutralize her effects and transform the bliss she generates into wisdom. Thus it goes through hand-holding "and so forth." As it is a big jump from hand-holding to sexual embrace, we must imagine that

Gyatso's "and so forth" covers several discrete stages. For example, there might be hugging, kissing, and eventually Vimalananda's image of seating her on our left thigh with our hand on her left breast and her right hand on our penis.

Only after all these graded exercises with an imagined consort does the practitioner take up the bodily work of actual intercourse with a fleshly consort. In this final stage, direct bodily arousal with lips, tongue, hands, breasts, and genital organs fuels a physiological charge that precedes the work of imagination. In all the previous exercises, imagination is used to move our physiology. Even if we court the danger of being so turned aside into lust as to fall into Matsyendra's sleep in the Forest of Women's Thighs through our imaginal activities, imagination has always taken the lead. Now, if we are to engage in actual intercourse, we really put our mastery of imagination to the test. The ultimate goal of Gyatso's meditation exercises is to enable us to transform the bliss of actual, physical intercourse into the spiritual path. The imagined goddesses, the level of their sexual abandon carefully graded, are only preliminaries. Each stands on a separate rung of Gyatso's ladder, enticing the practitioner upward toward "Indra's Heaven." Like the Buddha, Gyatso seizes the arrow of our lust and turns it into the means of our mystical attainment.

MAHAMUDRA

Gyatso's *Clear Light of Bliss* describes the central meditative practice of Mahamudra, one of the highest teachings of the Tibetan Vajrayana tradition of Buddhism. Literally, *Mahamudra* means "great seal" (Fischer-Schreiber, *et. al.*, 1989). Dowman translates *Mahamudra* as "the Magnificent or Sublime Stance"; he calls it "the ultimate aim of all practitioners of the Tantras," and cites Drukpa Kunley as a prime exemplar of this realization (Dowman, 1988: 152). He says that the goal of the work is to attain the "free space wherein action is called Non-Action," which means to be "in such harmony with the universe that it requires no effort or striving; spontaneous and uninhibited, it transcends our concepts of work or activity" (Dowman, 1988, xxxiv).

Gyatso breaks down the discipline of Mahamudra into three fundamental goals: (1) the attainment of "Spontaneous Great Bliss," (2) the attainment of "emptiness," and (3) the union of Spontaneous Great Bliss with emptiness. "Spontaneous Great Bliss" refers to an emotional and physiological arousal of kundalini which has been transformed from attached bliss to detached wisdom. It is still "blissful" in the sense that it is an aroused state. It is, in fact, the sexual component in the practice of Vajrayana ("the diamond vehicle path") in Tibet.[20] Gyatso gives a brief history of Tibetan meditation, arguing that his method of "inner fire meditation" is the central doctrine in all Tibetan forms of Buddhism (Gyatso, 1992: 36). We shall follow Gyatso's instructions only as far as they concern the first goal of attaining Spontaneous Great Bliss; for this is the achievement distinctive to the subtle-body rung of the diamond ladder.[21]

What we have been calling the rise of kundalini that activates the subtle body from within, Gyatso calls "penetrating the channel wheels" (chakras) with "subtle winds." In his view, the subtle body is activated only when at least one chakra is open so that cosmic winds coming from the outside can penetrate it and fill the entire subtle body with their power. Gyatso thus refers to an experience that is not at all foreign to what we have considered. For example, when the abdominal chakra (or "navel channel wheel") opens like a camera eye, we feel that a powerful force beyond our capacity to resist invades us from the body of our partner. It seems too much for us and threatens to destroy our integrity, our sanity, and our propriety. It leaves us feeling naked and undefended. All the protective barriers have fallen between ourselves and our partner, and we are in danger of being torn apart by instinctual forces. When the heart chakra opens, we again feel penetrated by forces that have the quality of a wind or air. All is "sublimed," and the experience is not so dangerous-feeling. But the impression of being penetrated by a force from outside our own body is undeniable. Thus Gyatso pays attention to the experience of open chakras without imagining kundalini as a serpent that sleeps at the base of the spine and needs to be awakened. He considers her manifestation at the several chakras that comprise the rungs of the internal ladder and how, once inside, she moves up and down the central channel.

Although Gyatso's system involves ten chakras, most of the work deals with four of them: navel, heart, throat, and crown. These, he says, are the only ones where knots occur (Gyatso, 21). The brow chakra plays an important role near the end of the process of realizing Spontaneous Great Bliss.

The essential practice in attaining Spontaneous Great Bliss is the yoga of inner fire meditation (*tummo*), in which a flame is created in the navel center which rises up the central channel

---

20 The "diamond vehicle" is, of course the "diamond body," the ultimate means of attainment, and what we are calling the internal diamond ladder.

21 In the next chapter we shall pursue Spontaneous Great Bliss further by considering related traditions that transform sexual practice into an erotic trance in which we and our partner become a pair of copulating divinities. Volume Two, Chapter Four will take up the topic of emptiness (Gyatso's second goal) through considering other traditions; and Volume Two, Chapter Five will take up Gyatso's highest goal (again through other traditions) of uniting Spontaneous Great Bliss with emptiness.

and melts the "drops" (i.e., opens the chakras) at the heart, throat, and crown. *Tummo* (also written *tumo* and *tunmo*) which means "Fierce One," is usually a "wrathful Heroine," i.e., a fiercely sexual goddess (Gyatso, 35). It is the Tibetan equivalent of kundalini. The wrathful heroine is the wanton divinity that Vimalananda warns us about, advising that we treat her as a mother if we believe we are not prepared for her to become our consort. Gyatso's method provides another means of taming the wrathful one. It directs our attention away from the imaginal goddess to the effects she creates within our subtle body: the flame that results in the navel chakra. Gyatso thereby reverses our natural tendency to stand before her in aroused horror, feeling our navel chakra yawning uncontrollably open and threatening to rip us to shreds. In effect Gyatso urges us to stop dancing around that crater of terror and pain, wondering how to stop a force that is greater than we are. He urges us to plunge right into its center and become one with the flame that wrathful heroine generates within us. Stop riveting your gaze on the challenger, and pay attention to the process that is going on within you.

To that end, we have to familiarize ourselves with the subtle body and its central channel (sushumna) in particular. For in normal consciousness, the winds travel through the side channels (ida and pingala) and generate the "gross thoughts" by which we construct the empirical world. Erotic trance occurs only when the winds move within the central channel. Then our gross thoughts and the empirical world they create are stopped, and we enter upon the subtle plane (Gyatso, 31). We might well recall in this context the woman described in the previous chapter who had to learn the hard way that just because the visions are *true* does not mean they should be taken "literally." What she might have realized as belonging to the subtle plane, she tried to apply "literally" to the empirical world; and this unhinged her, resulting in a couple of weeks of apparent psychosis. Gopi Krishna's problems very likely resulted from the same failure to distinguish clearly between the subtle plane of the central channel and the empirical world of the side channels. Note that the imagery of channels is a way of "anatomizing" states of consciousness. The anatomy of the subtle body is the mesocosm that "maps" the various levels of erotic trance and contrasts them with profane thinking.

INNER FIRE MEDITATION, PRELIMINARIES

Inner fire meditation begins with fairly standard preliminaries, including a mandala meditation in which one's "root guru"[22] occupies the central position, and a Buddhist prayer of intention to perform the inner fire meditation successfully for the liberation of all beings. After

---

22 The root guru is apparently the historical/legendary figure responsible for having developed the particular sadhana (spiritual practice) that one is following.

this, the mandala is dissolved into the root guru who is brought through the crown to the heart chakra, where he "dissolves into the indestructible wind and indestructible mind inside the indestructible drop in the center of the heart channel wheel" (Gyatso, 38). In short, we begin by identifying with the author of our tradition, who takes up residence within our heart chakra, which is our own home-base within the subtle body.

After some breathing exercises, the first task of Gyatso's method is to familiarize ourselves with the subtle body that is comprised essentially of channels, the "plumbing" through which the "mounted winds" travel. First the gross body is reduced in imagination to a transparent empty shell:

> First we regard our body as being in its normal form—made of skin, flesh, bone, blood, and so forth—and then we strongly imagine that all the contents of our body melt into light and gradually disappear into emptiness, leaving only our skin like an empty shell. Once this meditation is stable we imagine that our skin becomes clear and transparent, without any physical resistance, like a rainbow (Gyatso, 43).

Next the subtle body itself is carefully constructed in the imagination, beginning with the central channel. We may begin by seeing it as thick as an arm, but then it should be reduced gradually in size until it is "the width of a drinking straw." When the visualization of the central channel and two side channels has become stable for us, we begin to construct the chakras, each with a precise number of "spokes" or secondary channels. We begin with the heart chakra, which is always our home-base.

> We imagine that if we were to turn on a light it would shine down the corridors of the eight spokes of the heart channel wheel. We look down these spokes carefully, inspecting each one closely, and then conclude, "Now I have seen the eight petals of the heart channel wheel clearly" (Gyatso, 45-6).

Once we have the entire subtle body stable in our imagination, we proceed to "correct all the defects in the spokes," making them "smooth, soft, and supple" (Gyatso, 48).

Gyatso says that this training in clearly seeing the plumbing of the subtle body is very much like visiting a museum in which we systematically study all the rooms and exhibits, always returning to our starting point (the heart chakra) until we have the entire building in all its detail firmly in our memory (Gyatso, 50-1). In doing so, he clearly reveals the mesocosmic role of the subtle body. It is no longer something we imagine to be merely "inside us." Rather we reverse this common-sense point of view and take up residence within it. Our subtle body becomes an imaginal palace whose grand staircase is the central channel, and whose palatial rooms are the chakras. The movement of kundalini within this palace becomes a "wind" that we "mount" and ride. Kundalini is no longer a vague and uncontrollable force surging through us in response to the threat of a wrathful and wanton heroine challenging us from without. Kundalini's movements become tractable when we learn how to ride and direct them. What kundalini does to us takes on a spatial significance, where the architecture of the subtle body becomes a kind of index for the level of her arousal. Precisely imagining a subtle body amounts to creating an alchemical vessel within which the forces of transformation can be controlled, slowed down, and pin-pointed with accuracy.

As we take up residence within the subtle body, we are very tiny, indeed. We are inside a drop which is inside a vacuole at the very center of the heart chakra, where the central channel runs through. We can see down to the navel center, where a fire blazes, and up through the throat chakra to the sahasrara, where a white drop of nectar hangs from the very crown of the head. The heart seems to be an ideal location. It is above the diaphragm and therefore curiously removed from the instinctual tumult of the lower chakras. And the upper chakras are too rarefied. Only in the heart chakra can we relate equally well to the sublime and the earthly.

INNER FIRE MEDITATION, AROUSAL

To view that flirtatious goddess who stirs our kundalini, we descend the translucent tube of the central channel to the vacuole at the center of the navel chakra. By placing our consciousness in the navel, we concentrate all the kundalini energy the wrathful beauty has stirred up in the anatomical region where we feel the danger, instinctual force, and fragmenting terror of the challenge. We are a vira, for we brave the challenger head-on. But we do not look directly at the seductive one. We let a more fleshly set of eyes take care of that detail. Instead, we pay attention to what is happening right here in the basement of our mansion. Rays of energy are streaming through the "spokes" of the navel channel wheel and converging with terrifying force upon the very vacuole in which we are sitting. It bursts into flame. We hasten back to the safety of the heart chakra. From our home-base vantage, it appears that a column of fire is rising up the central channel from below, and we know that it will eventually reach us.

The fire in the belly expresses very accurately the unhinging power of kundalini, as she is felt when we identify with our fleshly body and fear we may lose all control. Fire burns and destroys, but it also generates usable energy. If we were to stay in the navel, we would very likely be burnt alive—at least in the sense that we would lose our sanity. Undoubtedly, we spend most of our time in the drawing room of the heart chakra because it is far enough from the furnace that we can feel the heat without risking our destruction. The disembodied sublimity of the heart chakra allows us to feel the effects of kundalini in a rather blissful way. Kundalini changes us more gently.

Outwardly, the heart chakra is the region in which we find our union with that wrathful deity takes place primarily in the realm of feeling. People have described this to me in almost the same words I have used to describe it to myself. It is as though the two of us are comprised of mist. We enter one another in such a way that the molecules and droplets of our separate mists become thoroughly mixed into a single body of mist. The terror of being torn apart that belongs to the navel chakra no longer applies at the heart chakra. Some resistance has melted within us, and this is symbolized by the softening of the drop in the center of the heart chakra.

As the column of fire slowly rises below us, we feel the drop which surrounds us warm and soften. This opens the spokes of the heart channel wheel, and energy from the goddess streams in, focused right on the drop in which we sit. While our more fleshly body is experiencing the whirling fans of light and blissful union, we remain focused on the events taking place in the drawing room of the heart. The column of flame has encircled the drop, which is becoming more and more subtle. We seize our opportunity to mount the fiery wind of kundalini and ride to the throat and crown chakras.

Already we can begin to appreciate the advantage of imaginally constructing an interior palace of translucent tubing. We place different sorts of feelings in different rooms. We begin to sort out the emotional chaos brought on by the disturbing divinity. We allow our erotic trance to be driven by the flaming force of physiological arousal, and then because the several chakras are so refined in what they admit, we can tour our inner mansion and see how our favorite rooms have been transformed. In the heart we sort out feelings, in the throat make conceptual sense of them.

We have distinguished imagination from feelings and emotions, perhaps giving the impression that mastering the one might have nothing to do with the other. Now we see that the way of the antinomian hero does not need to be a crude facing down of force with force. True enough, heroes have to stand up to wrathful divinities. But when they do so, they need not remain unconscious of how kundalini is changing them. If they will imaginally construct a sort of distillation device such as Gyatso's tubular palace, they can begin to familiarize themselves with the various components of that emotional dragon that rears up within them as a sinuous column of fire.

To climb the interior diamond ladder—at least as high as the throat chakra—is to imagine a device (the tubing of the subtle body) to differentiate emotion and then make sense of it. In this sense it resembles the "cat-cracking towers" we use in the refinement of petroleum. Crude petroleum is viscous and sludgy because it is comprised of long multiply branched molecules that fail to disentangle quickly enough to pour easily. In this regard it is not unlike the undifferentiated emotion of raw kundalini as it is felt in the navel chakra. The raw petroleum is heated with catalysts[23] which "crack" the big molecules into smaller ones, which then vaporize and stream into the vertical tube of the "cat-cracking tower"—the heaviest ones settling near the bottom and the lightest rising to the top. Refiners separate the various components by relative size when they draw off the vapors at different levels of the tower. Gyatso's tubular palace works in precisely the same way, breaking emotional chaos down into its smaller and lighter components which are drawn off selectively in the several rooms of the internal mansion.

The difference between the refinement of emotion and that of petroleum, however, is that nothing leaves the system of the subtle body. Nothing is drawn off. The rooms are part of a single laboratory apparatus that lets nothing escape. What we learn in the heart chakra we take with us as we ascend to the throat. D. G. White (1996: 245-62) presents overwhelming evidence that the Hindu alchemists of the Middle Ages conceived of the subtle body's plumbing as a pair of long-necked flasks joined together at their mouths. The resultant long tube with a bulb at either end was sealed with rags and mud, which were said to represent the fleshly body. Just like the Western alchemists, they required a *vas bene clausum*, a well-closed vessel.[24] Kundalini is not to escape, either through ejaculation or through emotional tumult. Even saintly madness implies a squandering of valuable erotic energy. Every molecule of kundalini, from the most subtle to the most gross, is to be folded into the work.

INNER FIRE MEDITATION, NECTAR

Gyatso's tubular palace is a more elaborate apparatus than the medieval Hindu alchemist's pair of long-neck flasks. But it works pretty much the same way. This becomes particularly clear when we ride the hot wind of kundalini to the crown. Because none of her heat has been lost, kundalini can melt the white drop in the sahasrara until it begins to drip down the central channel in a long glistening strand "like the thread of a spider's web" (Gyatso, 67)—or perhaps like a delicate thread of prostatic fluid with a tiny drop bulging at the bottom. We who have learned to ride the wind of kundalini can also ride that drop down the central channel, as slowly as we wish to let it go. When we do so, we find that it brings joy to each chakra, a different quality of joy in each case. Gyatso fails to tell us what this joy is like. We are led

---

23 Catalyst: hence the "cat" in "cat-cracking."

24 The *vas bene clausum* is a major theme in Jung's writings on alchemy, in which he sees the analytic hour as the Bunsen burner to effect changes by heating up the patient's psyche. Ideally the patient and analyst will "contain" the emotions generated so as to learn from them. For example, discussing the work with third parties can let off too much steam.

to conclude that it adds an ineffable something to each chakra as it descends. A more refined form of kundalini enlarges and intensifies our experience at the levels of the throat and heart. When it slowly stretches down to the region of the navel, it catches fire and fuels a roaring blaze in our mansion's furnace.

The medieval alchemists said that semen, whose course is reversed through the practice of vajroli, rises through the tube of their subtle body just as vapors rise in their laboratory apparatus. When it reaches the crown, it is transformed into nectar through the copulation of Shiva and Shakti. As nectar drips down to the throat and heart, it brings bliss. If their two-bulbed tube was really a "well-closed vessel," nectar must have added to the solution that was heated in the lower bulb, and transformed the upward flow as it vaporized. Such, certainly, is the effect in Gyatso's inner palace. As nectar feeds the fire in the navel chakra, we can ride up the central channel more vigorously and experience yet another nuance at the heart and throat as we rise. For the flame is enriched with nectar. This time, however, we cause kundalini's sinuous fire to loop around the drop in the crown chakra and continue on as the central channel bends forward and down toward the brow chakra.[25] Here, at the third eye, the flame that begins at the navel gives rise to the vision of a great mandala in which all the Buddhas are seen as coupled heroes and heroines "in single-pointed embrace" (68).

Surely Padma Sambhava (Pema Heruka) and his favorite consort, Yeshe Tsogyel, will be among those naked copulating heroes and heroines, for Padma Sambhava is the most important Buddha (enlightened being) Tibet has known. Probably they are the central couple in a sexual chakra ceremony of coupled divinities. The vision we enjoy when we ride the fiery wind of kundalini to the ajna chakra resembles very closely that testimony from Promode Chatterjee we saw in the first chapter of Volume One. Chatterjee had the privilege of being witness to an Aghora sexual chakra performance that took place in a cremation ground (smashan) during a thunder storm. He was very impressed with the holiness, sweetness, and ecstasy of the event; and, then near the end, a flash of lightning revealed the divinity of the scene: "light-figures of naked gods and goddesses in the midst of their divine play, surrounding a large statue of Hara and Gauri, as still and profound as the Himalayas" (McDaniel, 1989: 124). This vision that greets us from the observation deck of the subtle body's third eye is undoubtedly a variation on what the Buddha's half-brother, Nanda, observed when he was transported to Indra's Heaven.

---

25 This is clearly a different arrangement of the chakras than we have considered. Hindu Tantra generally prefers to place the *ajna* chakra on the central channel between the throat and the crown, while Buddhist Tantra places it on an extension of the central channel, which turns at the crown chakra and then proceeds down the front of the face—more in keeping with the laboratory discoveries of Lee Sannella and Itzhak Bentov.

SPONTANEOUS GREAT BLISS

In Gyatso's account, we watch this mandalic scene of divine sexual union with intense interest, as one by one, the couples experience great bliss and melt into light. The separate drops of light melt into a single one that we draw into the third eye and ride up the central channel back to the crown chakra. There it dissolves into the drop of nectar hanging from our crown so that it becomes "completely identified with the essence of all the Heroes and Heroines" (Gyatso, 68). The vision of a divine subtle plane of sexual union informs and gives new meaning to what formerly was undifferentiated nectar. Only now that we have enriched the nectar with divine vision do we allow the fiery wind of kundalini to melt the drop. The elastic springiness of the glistening thread with its tiny, bulging drop at the end allows the unification of all the blissfully coupled Buddhas to bring great "joy" to the throat and heart centers and a huge increase of heat at the navel (Gyatso, 69).

However, now that the drop of nectar has been "distilled" through its contributions to each of the four main chakras and has been enriched with divine vision, we take it beyond the navel, all the way out to the end of the sex organ, where we hold it steady (Gyatso, 102). Although Gyatso does not say so, his account seems to imply that this is the moment when, in our intercourse with an actual or imaginal partner, we reach the stage of an "internal orgasm." For, in the practice of semen retention, it does seem as though the semen charges down the seminal ducts and out the urethra to poise precariously at the inner tip of the penis. At this crucial moment, if we are able to hold back from an explosive orgasm, ejaculation is stopped at the last possible moment, holds steady at the tip of the penis, and pauses there for what seems to be an eternal instant of motionlessness before "internal spasms" occur in the urethra. These spasms are called "internal" because they do not result in the discharge of semen. They mark the passing of the crisis, after which it seems as though the charge of semen begins to withdraw.

It is reasonable to think that Gyatso refers precisely to this male experience which occurs only during the practice of carezza. One feels that a tube that runs through the body and ends in the penis has closed down at the tip at the last possible moment; and after the crisis of an internal orgasm, the substance that fills the tube retreats. If vajroli does not actually amount to a "sucking up" of sexual fluids with the penis, the sensations just described would be a sufficient explanation for why the sexual/mystical practices of the Orient have generated the conviction that it does.[26]

---

26 In a more precarious experience even that the one just described, it is possible for both the man and the woman to detect a tiny emission of semen at the moment of the crisis, which is followed by the internal spasms which give the impression that the penis has reversed the flow. This set of

This means that the fiery wind of kundalini, after having united the divine vision with nectar, brings the substance of bliss to the very end of the penis where it is charged with the energy of an internal orgasm. The nectar of spiritual realization, now informed by the divine vision and charged with the ecstasy of orgasm, is ridden up the central channel of the subtle body, where it brings Spontaneous Great Bliss to each chakra. Each room of the internal palace experiences Spontaneous Great Bliss in its own unique manner (Gyatso, 102-3). Spontaneous Great Bliss combines the vision of the divine subtle plane with the raw energy of sex.

INNER FIRE MEDITATION, SUMMARY

This alchemical transformation of divinity with sex and sex with divinity is made possibly only when we detach from the wrathful and wanton divinity that disturbs us, and place our one-pointed attention on the changes she effects in our subtle body. The changes in us are at least as real as she is. But when our attention is attached to her, we remain ignorant of what is happening within ourselves. Gyatso directs our attention to the imaginal palace of our subtle body, where we can watch the disturbances generated by kundalini as if under a microscope. We find that new possibilities emerge as each chakra opens; and we find that each new level of experience we become familiar with adds to our experience of the others.

For those of us who have not practiced inner fire meditation, the process may seem all too abstract. But analogies are readily available. Note the difference, for example, between the terrifying panic that attends the first opening of the navel chakra and how this same energy becomes sublime when it has risen to the level of the heart. Once we have become familiar with this transition, our next meeting with the fierce consort who affects us so strongly will no longer be attended by such a frightening opening of the navel chakra. Our familiarity with kundalini has grown, and the sublime associations gained at the heart chakra will not be missing when the navel opens again. Now it opens with a warm, insistent vibration that corresponds very well to Yeshe Tsogyel's claim that she offered the mandala of her subtle body to the mandala of her guru.

The same sort of transition occurs when the brow chakra has opened and we have seen our consort as a divinity. I do not refer to perceptions of beauty and goodness, for these—impor-

---

natural impressions might well account for the wide-spread belief in sexual mysticism that commingled male and female fluids are absorbed by the penis. Vimalananda's words concerning the vajroli contest should be remembered in this context: "She releases a little of her secretion to him, just enough to lubricate his prostate; he releases just enough of his prostate fluid to rejuvenate her" (Svoboda, 1986: 288).

tant as they are—belong to the solar plexus. When we perceive our partner as a divinity, we are gripped by the reflex to worship. We have passed beyond the personal. When, after this, kundalini subsides to the level of the heart, the experience of the sublime has a new divine quality. The intermingling mists of the heart center are flavored with coupled divinities.

Gyatso, unfortunately, does not speak of these things. He is interested only in teaching us the technique of mounting the winds of kundalini and riding her up and down the central staircase of the subtle-body palace. He leaves it to us to learn what these things feel like. In the end this may be the best solution, for anticipating what an experience should be can interfere with our having it.

For example, Günter Nitschke (1995), a follower of Osho, otherwise known as the Bhagwan Shree Rajneesh, gives an overly simplified adaptation of Gyatso's meditation practice that makes no mention of the tubular palace. Perhaps this is the reason Nitschke's distinctions between the several states of consciousness we are considering seems vague and at times contradictory. Thus, when he describes an experience he calls an opening of the heart chakra, we may wonder whether it might more likely have been his throat, or brow that opened.[27] Nevertheless, it seems that something monumental did in fact occur:

> "I" disappeared and for the first time in my life "was." All that remained was the whole universe in the form of a dark-blue starry night-sky with one central red spot. The overall sensation was one of being bigger than the universe or at one with it, of liberation from my separate existence, from death (Nitschke, 1995: 38).

This was surely a little bit of enlightenment, the realization that an erotic trance was possible in which a vista "bigger than the universe" informed him of the smallness and illusory nature of the empirical world. But he confesses that it also became a block to his further progress. He waited in vain for this experience to occur again instead of remaining open to whatever might appear upon the subtle plane. It may be that Gyatso wants to avoid blocking our spontaneous experience of bliss by refusing to tell us what it feels like to him.

If so, I have perhaps corrupted the clean abstract lines of his book by identifying with the tiny inhabitant of the tubular palace and recounting my imaginal experience upon ascending and descending the central ladder. My account is much more vivid than his. He goes for pages and pages without mentioning the fierce and wanton goddess that appears to be central to his method. He dryly presents a series of imaginal exercises that are so abstract that the careless reader might well conclude that kundalini is raised not through an encounter with a wrathful deity but by "pure meditation"—setting up a standing wave in the aorta. If many of

---

27 He identifies the experience with his heart chakra on the authority of Osho, but reports no supportive evidence based in bodily sensations that accompany the opening.

his followers, however, have relied entirely upon a standing wave generated by the absolute stillness of sitting in meditation, Gyatso's references to wrathful heroes and heroines make it clear that doing the work without a wrathful opponent would function as a sort of preliminary exercise, a pursuit of "the first qualification." For there can be little doubt that the goal of inner fire meditation on the interior tubular palace is eventually to be used in the course of actual sexual intercourse with a fleshly but highly accomplished consort. *Tummo*, the Tibetan word that means both "inner fire" and "wrathful Heroine," (1) begins in sexual arousal, (2) adds the attainment of nectar, (3) informs that nectar with a vision of the divine subtle plane of ecstatic sexuality, and (4) completes the process with the orgasmic energy of a fully realized internal orgasm.

THE CONQUEST OF DEATH

These four elements lead to Spontaneous Great Bliss—a topic we shall pursue further in the next chapter by examining the mystical consorts' experience of divinization. But Spontaneous Great Bliss is only the first of three goals, the others being the achievement of emptiness and combining emptiness with Spontaneous Great Bliss. But even this third achievement, as abstract as it may be for us at this point, is not the end of the Mahamudra practice. For Gyatso, the purpose of building the tubular palace and becoming intimate with kundalini is so that he can ride out of his physical body at the moment of death upon the fiery life energy of his soul. To ride into death on the reptilian head of kundalini means liberation from the endless round of uncontrolled reincarnations, and gives to the enlightened being an extraordinary choice. Either she can attain Indra's Heaven for eternity, or she can choose the route of the Bodhisattva: to return to another incarnation as an enlightened one, a Buddha, and work for the liberation of all beings.

Those who learn to ride into death on the head of kundalini have, first, to be able to generate Spontaneous Great Bliss while alive and awake. But this is only the beginning of their work. Their next task is to learn to perform the same imaginal, emotional, and physiological task of riding kundalini while asleep. For this, they need to develop the throat chakra, which Gyatso claims enables the practitioner to obtain a deep and long sleep quickly and to have vivid dreams (Gyatso, 32). These are the necessary conditions for the practice of inner fire meditation while asleep. To be able to generate Spontaneous Great Bliss in one's sleep, then, amounts to a training exercise for the ultimate moment of death.

Thus Gyatso's method has to be seen in the context of *The Tibetan Book of the Dead* (Evans-Wentz, 1960), where the imaginal scenes (*bardos*) that threaten to trap the dying soul are read over the body of the deceased to raise the consciousness of the discarnate soul which is believed to be hovering in the vicinity of its putrefying body for several days after death. Obviously to recognize the moment of death as an opportunity implies an attitude completely foreign to profane consciousness and requires a formidable mastery of erotic trance. Recognizing a passing moment as an opportunity has been expressed vividly by Carlos Castaneda (1972) in his phrase "the cubic centimeter of chance." Life presents us with countless variations on our cubic centimeter of chance, whose ultimate moment is death. For example, the moment of waking from sleep and the moment of falling asleep each present us with a "cubic centimeter" of contentless thought which can be used to realize that we are not the empirical ego which talks to itself incessantly about the empirical world and the persona field's obsession with survival. There is also an empty moment between each pair of thoughts our ego entangles itself in. If we are attentive, we can catch that centimeter moment and use it to stop our internal monologue and the world it tirelessly sustains. When we work in waking life to catch hold of these countless cubic centimeters of chance, we are preparing for the ultimate opportune moment, the one our whole life is directed toward, the instant of death.

To become conscious in minute detail of what orgasmic bliss effects within us; to detach ourselves from the crude impressions of physical orgasm as they are felt in our genital organs and chakras; and to convert that ordinary bliss into detached wisdom: these sublime intentions of the Vajrayana tradition certainly introduce us to the spiritual potential of sex. If we thought Bregman (1982) expressed a wise skepticism regarding the alleged spirituality of "liberated orgasm," Gyatso shows us why she was right. If we wondered about the authentic spirituality of the mad saints and the antinomian heroes, Gyatso has given us a dependable yardstick for judging the spirituality of sexual practitioners. Indeed, it is possible for the psychic re-organization of the mad saints and antinomian heroes to stop at the level of the manipura chakra in the solar plexus, where one's eyes are opened to one's "essential being." Gyatso, however, bases all of his achievements upon the condition of our being able to sustain a lengthy habitation in the heart chakra; and his espousal of inner fire meditation during the state of sleep implies our gaining real familiarity with the throat chakra as well. In the last analysis, these are the reasons why turning to the internal ladder and learning to negotiate it takes us beyond the rung of scandal to that of the subtle body.

3

INTERCOURSE OF GOD AND GODDESS

Although at this point we have little idea what Spontaneous Great Bliss feels like, several principles have been discovered. (1) Tantra aims to give a powerful boost to spiritual practice by drawing upon sexual arousal. (2) Arousal itself is taken as the object of meditation. (3) Meditation employs the imaginal construct of the subtle body to "distill" arousal into its emotional and imaginal components and have them "condense" in the separate chakras. (4) Retaining the arousal intensifies and transmutes it in two ways designated by mysterious images: (a) Rising kundalini is said to melt a drop of nectar which falls through the chakras bringing them joy and heat. (b) The nectar itself is augmented when it becomes "imprinted" with the vision of a blissful and precise orgy taking place in "Indra's Heaven." (5) Spontaneous Great Bliss is generated when the imprinted nectar is boosted with an internal orgasm.

Gyatso's inner fire meditation very clearly expresses the essential nature of yogic practice, the "de-conditioning" of the ego.[28] He takes our attention away from the object that would naturally rivet us in a mixture of terror and lust and has us focus on the emotion itself, on the whole field of awareness that is occupied by that trembling lust. Forget status, possession, and loss. That wanton goddess is bound to leave you in ruins before she turns tail and reduces you to a raving mad saint. Your attitudes about her are illusory, but what she does to you is real. Pay attention to that, for that is who you are.

Yoga—whether it employs sexual practices or not and whether it is to be found in Hinduism, Buddhism, Taoism, or elsewhere—is always intent upon stopping the socially construed world. Miranda Shaw calls Buddhism "a strategy for deconstructing the unenlightened ego," and *Tantric* Buddhism "a means for men and women to deconstruct their conventional selves *together*" (Shaw, 1994:203). This "deconstruction" amounts to eliminating the distinction "between subject and object, between I and not-I" (Evola, 1992: 17).

---

28 "With a vigor unknown elsewhere, India has applied itself to analyzing the various conditionings of the human being . . . in order to learn how far the conditioned zones of the human being extend and *to see if anything exists beyond these conditionings*"(Eliade, 1969: xvi-xvii).

Gyatso, like all the other sources we have considered, finds sexual arousal gives yoga an indispensable boost. Nothing reveals the mutual implications of physiology and awareness better than sex. Nothing is more effective at disorienting our ego and consensus assumptions than a mixture of terror and desire. This is where we live. Start here. Vimalananda is characteristically emphatic: "Rather than seek to extirpate their emotions as Yogic practitioners do, Tantrics magnify their emotions and transfer them entirely to a deity, a personified cosmic force" (Svoboda, 1986: 14). Shaw quotes the Tibetan master, Tsongkhapa (1357-1419): "Bliss is gathered by passion. Therefore, unite profusely. One attains [realization] by virtue of being passionate; otherwise, spiritual ecstasy will not arise" (Shaw, 1994: 169; Shaw's brackets). These texts make it clear that sexual arousal is being employed as a tool that provides a huge boost of energy to the deconstruction project.

The translator of Yeshe Tsogyel's adventures in eighth century Tibet, Keith Dowman, says, "Strip *yoga* of its arcane terminology and there is a simple meditation technique; stimulate desire and then use it as the object of meditation and it becomes Awareness" (Dowman, 1984: 249). Here is how the tool is used. Once consensus reality has been called into question by a strong arousal that sends us into erotic trance, the practitioner of sexual yoga directs attention away from merely bodily arousal to our erotic consciousness, our "desire." It is natural and naive for us to attend to the individual who has aroused us or to our bodily tension that seeks immediate release. These disturbances in our consensus-world functioning distract us from the proper object of meditation, our aroused consciousness. For only meditating on what is effected in us through the arousal will enable us to elevate mere human pleasure to "bliss." In tenth century Kashmir, the man who described the feces-smeared Trighantika, Abinavagupta, scorned that exalting brute for thinking there was anything of truly transcendental power in sexual fluids and feces. He directed Tantra's gaze inward—away from material manifestations of arousal—to the consciousness itself that has been aroused (D. G. White, 1996: 136-8). Abhinavagupta says:

> [As to those] who have not increased their virile efficacy within and do not leave any room to the pleasure of the God of love, they remain like rocks when facing a beautiful maid and hearing her melodious sound, deprived as they are of inebriation and bliss.
>
> . . . Lack of virility is lack of life, lack of the power to wonder (Silburn, 1988: 161).

To counteract the male bias in Gyatso and Abhinavagupta, we might consider the teachings of a female guru from eighth century Tibet, Sahaja-yogini-cinta (Spontaneous Yogini Who is Like a Jewel). Her very name includes the word *spontaneous* (*sahaja*), the essential element in Spontaneous Great Bliss. Spontaneous Jewellike Yogini teaches that "ecstasy is inseparable from embodiment and embodiment is inseparable from gender" (Shaw, 1994: 183). "Spontaneous" bliss depends upon gendered sexuality:

> In order that one may realize one's inner state,
>
> Which is spontaneous (*sahaja*), naturally pure, and nondual,
>
> The inner self manifests here as man and woman.
>
> One's own self, creative by nature,
>
> Enacts reality through bodily expressions (Shaw, 1994: 183).

Sahajayoginicinta was the daughter of a noble or merchant family, possibly a court retainer, courtesan, or dancer, who had a Buddhist education. At some point, however, she left high society to become the consort of a low-caste pig farmer (Shaw, 191). She relinquished the standards of consensus reality for a consort with whom she could transform arousal into bliss. The text she composed, "Realization of Reality through Its Bodily Expressions," was evidently taught to a group of Tantric women who were by no means novices (Shaw, 193).

> Like the jewel that is her namesake, the illustrious yogini has many facets. She is a visionary revealer of Tantric teachings received in a deep meditative state. She is a skilled rhetorician who dazzles her audience with a sensuous and exuberant vision of Tantric sexuality. She is a skilled homileticist who motivates her audience to religious discipline, exhorting them that worldly pleasures are impermanent and ultimately unsatisfying. She is a subtle philosopher who spins and unravels the theoretical intricacies of her position. The women in her audience were rewarded for their attendance at her discourse by a striking and perhaps unique portrait of how a Buddha responds to passion, expresses love and desire, and engages in the transcendental pastime of erotic play (Shaw, 1994: 192-3).

Spontaneous Jewellike Yogini describes the standard practice of yogic intercourse (maithuna) in which the male Buddha stands or sits unmoving as the female Buddha wraps her limbs about his body, kissing him "with a variety of kisses," and generating "intense bliss" through her constant movement. They gently scratch one another to prevent "drowsiness and ordinary passion." The goal is to overcome "the subject-object dualism of ordinary experience until "one ceases to know who is the other and what has happened to oneself." They are "mindful only of pleasure" (Shaw, 186-7). This "human pleasure" or "bodily bliss" is taken as the "support" or "object" of meditation in order to elevate it out of the profane realm of experience and bring it to the transcendent sphere:

> Human pleasure, with its identifiable characteristics,
>
> Is the very thing that,

When its characteristics are removed,

Turns into spiritual ecstasy,

Free from conceptual thought,

The very essence of self-arising wisdom

(Shaw, 1994: 188).

Spontaneous Jewellike Yogini reveals the essence of Gyatso's practice. The sensual pleasure of sexuality and the spiritual goal of sadhana are only apparently opposed. The spiritual object can be reached through anything, but especially anything that arouses us and leads us by erotic trance onto the subtle plane. "The senses no longer desire to wander in the desolate cities created by hunger and desire when they can be opulently entertained in palaces spun of bliss and luminosity" (Shaw, 1994: 188).

Eight centuries later and thousands of miles to the West, Pico della Mirandola arrived at a very similar conclusion, which he referred to as the *mors osculi* ("death by kiss"). By "death," he meant "corporal extinction" in a state of erotic trance that he called "intellectual ecstasy." The partners' kiss enacts the ecstatic union by which they pass beyond profane existence and attain spiritual realization (Couliano, 1986: 57). There is another strange parallel between Tibetan Buddhist spirituality and the Italian Renaissance. Pico belonged to a tradition that employed imaginal mansions. The discipline of constructing and maintaining a complex internal building filled with rooms and passageways was used as an aid to superior feats of memory. Every item to be remembered was placed in a specific location within a specific room of the mansion so that the practitioner had only to walk through the internal palace to recollect whatever was desired. "Lustful images" in those rooms were particularly efficacious (Couliano, 1986: 63). They gave an emotional and physiological boost to memory. One could perhaps clothe the lustful image with matters to be recalled at a moment's notice.

THE DIVINE FEMININE

Feminist scholar, Miranda Shaw (1994) gives us a Spontaneous Jewellike Yogini who appears to agree in all essentials with Gyatso and to articulate doctrines that are so typically human that similar practices have been discovered in other cultures and at other times. Shaw never reveals whether the great yogini employed the tubular palace meditation. Perhaps she employed a simpler variant. For the Tantric traditions are unshakable in their conviction that men and women are opposing forces; and men have different needs than women. We have already considered Eliade's observation that the naked woman, when seen in a ritual context, embodies cosmic mystery. Hinduism calls this Shakti, which is sometimes merely the name given to Shiva's consort, or the consort of any god, in which case Shakti is the god's power conceived as an other to which he must learn to relate. Thus the male god's relationship to his Shakti is analogous to our relationship with kundalini-shakti.

> Shakti ("power") is the dynamic or creative principle of existence, envisioned as being feminine. This concept is intended to explain how the undifferentiated singular Reality can produce the multidimensional cosmos with its infinite forms. The transcendental static principle, personified as Shiva, is in itself incapable of creation. As a popular doctrinal maxim has it: "Shiva without Shakti is unable to effect anything." Shiva apart from shakti is likened to a corpse. The *Shiva-Purana* (VII.2.2.10) resorts to this poetic metaphor: "Just as the moon does not shine without moonlight, so Shiva does not shine without [the principle] of *shakti* (Feuerstein, 1990).

Thus the male is unmoving and impotent without the dynamism of the female. The male contemplates in stillness the dynamic female who arouses him. Without her spontaneous activity, he is like a corpse (shava). Without Shakti, Shiva is shava. On the ritual level this mythic doctrine is enacted by the male practitioner's remaining motionless while the woman moves with utter freedom. But the mythic doctrine is based in physiology; for when the man is active, he more readily arouses himself past the point of no return, precipitates an ejaculation, and loses his ability to maintain his arousal. When he takes the position of the unmoving Shiva and his consort moves freely like Shakti, arousal is heightened while the danger of an ejaculatory ending of the ritual intercourse is reduced. O'Flaherty (1973) makes it clear through an immense collection of mythic texts that Shiva's unmoving participation in intercourse with Shakti amounts to an alternate expression of his role as the God of Yoga. Whether sitting in a cremation ground smeared with ashes and meditating in isolation, or engaged with his consort in semen-retaining intercourse for a thousand years, the God of Sex and the God of Yoga are one and the same.

In his history of Chinese sexology, Wile notes that in the late alchemical texts male sexual energy, unlike that of the woman, is unstable and can only be usefully aroused when "fused with feminine essence" (Wile, 1992: 50). "Men must control both their passions and naturally active *ch'i*, whereas women also must still their desires, but stimulate their *ch'i* to overcome the natural stasis of *yin* [the feminine principle] and release the *yang* [male] principle" (Wile, 50). This seems to agree completely with what we have understood about carezza. The male has to control his unstable arousal so as not to have it end prematurely in an "external" or "explosive" orgasm. Although women, too, are subject to external orgasms that sap their arousal and require a period of recuperation, women "implode" more easily than men and enjoy a seemingly limitless capacity for multiple orgasms. Control is necessary for women but more easily attained.

When the Chinese (and Indian) sexologists say that the woman has to stimulate her ch'i—the "life energy" that is likened to breath, cosmic energy, and "the body's neurohormonal system" (Fischer-Schreiber, 1989)—they imply that arousal itself is the means of consciousness-changing. Indeed, a series of internal orgasms not only sustains arousal but increases it. [29] For while the male stills himself like Shiva to gain control, the woman lets loose like Shakti. Making the transition from spasm reflex to eros much more easily, the intensity of the woman's erotic trance fans the fire of the man's arousal and guides it in the direction of eros. Her Shakti temperament, based in physiology but centered on the subtle plane, inspires her partner and draws him along in her wake. Indeed a man's progress in Tantra is marked by stages in his relationship with women (Shaw, 1994: 43).

The woman's superior emotional aptitude and sensitivity to the subtle realm is universally insisted upon. But in the Tantric tradition—apparently the only one that permits them to function as gurus[30]—women are acknowledged as specially equipped to lead the way. A popular story in the *Yoga Vashishtha* describes how Queen Chudala leads her husband to the highest states of awareness and back again: "Sometimes as she traveled through the other universes that co-exist with our own, she would see the women *siddhas* (perfected masters) moving through the sky on the way to rendezvous with their sage husbands" (Johnsen, 1994: 17). Not being bound by their physiology in the same way as men, women pass back and forth easily between the empirical world and the subtle plane.

> Although Tantric literature offers only passing glimpses of women's (and men's) magic powers, these reveal a religious landscape in which women roamed freely and stepped lightly across the threshold between the world of ordinary reality and the realm of magic wherein thoughts are real, appearances are symbolic, and objects mirror the creative capacities of the mind (Shaw, 1994: 80-1).

---

29 Indeed, the copious welling up of prostatic and vaginal fluids may even be an index of an arousal that has become more erotic than spasmodic, as Paschal Beverly Randolph seems to have believed (Deveney, 1977). Evidently the feces-smeared Trighantika, who knew the nature of lust, had arrived at the same conclusion—although he valued the fluids themselves as magical substances, rather than as a physiological by-product of a change in consciousness.

30 "The permission that a woman become a guru is, as far as I know, peculiar to the Tantric tradition" (Dimock, 1989: 98).

Vimalananda says this female superiority is a function of the woman's closer relationship with her emotions which gives her a facility in achieving emotional ecstasy (Svoboda, 1986: 238).

Very likely it is this female trait that underlies a theme Miranda Shaw has identified. Men are required to honor and worship their consorts as goddesses, while women are to accept this worship and know that they themselves are divine (Shaw, 1994: 179). A number of tales describe how men gradually learn to shift their awareness so as to perceive the divinity residing in serving women, goat-herders, and the like (Shaw, 43-4). Typically the man deconstructs his ego through entering an erotic trance in which his partner's divinity is unmistakable. His erotic trance gives him no choice but to worship her. Few texts describe a woman worshipping the man; and those that come close—such as the story of Yeshe Tsogyel and Pema Heruka— inevitably involve a man of higher attainment who serves as the woman's guru. Kinsley (1997: 247) says that worship of the woman as goddess is "persistent" in Tantra, and describes a ritual in which the man gradually converts his flesh-and-blood partner into a cosmic goddess.

Another physiological reality underlies these mystical doctrines. With youth, the male's potency is at its height and he is able to ejaculate several times a day—perhaps three or four times in succession with a recuperative interval of only ten to twenty minutes. His youthful ability to retain his semen, however, is generally quite limited. He may in fact be liable to premature ejaculation. Meanwhile the young woman generally requires a fairly lengthy period of arousal before being capable of orgasm. This situation gradually changes, so that by middle age women are more easily aroused and more capable of multiple orgasms. At the same time, the man's arousal has slowed down, and he is less able to ejaculate several times during a single episode of intercourse.[31] Thus the practices of sexual yoga are more naturally employable by middle-aged partners than by youthful ones.[32] Such changes in physiological function correspond very well to the psychological differences between what Jung calls the first and second "halves" of life. He argues that in the first half of life, we are all required to develop a strong and

---

31 In my psychological work with middle-aged men and women, I find it not uncommon for women to complain that they have become sexually "insatiable," believing that something is wrong with them, and for men to express great fear that their potency is gone and that they will never be capable of satisfying partners whose new-found sexual aptitude intimidates them. Such individuals are fighting their physiology as well as their psychology.

32 It is no accident that sexual initiatrixes are generally women in their middle years. Although they are not likely to attain their distinctive skills and wisdom without years of practice, their ability to initiate others requires a lengthy physiological, emotional, and imaginal maturation. It appears that the best Bhairavis are between the ages of forty-five and sixty-five. This fact was clearly recognized by Noyes' Oneida community in their initiating of the young by elders with spiritual and physiological attainment.

flexible ego that is capable of dealing effectively with the empirical world. However, around the age of forty the central concern of life shifts and it becomes necessary to explore the spiritual dimensions of human existence. The merely personal ego has to be transcended through developing a conscious relationship to the self.[33]

This amounts to a Western formulation of the standard Hindu expectation that after we have acquitted ourselves of the duties of "householders," we should relinquish the concerns of the empirical world in order to pursue spiritual advancement as sannyasins:

> [The *sannyasin* is] one who has renounced the world and lives totally without possessions solely for the realization of liberation (*moksha*). The *sannyasin's* lack of possessions consists not only in total material poverty but also in what Christian mysticism calls the "poverty of spirit," that is, freedom from such dualistic notions as good and evil, desire and repulsion, fear and greed (Fischer-Schreiber, 1986).

Vimalananda says *sannyas* literally means "coma," and that sannyasins are "comatose to the world" (Svoboda, 1997: 29). A pair of sexual yogic partners are sannyasins insofar as they have renounced the profane world as the center of their interest. But unlike the picture of sannyasins we encounter in an introductory text on Hinduism, such partners do not renounce sexuality altogether. What they renounce is the propagation of children that would entangle them again in the work of householders. They take up sexuality as the engine of consciousness changing, learn carezza, and practice "amatory" intercourse as a means of entering an erotic trance that leads them to the subtle plane. Then, taking their aroused consciousness of the subtle plane as the object of their meditation, they work to transform bodily pleasure into bliss.

THE NATURE OF NECTAR

Such is the foundation of all sexual yoga, including that of Gyatso. But when Gyatso describes the attainment of Spontaneous Great Bliss, he tells us that there are three stages in the work. The first is what we have just considered: redirecting our focus from bodily tension and excitement to aroused consciousness. With this move, awareness occupies the center of our attention. The second stage involves transforming this initial blissful awareness with "nectar";

---

33 "In the second half of life, the accent shifts from the interpersonal or external dimension to a conscious relationship with intrapsychic processes. Dependence upon the ego has to be replaced by relationship to the self; dedication to outer success modified to include a concern for meaning and spiritual values. Jung's emphasis for the second half of life is on consciousness of a sense of purpose" (Samuels, et.al., 1986).

and the third stage "imprints" the nectar with a vision of blissfully coupled divinities. Gyatso employs vague and obscure images to describe the second and third stages. It will now be our task to examine these one by one, beginning with nectar.

The only dependable information Gyatso gives us concerning nectar is (a) that it resides naturally in the crown chakra (sahasrara), and (b) that it contributes a new experience of "joy" to the throat and heart chakras and additional "heat" to the navel center. The crown chakra, therefore, adds something perhaps ineffable that intensifies and transmutes our experience of the other chakras. Since each chakra represents a specific "level" of attainment in erotic trance, our most reliable approach to understanding the nature of nectar will begin with a differentiation of the several trance states.

If we consider the levels of trance in terms of how we see our consort, we can distinguish first between profane consciousness and erotic trance. In profane consciousness, when kundalini sleeps in the muladhara, we may find our consort attractive, interesting, and fun to be with. She or he is an exceptional individual but very much a human personality and denizen of consensus reality. The large transformation that occurs when kundalini awakens transforms our consort into an earthly Venus or Adonis. Now we are in erotic trance and dwelling on the subtle plane. But erotic trance is not a single thing, for it manifests differently at each of the chakras. The consort who arouses our navel chakra inspires terror in the face of an ego-destroying adventure that we may not be up to. At the solar plexus, we are no longer paralyzed in fear but have broken through to an important vision of "essential" significance. What we know of our own essential being is something to build upon; and our familiarity with our partner's essential being gives our relationship stability. At the level of the heart a much more sublime experience occurs, and we experience ourselves and our partner as airy beings, bodies of mist capable of thoroughly interpenetrating one another and becoming one. At the throat center we perceive various dimensions of this oneness and become able to conceptualize it for ourselves. This capacity to think and articulate is now directed to "ethereal" realities—more basic, true, sublime, and lasting than those of the empirical world.

Placing the brow chakra on an extension of the central channel, Gyatso's tubular palace meditation takes us directly from the throat to the crown. We can only think that the leap in level of erotic trance between the throat and crown must be analogous to that between the navel and heart—a vast transformation. The alchemical notion of nectar (amrita) in the crown chakra that is caused to drip downward and affect one's whole being through the arousal of kundalini is by no means unique to Tibet:

> In the literature of *hatha-yoga*, the word *amrita* . . . refers to the nectar of immortality that trickles down from an esoteric center in the head and is wasted by ordinary mortals because they do not know its secrets. The intrinsic connection between this nectar and immortality is

succinctly captured in the *Kaula-Jnana-Nirnaya* (XIV.94), which poses this question: "How can there be immortality (*amaratva*) without [the flowing of] the nectar [*amrita*]?"

. . . The *Hatha-Yoga-Pradipika* (IV.53) states that the whole body should be flooded with this ambrosia, which produces a superior body endowed with enormous strength and vigor and which is free from disease. This practice also prevents aging and bestows immortality as well as the eight magical powers (Feuerstein, 1990).

In the epilogue to his book on medieval alchemy, D. G. White (1996) describes his search for a living, practicing alchemist in India. He had two possible near misses. One turned out to be a man who had died twenty years before at the age of seventy-five—by no means immortal but remembered as having appeared no older than twenty-five at his demise. The reality of nectar is taken seriously—even literally—by many. White says that India is filled with stories and rumors of "semen-headed yogis" (D. G. White, 1996: 483). For semen is the usual source of nectar—semen that has been raised by kundalini to the cranial vault for transformation:

In her rise through the yogic *cakras*, the *kundalini* serpent is said to dance with the yogin. And, at the end of her rise, it is the yogin's own sexual fluid which, carried upward through her body, is transformed into immortalizing nectar. As a conduit for the yogin's semen, the female *kundalini* may be likened to the female sexual organ; . . . (D. G. White, 1996: 309).

Gorakh (or Goraksha), whom we saw earlier as the disciple and savior of his guru Matsyendra who had fallen into deathly sleep in the Forest of Women's Thighs, was "one of the greatest masters of *hatha-yoga*" (Feuerstein, 1990). Gorakh lived in the ninth or tenth century and has left us several Tantric scriptures. His remarks about nectar reflect the common mythological doctrine that nectar is produced by the mating of the Sun of Shiva (semen rising from the blazing fire at the navel) with Shakti, who resides in the Moon of the cranial vault. The upturned mouth of the interior Sun in the navel chakra, "whose essence is fire," hungers for the nectar dripping from the moon (D. G. White, 1996: 482). In the *Goraksa Sataka*, Gorakh speaks "of a pool (*dhara*) of lunar water in the cranial vault, which the yogin is to drink, lest it fall into the sun in the lower abdomen" (D. G. White, 1996: 481). In another passage, jauntily translated by White, Gorakh says:

Now that you've pierced [*bedhya*] the lotuses six,

Go and drink that nectar mix . . .

Semen is yoga, semen is what pleases;

Semen averts the sixty-four diseases.

> The rare dude who pierces semen's mystery,
>
> He's the creator, he's the divinity
>
> (D. G. White, 1996: 320-1).

Here it is clear that the six chakras (lotuses) constitute a set and that the crown chakra stands above them, not only in empirical space through its placement at the top of the head, but also in significance. The cranial vault is the place where semen, retained in carezza and made to flow upward by the rising kundalini, is itself transformed. On its way up to the crown, it effects real changes in the lower six chakras; but these are nothing in comparison to what *nectar* can accomplish. Nectar brings "immortality"—makes us the "divine creator"—and introduces a host of secondary but related changes such as strength, vigor, and immunity from disease. No doubt many take this claim of immortality in a literal and empirical sense. Certainly that old exaggerator, Vimalananda, seems to do so when he says that his Bhairavi was able to appear as a fifteen-year-old girl even though she was actually so old she had to lift her eyelids with her fingers. She "had made herself immortal" by ingesting mercury. D. G. White makes it clear that the "mercury" which brings immortality is semen transformed through the "sulfur" of menstrual blood: an alchemical procedure that may take place either in the laboratory or in the body of the yogin-alchemist. The two processes are parallel in all respects and symbolize one another.

Because there appear to be no historical figures who attained literal immortality—or lived even four hundred years—we have to take such stories symbolically. Real immortality means release from samsara, the eternal round of birth, death, and rebirth. It means leaving the empirical and profane world forever. It describes a state of erotic trance. When kundalini has risen to the cranial vault and either melted the drop of nectar or else brought the semen of Shiva into union with Shakti's "pool" of sexual fluids, erotic trance undergoes its most profound augmentation. Whether or not the yogin actually feels or imagines a liquid dripping into his throat, the activation of the crown chakra so transforms the nature of erotic trance that Indians, Tibetans, and others have for centuries resorted to the imagery of nectar and ambrosia to account for it.

DAKINIS

But what can we point to in the experience of even a single yogin who has drunk nectar to make this process intelligible for ourselves? What happens when an individual forsakes the empirical world and becomes immortal? We get some hint of the beginning of this journey in the many stories about kings who have been converted to the Tantric path by a pair of lewdly dancing dombis, who awaken him to sexual practices that lead to immortality (D. G. White, 1996: 308-9). Dombis are the most skillful and desired of Tantric consorts, initiatrixes who appear to be as "enchanted" as Vimalananda's Bhairavi. They are superhuman beings capable of shape-shifting, and they are terrifyingly indecent, alluring, and challenging. In Tibet, dombis are called dakinis; and "the Dakini principle" describes the ever-changing flow of kundalini (Allione, 1986: 32). The dakini (masculine: daka) changes our lives by transforming all of our experiences, by appearing "at crucial moments to destroy the fixed ideas of the practitioner" (Allione, 1986: 37). Trungpa Rinpoche describes the dakini as a dangerous challenger:

> The playful maiden is all-present. She loves you. She hates you. Without her your life would be continual boredom. But she continually plays tricks on you. When you want to get rid of her she clings. To get rid of her is to get rid of your own body—she is that close. In Tantric literature she is referred to as the dakini principle. The dakini is playful. She gambles with your life (Allione, 1986: 38).

Dakinis are, in fact, so fearsome and indecent that the uninitiated in Nepal use the cognate word *dankini* "as an expletive or slur on a vile woman, a witch, enchantress, or manipulator of the spirit world and a seductress who abuses her sexual powers" (Dowman, 1984: 258).

The positive value of a dakini is that she can awaken in us "the universal urge to enlightenment" whereby we penetrate "to the true meaning of doctrines too profound to yield their secrets at the everyday level of consciousness" (Blofield, 1987: 114). But the dangers are considerable, as Vimalananda insists regarding the Hindu category of seductive beings called yakshinis (masculine: yakshas):

> There is a type of spirit [Yaksha] who comes to a woman and makes her fall into a stupor, what we call the state of *Tandra* in Sanskrit, and then enjoys sex with her. If you were to watch it, and I have watched it, you will see her lying on the bed, twisting and turning, oozing, enjoying orgasms, and what-have-you. In fact, she will find it much more satisfying than physical sex, because he has no body to tire out, and he makes her enjoy much more than any man could. . . .
>
> . . . And believe me, a Yakshini can make you enjoy sex. If you do this five or six times the Yakshini will come to you on her own and force you to copulate with her and extract all your energy. And you can't get free of her; It's next to impossible. When you die, you become one of the fraternity of spirits, of an order lower than even the Yakshini, and you will have to work your way up from there, roaming about. You don't even have to copulate with her; just kiss her—once only—and you are finished, done for (Svoboda, 1986: 195-6).

Beings of this sort would seem uniquely qualified to build a fire in the navel chakra. We need the challenge a wrathful heroine with the wiles of a dakini if the fire at our navel is going to boost us all the way to the cranial vault and make nectar. Thus when Yeshe Tsogyel masturbates to awaken kundalini, she enters an erotic trance in which her guru Pema Heruka appears to her as a daka (male form of dakini). A wrathful daka would surely be able to turn any heroic meditator into an intensely writhing snake. A mad saint would simply writhe helplessly. The heroic saint, however, becomes conscious of the serpent as "other." Yeshe follows Jung's advice: "It is wise not to identify with these experiences, but to handle them as if they were outside the human realm. That is the safest thing to do—and really absolutely necessary. Otherwise you get an inflation" (Jung, 1996: 27). As the serpent power rises to possess her, another dragon surges forth from within, the life energy of her soul. It gives her the strength and spontaneity to engage with that daka-conjured serpent. Not merely to stand up to kundalini but to dance with her. As Yeshe writhes, the kundalini of her soul is racing like lightening up the staircase of her tubular palace.

Next the Sun of Splendor lights up the sky. The drop of nectar has melted. The semen of Shiva has penetrated Shakti's lunar pool. The wrathful daka, whose abusive and rapacious vajra sits within her writhing lotus throne unmoving as a god in a sand painting, and whose scornful laugh just moments before ruptured them through onto the sublime plane of the heart chakra, now unites with Lady Kundalini in the cranial vault. Bliss supervenes.

THE NATURE OF BLISS

Unfortunately *bliss* is a very abstract word. It connotes an experience of very pleasant but ineffable sublimity; and although in this context it is a bodily experience, it is not merely a physical sensation but carries with it a large component of something vaguely transcendental. We who live most of our lives in the empirical world cannot be sure we have ever experienced the sort of bliss the mystics speak of. If we have been fortunate enough to have felt the fans of the heart chakra spin and have been led to refer to this experience as "bliss," the substantial augmentation deriving from the crown chakra suggests a body-mind state that exceeds the bounds of our experience. In fact, the only indication we have regarding the content of nectar's bliss is the imaginal appearance of the mystic's consort, before and after nectar's contribution.

Once nectar has dripped slowly down to the region of the throat and heart, the consorts find they are sharing a sublime oneness no longer with a wrathful daka or wrathful dakini but with a blissful consort of superhuman power, wholly unanticipated spontaneity, and timeless significance. Dowman defines the dakini according to the following lines of the *Great Paramita Sutra:*

> Indescribable, unimaginable Perfection of Wisdom,
>
> Unborn, unobstructed essence of sky,
>
> She is sustained by self-awareness alone:
>
> I bow down before the Great Mother of the victorious ones,
>
> > past, present, and future
>
> > (Dowman, 1984: ix).

Dowman comments, "Desireless, blissful wisdom is the essence of all desirable qualities, and unobstructed going and coming in endless space." This is a very "Buddhist" formulation, reminiscent of the Buddha's own title, *Tathagata*, which may be translated, "Thus come, thus gone." Such phrases reflect an unimaginable subtlety and a spontaneity that implies transcendental intentions. If we have been able to stretch our language to suggest something intelligible about the experience of the heart chakra, nectar from the crown challenges our capacity to find words. We have to begin to speak in comparative analogies: if the sublimity of the heart chakra seems to transcend everything we associate with corporality, then the nectar of the crown transcends sublimity.

> The *dakinis* leap and fly, unfettered by clothing, encircled by billowing hair, their bodies curved in sinuous poses . . . enlightened women who can spark a divine experience of reality with a precisely aimed word or gesture . . . their exuberant air of passion and freedom communicate[s] a sense of mastery and spiritual power (Shaw, 1989: 3).

> The best type of *dakini* is one whose awareness is so transcendently lofty that her mind is free from worldly thoughts and flows in a natural and spontaneous stream, a level of attainment known as *sahaja* realization, or "enlightened spontaneity" (Shaw, 1989: 170).

The blissful dakini (and daka), therefore, represent the "ever-changing flow of energy with which the yogic practitioner must work in order to become realized" (Allione, 1986: 25). The absolute spontaneity which these beings make possible is often compared to the open and unobstructed space of the sky—hence the frequent description of the blissful dakini as "sky dancer."

All dakinis, whether blissful or wrathful, are to be found on a distinctive level of the subtle realm, what we might call the dakini plane. The difference between them—that is whether we see them as full of bliss or wrath—depends upon the admixture of nectar to our erotic trance.

Their appearance as blissful or wrathful depends upon us, upon the level in our subtle body to which kundalini has risen. If we have been privileged to encounter a daka or dakini, kundalini is awake. If the spirit beings appear wrathful, kundalini has not yet risen to the cranial vault. If blissful, we have experienced the ineffable augmentation of nectar's bliss.

Objectively speaking, we can say that *in themselves* there is no difference between a wrathful dakini and a blissful one. It is the same dakini, whose appearance reflects the state of our consciousness. She is wrathful when her spontaneity strikes fear in us. Everything that she is and stands for challenges the stolid illusions of the empirical world and the persona field. When we see her as wrathful, we are feeling a challenge to the comfortable realities of our habitual existence in conventional reality. She puts our ego's point of view in crisis. When she becomes blissful, we have dropped our dependence on ahamkara, our memory of what constitutes "me and mine." We have entered the dakini plane without presuppositions—without the safety net of what we have dependably come to know. We have embarked upon a subtle-plane sojourn without reserve, without fear, in total acceptance and spontaneity.

SPIRAL PROGRESS ON THE LEFT-HAND PATH

When we consider the more conventional saints, the ones who say nothing of any indecent sexual component in their spiritual practices, we are led to think that they proceed on an ever-upward path: perhaps from profane consciousness directly to the plane of blissful dakinis and dakas and then onward and upward to the blissful gods and goddesses. Tantra's left-hand path aspires to the same ascent, but it does so by first dipping downward into the realm of the disturbing shadow, where a rush of sexual arousal and terror gives the practitioner a powerful boost of energy. By way of analogy, we may consider how earth-born space vehicles are given a boost from the gravitational field of a planet or the sun. The gravity—or "eros," as Isaac Newton called it in his notebooks (Berman, 1981)—of the heavenly body threatens the vehicle with final destruction if it should succumb entirely and crash upon the surface or burn up in the furnace of the star. But by skillfully employing that erotic gravity and maintaining a precise balance of nearness and distance, the space vehicle increases its acceleration by swinging around the danger in a half-arc that propels it onward with the force of a celestial sling-shot.

Such is the technique of the Tantrikas. They make no attempt to deny or circumvent the disturbing and potentially destructive effects of the wrathful dakini or daka. Instead, they enter directly into the disorienting realm of the shadowy spirit beings so as to build a roaring conflagration in their navel center. It is a dangerous practice, for they risk being shattered or burnt to a cinder in the heat. But when used skillfully, when employed as the most natural and straight-forward source of psychological and physiological boost, they use the wrathful dakini's disturbing power to propel themselves into the region of nectar's bliss. Like gravity-employing space vehicles, they calculate the danger in full consciousness. Instead of succumbing to the wrathful dakini's power helplessly and unconsciously, and thereby losing their awareness in a shattering crash, they redirect their attention to the dragon of their soul's life energy. Riding the serpentine head of kundalini as she streaks up the central channel of their interior palace, they attain the cranial vault where nectar transmutes their arousal to bliss. At this point the dakini is no longer a wanton and dangerous challenger. Her unfettered spontaneity ceases to be a threat and becomes an invitation to the dance. Nectar gives us the freedom of the open sky. We have dropped all presuppositions. We have ourselves attained the spontaneity of the daka or dakini.

The left-hand path generally describes itself as "the most natural," "the fastest" and "the most immediate" course to enlightenment. It argues that the dragon of desire is not to be overcome, extirpated, or rendered harmless. Rather it is to be engaged and redeemed. In effect the left-hand path urges us to begin where we are. If we find something exciting or disturbing, we are not to ignore it or attempt to vanquish it with ascetic practices such as fasting and self-flagellation. Rather we are to see what that disturbance does to us and direct our attention specifically to the consciousness it induces. For that aroused consciousness is the first appearance of kundalini. It is the source of a boost which we can ride into higher levels of erotic trance.

The tubular palace meditation of Gyatso lays out for us a path in several stages by which we: (1) leave profane consciousness by means of an emotional and physiological disturbance which takes the form of a wrathful daka or dakini; (2) engage with the wrathful one by directing our attention to the flame induced in our navel chakra; (3) ride kundalini in her first upward climb to release nectar and transform the wrath into bliss; (4) descend the central channel with the nectar to gain a new boost of wrathful energy and leap from the dakini plane to the divine plane at the navel chakra, where a wrathful god or goddess is encountered; (5) ride kundalini up to the observation deck of the ajna chakra to obtain a vision of blissful gods and goddesses in sexual embrace on the strength of the nectar-augmented flame in the navel; (6) achieve Spontaneous Great Bliss on a final trip through the tubular palace when the impressed nectar is boosted by an internal orgasm.

Omitting the last of these, I have diagrammed this "Spiral Progress on the Left-Hand Path" in Figure 1. In the center of the chart are Yeshe and Pema, two human individuals, each with a personality, a history, and a persona-field identity in the profane world (#1). As their consciousness is aroused to the dakini plane by the fire at their navel, Yeshe loses her human personality and becomes a wrathful dakini engaged with Pema's wrathful daka (#2). Remaining on the dakini plane, represented in light gray, they employ a boost of navel fire to attain nectar and become blissful daka and blissful dakini (#3). When they ride the descending nectar to the navel's fire, the dakini plane is ruptured; and they break through to the divine plane, where they become wrathful god and goddess for one another (#4). Finally, a boost of nectar-enhanced fire takes them back up through the tubular palace to the brow chakra, where they obtain the vision of nectar impressed with divinity and become blissful god and goddess (#5).

The wrathful gods and goddesses resemble the wrathful dakas and dakinis but are immeasurably more powerful. We have revisited Vimalananda's advice to Svoboda many times: the strategy is to attract an "enchanted woman," presumably a dakini, and then resist her advances so as to attract a wanton goddess. Now that we have Gyatso's structure to sort out the five stages running from ego-consciousness to the encounter with blissful deities, we can better appreciate what the old exaggerator had in mind.

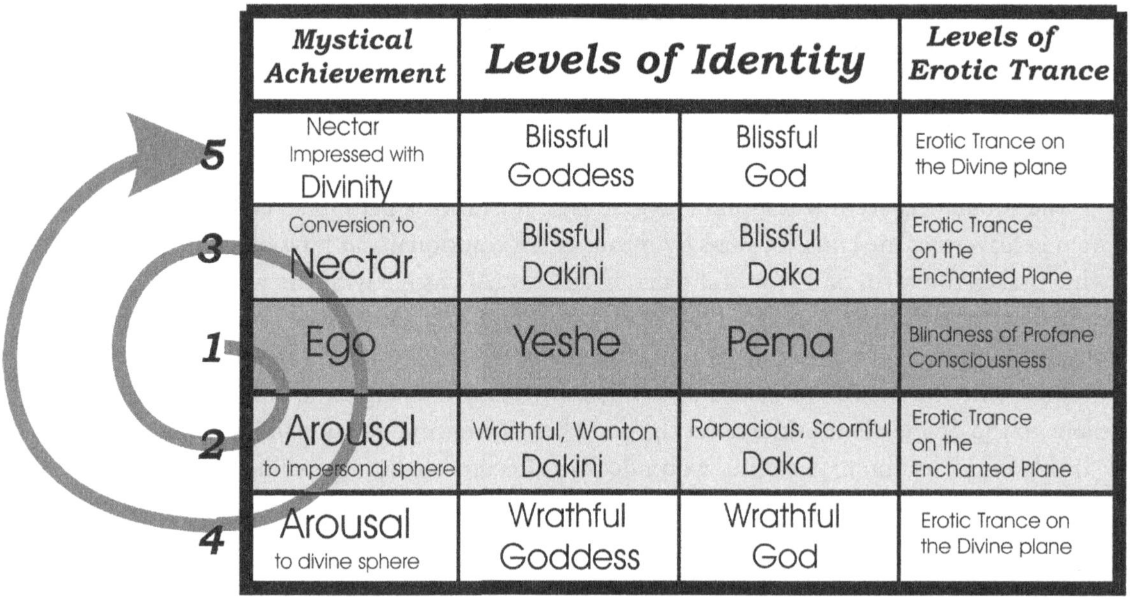

Mystical Achievement	Levels of Identity		Levels of Erotic Trance
5 Nectar Impressed with Divinity	Blissful Goddess	Blissful God	Erotic Trance on the Divine plane
3 Conversion to Nectar	Blissful Dakini	Blissful Daka	Erotic Trance on the Enchanted Plane
1 Ego	Yeshe	Pema	Blindness of Profane Consciousness
2 Arousal to impersonal sphere	Wrathful, Wanton Dakini	Rapacious, Scornful Daka	Erotic Trance on the Enchanted Plane
4 Arousal to divine sphere	Wrathful Goddess	Wrathful God	Erotic Trance on the Divine plane

Spiral Progress on the Left-Hand Path

Figure 1

WRATHFUL GODDESSES

The main wrathful god in Hinduism is Shiva, whom we have described in some detail. McLean says the Shiva of folklore is an old reprobate who "spends all his time high on bhang and datura," chasing prostitutes and young girls (McLean, 1998: 62). He delights in over-turning all the distinctions between the moral and immoral, the pure and polluted. He loves cremations grounds (a place of transit between the worlds), smears himself with ashes, and is generally to be found naked, with matted hair, wild eyes, and an erect penis.

Wrathful goddesses, however, are much more numerous. Most are consorts of Shiva. In *Tantric Visions of the Divine Feminine* (1995), David Kinsley has done the spade work in as-sembling pictures of the "Ten Mahavidyas," each a symbol of defiant female independence in a society that severely restricts women's freedom (Kinsley, 1995: 70). Although there are always exactly ten goddess of "Great Knowledge" (Maha-Vidya), their names are not always the same in every list. We shall briefly mention four of them.

The best known of these wrathful goddesses and never omitted from any list is the Black One, Kali. Kinsley says that she is primarily a woman who "deconstructs" the categories of cultural consciousness, "inviting all those who would learn from her to be open to the whole world in all its aspects" (Kinsley, 83).

> Although [Kali] may be said to serve order in her role as slayer of demons, more often than not she becomes so frenzied on the battlefield, intoxicated with the blood of her victims, that she herself begins to destroy the world she is supposed to protect. Thus, even in the service of the gods she is dangerous and likely to get out of control (Kinsley, 74).

Kali's nakedness displays her sexual readiness, her unbound hair implies a state of pol-lution, very likely menstruation (Kinsley, 84); her necklace of skulls and skirt of arms char-acterizes bloodthirstiness and her dismemberment of our ego. Her black color "represents transcendence over any manifested thing" (Kinsley, 30). Often her blackness is covered in sparkles, representing "the gods [that] arise from her like bubbles from the sea, endlessly ap-pearing and passing away, leaving their source unchanged" (Kinsley, 76). Thus her shameless and indecent appearance is merely a wrathful illusion behind which lurks the eternal and unchanging (blissful) reality. Although this profound mystical significance is widely known, Kinsley reports that a great many Hindus are uncomfortable "with her outrageous, shocking features" (Kinsley, 91).

Chinnamasta, another naked and shameless goddess, is generally pictured with a knife in one hand and her own severed head in the other. Three streams of blood fountain up out of her neck and fall into the mouths of two naked woman disciples and into the mouth of the head Chinnamasta holds in her hand. According to one tradition, she becomes so intoxicated drinking the blood of her victims that she loses control and cuts off her own head (Kinsley, 149). In another she blows her head off by absorbing the sexual energy of copulating human couples whom she stands upon or straddles. Kundalini rises up within her so forcefully that it cuts the knots in all the chakras—something she can do for us—and tears off her head, rendering her egoless (Kinsley, 159).

Dhumavati is a widow sitting in an unhitched chariot, therefore, "a woman going no-where, the ultimate symbol of all that is unlucky, unattractive, and inauspicious" (Kinsley, 182). But sometimes she is presented as attractive, in which case she embodies the most threatening of women in Hindu society, for widows are believed to be driven by unsatisfied sexual longings they have no reason to resist (Kinsley, 190). The goddess Bhairavi, after whom sexual initiatrixes are named, loves anger, jealousy, and every form of selfish emotion and activity. Righteous behavior by humans weakens her power (Kinsley, 170). Two of her titles refer to her favorite indecencies: She Who is Fond of Semen and Menstrual Blood, She Who is Worshipped by Those Who Worship with Semen (Kinsley, 172).

NANGSA OBAM

Tsultrim Allione, an American woman who is an initiate in Tibetan Buddhism, illustrates the achievement of wrathful divinization with her detailed account of a Tibetan folk drama that depicts legendary events from the eleventh century, a time of Buddhist revival in Tibet (Allione, 1986: 66-128). The story of Nangsa Obam displays many typical features of Tantric stories from India and Tibet in that it concerns itself with a woman whose predilection for mystical attainment, evident from birth, was temporarily thwarted by an early marriage. In Nangsa's case, her parents were themselves devout Buddhists who "did extensive practice without interruption, and without thought of personal gain" (Allione, 66). They resisted all Nangsa's suitors until the King of Rinang insisted upon marrying her to his son, Dragpa Sam-drub, and threatened Nangsa's parents with death if they did not accede to his request. Thus she was married against her will but eventually found a way to escape from court to become the mystical consort of the Great Lama Sakya Gyaltsen, who recognized immediately that Nangsa was a great dakini.

Soldiers were sent to Gyaltsen's monastery to seize Nangsa and bring her back. They found the pair in ritual sexual embrace. Their accusation that the great lama had "sullied" the king's wife was cut short when they themselves suddenly entered erotic trance and saw the two mystic partners flying off from the earth in the form of yab-yum, sexually coupled divinities. The highly attained mystic consorts had become the dark-blue wrathful god, Cakra Sambhava and his consort Vajra Yogini. The soldiers' minds were opened, and the report they brought back to their king inspired him to give up his worldly life and practice dharma.

This is clearly a story of lust and the spiritual attainment that may be based upon the fire sexual arousal generates in the navel chakra. The worldly figures of the king and his son have experienced a peculiarly compelling sort of lust whereby the object of their attentions, the saintly Nangsa, stands out above all women. Thus far, their judgment agrees with that of Lama Gyaltsen. But being tethered to the world of social and political gain as well as bodily pleasure of an "attached" and purely instinctual sort, they are incapable of properly valuing the beautiful and graceful adolescent woman who has so powerfully won their admiration.

The soldiers, therefore, are brought in by the story-teller as rude and wholly believable witnesses. Nothing in their prior experience prepares them for a physiological and emotional atmosphere of such spiritual power that their brow chakras are opened and they see the adulterous liaison of their once esteemed princess and a raunchy guru on the plane of wrathful deities. According to this wide-spread literary device, what appears merely immoral and polluted to the eyes of the profane ego is in reality a sublime and holy event. The spiritual reality of ritual intercourse is so compelling that even the lowest of the uninitiated cannot resist its influence, and they themselves undergo a rupture of plane as their consciousness is elevated in a moment from the profane level to the divine stratum of erotic trance. The break-through they experience is far more abrupt than that of Promode Chatterjee, when he was privileged to witness an Aghori chakra ceremony in a smashan during a thunder storm. For Chatterjee had evidently been a sympathetic by-stander from the start, and his testimony that what he had witnessed was not lustful but sublime indicates that his heart chakra had been open during most of the night. Thus in that stoke of lightning, when he saw the Aghoris in the form of a sexual mandala on the divine plane, kundalini had only to rise from the fourth chakra (heart) to the sixth (brow). The soldiers of Rinang, however, shifted abruptly from a condition in which kundalini was asleep all the way to the observation deck of the brow chakra.

Sufism tells similar stories about the awakening of observers who are prepared to condemn indecent sexual practices until their own consciousness is suddenly elevated. One of the most famous of these incidents concerns Ahmad Ghazzali, the brother of the great philosopher who justified Sufi practices through rational argument based on the Qu'ran, Abu Hamad Ghazzali (1058-1111). Ahmad Ghazzali was therefore a contemporary—albeit geographically and culturally far removed—of the events in the folk drama of Nangsa Obam. According to the story, Ahmad Ghazzali was a practitioner of what Sufism calls "the witness game," in which a naked "beardless youth" is employed as the object of meditation in order to elevate the meditator through an emotional and physiological boost to the divine plane of consciousness.[34]

---

34 The three great poets of the Witness Game are Ahmad Ghazzali, Fakhruddin 'Iraqi, and Ahwhadoddin Kermani (Wilson, 1993: 57).

[His friends] found [Ahmad Ghazzali] seated in his cell-retreat, staring at a young boy, with a single rose on the floor between them. "Have we disturbed you?" they asked. Ghazzali replied *"Ay w'Allah"* ("By God!")—and all the company thereupon fell into a "state"[35]; that is they attained some measure of non-ordinary consciousness or ecstasy (Wilson, 1995: 95).

When profane witnesses[36] see through the appearance of an adulterous affair between lama and princess to its hidden divine reality, the story seems to provide "objective verification" that the liaison between Nangsa and Gyaltsen transcends the good/evil distinctions of the persona field. If this seems to constitute an exaggeration worthy of Vimalananda, the reader is asked to withhold judgment until we address the issue of mystical influence from one individual to another in Volume One, Chapter Six. At this point in our argument, it is enough to agree that the soldiers' witness serves as a testimony from the Buddhist community of faith that it is not only possible but expected that accomplished practitioners can attain a subjective identity with their deities when erotic trance carries them to the divine plane.

In fact Vimalananda himself agrees with Ibn al-'Arabi that if you think you see "the Reality Itself" you have no gnosis; the mystic with real gnosis knows that it is his own essential self that is seen: "What you will see is not the real deity; it is your own creation, from your own astral body" (Svoboda, 1994: 124). This means that Nangsa and Gyaltsen, when they experience themselves as a wrathful yab-yum, encounter the divine dimension of their own subtle body, as it manifests through the medium of their navel chakra. At the same time, their svadhisthana arousal induces a similar stirring in the navels of the soldiers. What the soldiers see may not correspond in all respects with what the consorts themselves experience. The two experiences are alike only in the fact that it is a wrathful yab-yum that is enacted by Nangsa and Gyaltsen. Their limited personalities have been "effaced" in favor of the wrathful divine dimension of their own being (Svoboda, 1986: 16).

He forgets who he is, and she forgets who she is. He says, "I am Lord Shiva in the form of Bhairava (the Fearful Lord), and this is my Shakti, my Bhairavi." She thinks, "This is my Lord Shiva, and I am His Grand Consort, His Bhairavi (the Fearful Goddess)" (Svoboda, 1986: 271-2).

---

35 The ladder of divine ascent in Sufism is described in terms of well-defined "states" of mystical consciousness and "stations" of attainment. "State" and "station," therefore, are technical terms.

36 Lest the reader be confused, it should be noted that the "witness" of the witness game is the beardless youth who bears witness to the Reality of God that resides in every created being. My use of *witness* in this sentence refers to the ordinary meaning: the soldiers and Ghazzali's friends are witnesses of transcendent realities in this ordinary sense.

The central issue in the Tibetan folk drama hinges on the meaning of lust. The profane consensus, which thinks it knows what lust is, is confounded by a vision of lustful deities. The king and prince believe they have "normalized" their lust by bringing it into conformity with society's horizontal value system, "till death do us part." Nangsa and Gyaltsen also manifest lust in the sense that their mutual erotic trance demands carnal expression, and pursuing that mystical impulse appears indecent and scandalous to profane eyes. Although we have subtle-plane testimony that their "sexual acting out" achieves divinization, it is still lustful insofar as the activation of their respective navel chakras predominates. The lustfulness of their encounter persists in the image of intercourse between wrathful god and wrathful goddess.

As a wrathful yab-yum they ascend into the sky and disappear from the soldiers' view. Wrathful god and goddess ascend to the blissful sector of the divine plane, and the soldiers' gaze is incapable of following. For the soldiers, we have to assume, are familiar with the terrifying and seductive nature of sex but not yet of its blissful potential. Thus the wrathful yab-yum disappears before their eyes as Nangsa and Gyaltsen are transformed in their own experience into blissful god and goddess.

BLISSFUL GOD AND GODDESS

Gyatso's inner fire meditation does not address the stage in which the partners become wrathful deities. He speaks only of the intensification of the navel fire when the slowly falling nectar reaches it. In his account, we do not encounter divinization until the penultimate moment of the meditation, when the nectar-enhanced fiery winds carry us to the observation deck of the ajna chakra. There three events take place in succession: (1) we witness a mandala of yab-yums; (2) one by one these yab-yums melt into a drop of blissful light; and (3) the many drops condense to a single one which we absorb through our third eye. In the stage of witnessing, those deities are not yet me and my partner. The potential divinity of our own being is still projected. At the second stage, the image becomes extremely abstract—mere drops of blissful light. But the fact that we can know those drops *as bliss* implies that the vision has done something to us. Like the soldiers witnessing the wrathful yab-yum of princess and lama, our witnessing the bliss of the deities in the mandala effects an emotional change in us. It elevates our erotic trance to the point that we have an implicit awareness of bliss within our own bodies—much as the soldiers attained an implicit awareness of spiritualized lust. They themselves did not become mystics, but they were so affected that the report they brought back to their king persuaded him to embark upon the mystic path. Finally, in the third stage, when we absorb the condensed drop of divine bliss and fuse it with the nectar in our cranial vault, divine bliss is within us and has become a component of the fiery winds that climb the central staircase of our subtle body.

The fact that one actually becomes a blissful deity united with a blissful divine consort is declared in unmistakable terms by Yeshe Tsogyel when her union with Pema Heruka reaches this stage:

> Out of the bliss-waves of the forehead center of our union, in the sphere of intense experience of Awareness of joy, arose a white paradise divided into thirty-two lesser pure lands. In each of these pure lands was a white Heruka in mystic union with his Consort surrounded by hundreds of thousands, an incalculable number, of Herukas and their Consorts identical to the principal. In the centre of this vast *mandala* was the Master of all the Herukas, the principal Heruka and Consort into whose Awareness of joy I received initiation. Through this joy the passion of anger was purified, the body cleansed of all traces of habitual action and reaction patterns, insight was gained into the elements of the path of application, and I was enabled to act for the benefit of the seven worlds of the ten directions. At this level I was conferred the secret initiatory name, Tsogyel the White Goddess of Pure Pleasure (Dechen Karmo Tsogyel) (Dowman, 1984: 40-1).

In Yeshe's account, the paradise vision is recognized as a projection of the "bliss waves" she shares with Pema Heruka. It has been an unconscious component of the intense awareness of joy they share, and first becomes known in projected form as a vision. She sees a mandala divided into thirty-two parts, each part ("pure land" or "Buddha paradise") is itself a mandala with countless yab-yums.[37]

Thus she clarifies the nature of the brow-chakra vision. It is an image to describe her bliss. Gyatso's nectar of unspecified bliss unfolds its contents as a mandalic vision when the brow chakra opens. This is the witness stage of the inner fire meditation. It is followed by awareness of the joy that is experienced by the principal heruka and consort. This corresponds to Gyatso's second stage of appreciating the bliss of each of the couples and combining them into a single drop of bliss. Evidently Yeshe absorbs this awareness, for she says that it initiates her. It reforms her into its shape, much as Gyatso's nectar is "imprinted" with the divine vision. When "the body is cleansed of all traces of habitual action and reaction patterns," ahamkara, the memory of "me and mine," is abolished. She loses her personal identity and becomes the White Goddess of Pure Pleasure.

---

37 The herukas of the vision are not necessarily Pema Heruka, for a heruka is simply "the male personification of yogic power" (Evans-Wentz, 1967: 174). Shaw (1994: 28) says herukas are wrathful deities, but in one place Yeshe says the herukas banished the wrathful deities (Dowman, 1984: 2). In any event, it is clear that the passage in question deals with a vision of blissful divinities.

Gyatso presents the inner fire meditation with economy of expression. He wants us to know exactly how it is done and what we are to take as the object of our meditation at each stage of our ascent and descent through the tubular palace. He evidently assumes that his disciples are steeped in Tibetan Buddhist teachings and familiar with the sorts of stories the great saints of the tradition have left us, like Yeshe Tsogyel's autobiography. For this reason, he does not dwell on the imaginal stages the practitioner employs to identify with her deity. His attention is directed exclusively to the subtle body and the rise and fall of kundalini within its central channel. To understand more fully what he is teaching us, we have to round out his account with complementary material from the Tantric tradition.

It is important to recall the gender differences stressed by Shaw—that men must worship their consort as a goddess and women must accept that worship and their own implicit divinity. Nevertheless, it is not possible for the man genuinely to worship nor for the woman to accept worship unless both parties are in a very high state of erotic trance. We find our consort worshipful not by some trick in a ritual that is manipulated by our ego. Rather we do so by cultivating erotic trance, retaining our aroused consciousness, and bringing it deliberately or by accident to the level of the brow chakra. When the third eye opens onto the divine plane, our consort simply *is* divine, regardless of our conscious intentions; and we have no option but to worship her.

In illustration of this principle, we might consider a myth wherein the goddess Parvati succeeds in redirecting Shiva's yogic attention. Neither her voluptuous beauty nor divine wiles has any effect upon the disreputable God of Yoga until she relinquishes her aim of rousing him from meditation and decides to join him on the subtle plane. She leaves him in his smashan smeared with ashes and returns to her mountain home,[38] where she covers herself in ashes and enters meditation, remaining as unmovable as Shiva for many years.

> Deep in his meditation, Shiva began to sense an extraordinary shakti, a divine energy more powerful and sublime than anything he had ever experienced before. To his shock he realized that it was a growing field of consciousness as perfect and extensive as his own. What could possibly be the source? He opened his three eyes and there on a distant peak he saw a yogini sitting immovable as the mountains themselves, covered with dust, her mind merged in the absolute. In that instant the great renunciate and lord of all yogis fell madly in love (Johnsen, 1994: 92).

This myth implies that even a goddess has to enter erotic trance if she is to attract the attentions of her deity and bring about divine union. Shiva is inaccessible on the plane of mere pleasure. If distracted for a moment by Kama, the God of (ordinary) Lust, Shiva incinerates

---

38 *Parvati* means "Goddess of the Mountains."

him with a single glance from his third eye. Only an erotic trance as profound and extensive as his own can catch his attention and fascinate him. The union of Shiva and Parvati that follows takes place on the plane of blissful god and blissful goddess and results in a thousand years of semen-retaining dalliance in which yoga and maithuna (ritual intercourse) are one and the same.

Thus when Vimalananda instructs Svoboda in the practice of *avishkara* (the worship of deities called into one's own body), we have to follow the neat steps he lays out without forgetting the central importance of the divine plane of erotic trance. The old exaggerator says we must start by "losing" our personal identity, so as to create a "spiritual vacuum" into which the god may enter. This already implies a level of erotic trance at least as far from profane consciousness as the wrathful dakini plane. Then we are to identify with the deity in an outward manner by donning the god's garments and accessories. Surely this is an imaginal activity that will bear no fruit if performed on the plane of ordinary awareness. To properly appreciate Vimalananda's teaching, we have to be able to stabilize an imaginal construction of ourselves clad and accoutered as an icon of our deity—a feat that might be compared to Tibetan mandala meditation. But this imaginal exercise is only preliminary to the next stage, in which we identify directly with the deity "with no thought for physical details." We have enabled our deity to acquire a living presence through our mastery of imagination. Then we drop the subject/object distinction between ourselves and the god. Gyatso's depiction of this stage provides a useful detail; for in directing our attention to the bliss attained by each visualized yab-yum, he makes it clear that what unites us with our deity is an emotional reality that can be attained exclusively through a very high level of erotic trance. In Vimalananda's last stage, one has become so familiar with the deity that the god comes at our "merest thought." Although at first the god comes when he or she wishes to do so, our increasing mastery of erotic trance brings us to the point where the deity comes and goes as we desire (Svoboda, 1986: 213-4).

If read cautiously, Vimalananda's instructions make a good deal of sense. In mysticism nothing is possible unless we first become familiar with erotic trance. Further progress requires mastery of the trance state in all three of its dimensions: physiology, emotion, and imagination. The method outlined to Svoboda assumes that the practitioner has already accomplished a great deal in the realm of bodily and affective arousal before taking up imaginal exercises. For the subtle body is discovered through physiology and emotion. It is mastered through imagination. The work of imagination takes us beyond the rung of scandal to the subtle-body rung. Further mastery of imagination employs the subtle body to effect apotheosis, our own divinization.

4

EMPTYING INDRA'S HEAVEN

When we considered the story of the Buddha's half-brother, Nanda, and his sudden transport into Indra's Heaven, we were unsettled by the end of the tale. Nanda's interest in his fiancée paled before those shining maidens, blissfully cavorting in a "Pure Land."[39] He immediately joined the company of the Buddha's monks—forswearing his wedding and, indeed, all the earthly joys of sex so as to save himself up for the subtle intensity of a congress that transcends the fleshly body. We wondered how pure and high-minded a vow of chastity could be that merely postponed sexual longing to a distant future.

The notion of erotic trance, however, has enabled us to understand that Nanda's mystic journey did not move him from one place to another but rather between two modes of seeing. One who has gained a certain mastery over the rise and fall of kundalini finds nothing improbable or postponed about Indra's Heaven. Trance takes place in an eternal "now" involving both body and mind, an utterly convincing vertical rupture of plane. The third eye of the brow chakra opens upon a mandala of coupled divine consorts enjoying Spontaneous Great Bliss. For a timeless moment, Nanda had been there—as much inside Indra's Heaven as it was inside him, drawn in through his ajna chakra and impressed upon the nectar dripping down the central channel of his subtle body. Even if he was left with no way of explaining the event, its vivid truth revalued all his values. Nothing less could serve as foundation for his daily life.

A process beginning in our physiology that generates emotional and imaginal realities invested with "involuntary belief" overshadows and reinterprets human life in a mythic manner. Down through the history of humanity—with the possible exception of the last two or three hundred years in the West—mythic realities have proven more comprehensive, coherent, and convincing than the space/time facts of everyday life. Furthermore, it is not simply that myth has had a greater explanatory power, nor that there is a larger reality waiting for us after death.

---

39 "Pure Lands": Iconographically represented aspects of the awakened state of mind in the stage before nirvana; in folk belief, geographically localized places of bliss (Fischer-Schreiber, *et.al.*, 1989). The story of Nanda, although evidently a folk-tale, evokes the more profound perspective of the Buddhist practitioner.

Both body and world are turned inside out in a single inversion of awareness. The empirical world is dissolved into and replaced by a celestial mandala, the passage of temporal moments into an eternal now, our all-too-solid flesh into a tubular palace of universally valid and localizable types of ecstasy. The human being who directs attention to subtle sensations and states of consciousness that have no place in our empirical world finds another dimension of reality, one that makes sense only in the context of luminous beings, the gods of mythology.

Our climb up the diamond ladder of sexual attainment is marked by a series of reversals, each revealing a reality more hidden than the last. Opposing the mechanical, spasmodic release of external orgasm reveals the power of eros. Exploring erotic longing reveals the arbitrary character of society's rules. An antinomian stance reveals the dragon of the soul's energy as an immanent surging forth of unthinkable power. Acquainting ourselves with that serpentine power reveals that the ladder does not lie outside us but is in fact our own subtle body. Imaginal mastery of the subtle body reveals the immanence of Indra's Heaven as a Spontaneous Great Bliss that lies within the reach of anyone who takes it seriously enough to submit to its discipline. The nectar of the sahasrara chakra is both physiological and mythic, and so is the "Pure Land" of coupled divinities.

From the moment a subtle plane of human experience becomes available on the rung of carezza to its culmination in Spontaneous Great Bliss, mythic realities have progressively become more well-known and reliable. Empiricism has been replaced by myth. To ascend beyond the rung of divinized coupling, however, another sort of replacement or inversion must take place. Gyatso alludes to this when he tells us that the practice of Mahamudra has three goals: Spontaneous Great Bliss, emptiness, and the fusion of emptiness with bliss.

Because the notion of emptiness is so foreign to our everyday consciousness and even to mythic consciousness, we have avoided the topic until now. Called *shunyata* in Sanskrit, "emptiness" is the name Buddhism gives to ultimate experience. In its earliest expression, it was called the doctrine of "no-self" (*an-atman* in Sanskrit). As a first approximation of what emptiness means, we might say that just as mythic consciousness asserts and demonstrates that the physical entities of empiricism are transcended by the imaginal objects of myth, so the awareness of emptiness transcends mythic objects. No object—either empirical or mythic—enjoys ultimacy. Both subject and object are transcended. If in mythic consciousness, I transcend the empirical ego to discover my identity with the divine ("Thou art That"), emptiness transcends both the Thou and the That.

Although brief descriptions of emptiness are inevitably misleading, they do point us in a useful direction. One classic approach to emptiness employs the standard Hindu doctrine of three states of consciousness. The *waking state* corresponds to the subjectivity of empirical consciousness; the *dreaming state* to mythic consciousness; and *dreamless sleep* to the undifferentiated unity of shunyata (Govinda, 1969: 23).[40] Eliade explains that the practice of breath control in yoga is designed to enable the yogin "without renouncing his lucidity [to] penetrate the states of consciousness that accompany sleep" (Eliade, 1969: 56). The main disadvantage of this approach is that it seems to imply that emptiness is an extraordinary sort of "object" that can be seen: "the rainbow-like insubstantiality and illusory nature of all phenomena" (Shaw, 1994: 24); or "a limitless sea of undifferentiated continuum" (Khanna, 1981: 30).

But Buddhism contends that emptiness is not an object at all. Rather it is "a term used to shift [our] mode of apprehending 'existence' and 'ultimate reality'" (Streng, 1967: 21). Emptiness has to do with our "manner of perceiving." Whereas mundane truth is "based on intellectual and emotional attachment," emptiness represents "a quality of life experienced in "complete indifference to the construction or cessation of 'things'" (Streng, 39). Japanese Buddhist philosopher, Keiji Nishitani, calls emptiness a return to the world of primary fact:

> We usually take the world as an extended environment that envelopes us and serves as our field of behavior. And from there, as it happens, we go on to think up another, invisible world behind that first one. But neither of them is the world in its suchness. Neither of them is the world we actually live in. The very fact that we can consider our extended environment to be a world, and then think up a supersensory world behind it, happens in the first place only because we actually live in a world of primary fact (Nishitani, 1982: 127).

Nishitani implies that what we have been calling the empirical world and the persona field that comprise mundane consciousness, as well as the invisible world that serves as the object of mythic consciousness, are secondary creations. Emptiness is not something we have to go out and find; it is rather an inherent perspective we have forgotten and must come back to.

It seems maddeningly contradictory to think that Buddhists spend years of study and meditation only to "return" to "a world of primary fact." We are reminded of koans and Zen stories like the following.

> Before beginning my study of Zen, when I looked out at the world I saw mountains, trees, and rivers. After three years of sitting in meditation, I no longer saw mountains, trees, and rivers. But now that I have studied Zen for thirty years and believe I have really come to understand it, when I look at the world I see mountains, trees, and rivers.

How are we to imagine the difference between the first state and the last? When "ultimate reality" is presented in *mythic* terms, symbols are employed to point to a transcendental ob-

---

40 Govinda's schema is somewhat oversimplified. According to the Mundakya Upanishad, there are four levels of consciousness. The fourth, *turiya*, would more properly be assigned as an equivalent of emptiness. We will discuss this later. For now, Govinda's description will suffice.

ject: Indra's Heaven; Father, Son, and Holy Ghost; the all-pervading brahman or shakti. Emptiness, however, is not a symbol that points to an object. To shift our mode of apprehension, it employs paradoxes that frustrate empirical and mythic ways of thinking. Emptiness is not a higher level of erotic trance. According to Gyatso, we first perfect erotic trance to the point of achieving Spontaneous Great Bliss. Then we enter that heightened state in the mentality of emptiness. Therefore, if we are to understand how sexual mysticism advances from the divinized rung of the ladder to that of emptiness, we will have to immerse ourselves in some of these paradoxes.

EMPTINESS AS PRIMAL EXPERIENCE

Returning to the world of primary fact implies that we were once there but that we have left it and forgotten it so thoroughly that the very idea of returning sounds like nonsense. Nishitani says we have cut ourselves off from the world of primary fact by locking ourselves up in "the citadel of the self" (Nishitani, 1982: 9). We are utterly convinced of our separateness from the people and things around us, living an "internal life" inside our heads and peering out through the windows of our eyes at others who are likewise opaque and hidden within themselves and at objects which are "dead things." The Buddhist doctrine of "no-self" is aimed precisely at this "common sense" standpoint whereby our being a "self" cordons off the world from us, making it everything we are not. We become mere observers, set at a distance from what we observe, gathering data from our sense organs as though they were coming in over telephone wires.

Obviously Buddhism would not have arisen in the East if the citadel self had not already been a problem there some 2600 years ago. But in the West over the last three or four centuries, it has become especially acute. Descartes formulated our imprisoned self in his *Meditations*, having determined that his own subjectivity was the beginning point of certainty ("I think, therefore, I am") and then sought to justify his knowledge of the world outside that self. Newton articulated a clockwork universe of dead objects acting upon one another according to mathematical laws of causality. We have all been born into this world that we know primarily in terms of abstract concepts worked out by rational "selves" located somewhere inside of brains that we conceptualize in terms of "hard wiring." We are suspicious of our emotions and imagination because their fuzziness and bias interfere with the clarity of our abstract concepts.

Before the seventeenth century, however, even educated Europeans were by no means so clear in distinguishing sensory knowledge and imagination. Alchemists, for example, treated their metals, salts, and liquids as spiritualized matter. They lived in a world of mystical participation with the substances in their laboratories and knew the experiments they performed in their retorts were also going on within themselves.[41] Even Isaac Newton was an alchemist; and his original conception of gravitation, the great driving force of the universe, was that all physical bodies are drawn to one another by eros—although he had to conceal this imaginal view in order to gain acceptance for his theories (Berman, 1981: 124). C. G. Jung, who opened the field of alchemy for modern scholarship, speaks of a "great schism" that occurred in Western culture at the time that alchemy gave way to modern empirical science. Imagination was sundered from measurable and repeatable observation and fell into disrepute (Jung, *CW 14*). A naive mystical participation of subject in object and object in subject, gets us closer to the world of primary fact than abstract concepts reckoned in the citadel of the self.

> Participation is self and non-self identified at the moment of experience. The pre-Homeric Greek, the medieval Englishman (to a lesser extent, of course), and the present-day African tribesman know a thing precisely in the act of identification, and this identification is as much sensual as it is intellectual. It is a *totality* of experience: the "sensuous intellect," if the reader can imagine such a thing. We have so lost the ability to make this identification that we are left today with only two experiences that consist of participating consciousness: lust and anxiety. As I make love to my partner, I immerse myself in her body, I become increasingly "lost." At the moment of orgasm, I *am* the act; there is no longer an "I" who experiences it (Berman, 1981: 76).

Berman makes it clear that *sometimes*—even for those of us who are not accomplished Buddhists—we have moments of leaving the citadel of the self and entering the world of primary fact. His book is not about mysticism but about the crisis of contemporary Western consciousness which prompts him to call for a "re-enchantment of the world." Nevertheless, his argument that we live in a derived world of concepts from which we must "return," echoes Nishitani's sentiments about the world of primary fact. It is also coherent with a wide-spread mystical theme according to which "enlightenment" is not some promontory we achieve by hard climbing but rather has to be "remembered." Our powerful tendency to take up residence in the fortress of the self causes us to overlook and forget moments when each of us has lived spontaneously and lost the artificial boundaries that support our subject/object dichotomy. One who is "awakened" or "enlightened," therefore, learns to recall what occurs in the gaps when the intellectual and social construction of reality falls away. By remember-

---

41 Jung frequently quotes the alchemical dictum, "*Ars totum requiret hominem*" (The art [of alchemy] demands the whole man [be involved in the work]) (e.g., Jung, *CW 12*: ¶ 6). The seventeenth century alchemist, Gerhard Dorn, warned that the practitioner would never succeed in making the "One" (the Philosophical Stone, the goal of the work) without first becoming "one" himself (Jung, *CW 14*: ¶ 753).

ing, cultivating, and expanding upon these moments, we are able to live more and more of the time in the world of primary fact.[42] This gives us a powerful hint concerning the Buddhist doctrine of emptiness.

That Berman chooses to give us a brief account of orgasm as a paradigm for mystical participation,[43] not only suits our theme of "sexual attainment," but also refers to a typical sort of gap in citadel-consciousness with which we are all familiar. Its universality suggests why Tantrism has chosen sexual practice as the shorter and more direct path to enlightenment.

OUR ORIGINAL COUNTENANCE

Zen speaks of "dropping body-and-mind," i.e., leaving citadel-consciousness so as to find the "original countenance" we had before our birth. Nishitani says, "This original countenance is present at the point that the world *worlds*, where one's treasure house opens of itself and one can use it at will" (Nishitani, 1982: 199). His phrase, "the world *worlds*," alludes to the philosophy of Martin Heidegger, who argues that human existence cannot be described in terms of an isolated subject in an environment of objects. Rather, human existence is "Being-in-the-world." The world is an inseparable part of our being. The world is in us and we are in the world. When the world "worlds" (does what the world does), it reveals us to ourselves. Jung, who was intemperately hostile to what he knew of Heidegger[44] and never mentions the

---

42 Daniel Odier's guru (to be described later on) says, "Without prior experience of awakening, no asceticism, no practice, no meditation bears fruit. Without awakening experience, there is no source, and since all of Tantric *sadhana* consists of returning to the source, one wanders, not knowing where to go. . . . Look into yourself deeply. Think about your childhood, your adolescence. An awakening experience is found there. No being exists on earth who hasn't had this fundamental experience" (Odier, 1997: 51).

43 Berman says "participation," not "mystical participation." I choose the latter phrase not only to be more specific, but also to allude to the writings of Lucien Lévy-Bruhl who describes "primitive mentality" with this phrase. He means that certain objects and events in ordinary life open upon a mythic world of "collective representations" to which the dichotomies of Western thinking do not apply (cf. Lévy-Bruhl, 1966).

44 In a letter to a graduate student in philosophy, Jung writes: "Heidegger's *modus philosophandi* is neurotic through and through and is ultimately rooted in his psychic crankiness. His kindred spirits, close or distant, are sitting in lunatic asylums, some as patients and some as psychiatrists on a philosophical rampage" (Adler, 1973: 331).

Buddhist doctrine of emptiness,[45] describes an experience he had in Africa which vividly illustrates the notion of "original countenance" and "the worlding of the world":

> To the very brink of the horizon we saw gigantic herds of animals: gazelle, antelope, gnu, zebra, warthog, and so on. Grazing, heads nodding, the herds moved forward like slow rivers. There was scarcely any sound save the melancholy cry of a bird of prey. This was the stillness of the eternal beginning, the world as it had always been, in the state of non-being; for until then no one had been present to know that it was this world. . . . There I was now, the first human being to recognize that this was the world, but who did not know that in this moment he had first really created it.
>
> [All this is in contrast to the "cheerless clockwork fantasy" of the Western world, which fails to understand that man] himself is the second creator of the world, who alone has given to the world its objective existence—without which, unheard, unseen, silently eating, giving birth, dying, heads nodding through hundreds of millions of years, it would have gone on in the profoundest night of non-being down to its unknown end. Human consciousness created objective existence and meaning, and man found his indispensable place in the great process of being (Jung, 1961: 255-6).

Jung's sense that he was the first being to recognize the world and by this means bring it into existence as a "great process of being" in which he participated certainly has all the marks of "primary fact." The world *worlds* as fodder and riverbed for the slowly streaming herds and at the same time becomes the "clearing" in which Jung's own Being-in-the-world finds its place as *Dasein* (Being-here). In this sense, his "original countenance" is revealed as the face before which the timeless primal fact of his humanity breaks through the "cheerless clockwork fantasy" of his European heritage. Evidently he felt himself brought to a new and more vital sense of life in the same moment that the world took on its eternal countenance, that state of "non-being" which was no longer a collection of objects, but the world in its "suchness,"

---

45 Although he usually asserted the gurus of India were too philosophically unsophisticated to know that there can be no experience if the experiencer (the ego) is overcome, less than a month before his death he remarked to Chilean journalist Miguel Serrano: "I have just finished reading a book by a Chinese Zen Buddhist. And it seemed to me that we were talking about the same thing, and that the only difference between us was that we gave different words to the same reality" (Serrano, 1968: 100).

An analogous point might be mentioned. In his study of mandalas spontaneously painted by his patients, Jung notes that the center is typically left empty—a striking contrast with the traditional mandalas of the Hindus and Buddhists, which generally place a divinity at the center. Jung believes that this indicates that God is a problem for us Westerners. Perhaps it also suggests that we are closer to an intuition of emptiness than we know. Compare this with the discussion of the crisis of nothingness that appears later in this chapter.

the point where everything "gathers together" and reveals a luminous and timeless oneness in which observer and observed are no longer sundered from one another. Jung lived that moment in the gap which moved the Zen master Rinzai to say, "If you meet the Buddha on the road, kill him."[46] If the Buddha is an "other" you can meet, he blocks your way to the emptiness of your own Buddha-nature. Nishitani comments: "We have to kill the self absolutely. And to do that is also to kill the Buddha, the patriarchs, and everything else, breaking through the field where self and other are discriminated from one another and made relative to one another" (Nishitani: 1982: 263).

Jung's experience reminds me of a timeless moment that occurred one afternoon when I rode a "whalewatch" ship out of Boston Harbor into Massachesetts Bay. As I stood at the rail, a porpoise suddenly broke through the surface of the water several yards away and swooped in a lazy sine curve parallel to our vessel, arcing alternately through air and water, keeping pace with us for a while before diving out of sight. Caught by surprise, the incessant chattering of my mind was brought to a halt, and something wordless was revealed. I was confronted with pure porpoise-hood. The magnificent being before me was simply "porpoising," living its porpoise nature in its uncluttered simplicity. As it porpoised, the sea and the air were brought to presence as the playground of its undulant, effortless surging. A moment before, the air had been as absent from my consciousness as it typically is, as the taken-for-granted medium that is forgotten when we look out at the world from the citadel of the self; and the sea had merely been the uneven floor of our vessel's passage. But in the first splash of its porpoising surge, my bottle-nosed companion porpoised sea and air into existence as the complimentary fluids of porpoiseful play. As body-and-mind dropped away, I, too, was porpoised. I felt the undulating flow in my legs and trunk, the enveloping plunge and light splashing free. In that brief episode, the two of us participated in a single primal world in which subject and object dissolved. There was no time to think, no opportunity to retreat to the citadel of my self. Only long after the porpoise had disappeared did it occur to me to wonder whether that air-breathing denizen of the deep had been as much "humaned" as I had been porpoised.

Also somewhat later I looked about and wondered whether any of the others standing at the rail had experienced what I had. Had I been the only one? Or may it have been the fact that we had all been porpoised, although only one or two of us noticed it? For this would

---

46 Rinzai Gigen: the Japanese name for the Chinese Ch'an (Zen) master, Lin-chi I-hsüan, ninth century, c.e. (Fischer-Schreiber, *et. al.*, 1989). Rinzai wrote: "If you meet the Buddha, kill him; if you meet a patriarch, kill him; if you meet a sage, kill him; if you meet your father or mother, kill them; if you meet your relatives, kill them. Only then will you obtain liberation and dwell in complete emancipated freedom, without getting emotionally caught up in things" (quoted in Nishitani, 1982: 262-3).

surely reflect the Buddhist doctrine that the world of primary fact is always present for all of us. We notice it—if at all—only "subliminally" and are rarely able to remember it. Even while being porpoised, we hide this primary fact from our consciousness by indulging in the same old static: "Oh, look, there's a porpoise! That's not a porpoise, it's a dolphin! My, isn't he close? He's so graceful!" Our exclamatory noise reveals a burst of excitement and energy. What *really* moves us: the porpoise as object to be photographed, or the porpoising that has invaded our being?

EMPTINESS AND THE LUCIDITY OF DREAMLESS SLEEP

A number of folkloric accounts of emptiness describe it from the viewpoint of an awe-struck and uninitiated outsider—the Tibetan biography of Machig Lapdron being an excellent example. In her previous life Machig had been a man initiated by a yogini, and her birth was attended by extraordinary signs. After years of study and practice, she was informed by a dakini that the Indian sage Topabhadra should be her consort. When she found him, however, he said he had nothing to teach her, to which she replied that the content of the teaching was of no importance; for to make a "*dharma* connection," any teaching would do. Their union produced so much light that Machig's landlady believed the house was on fire and opened the door. "She saw nothing except a room full of light and red and white spheres of light . . . She was afraid and fell into a deep sleep." Subsequently, Machig's antinomian sexual practice led to rumors that she had fallen from the ways of dharma, but in the end her evident spirituality won over her critics (Allione, 1986: 150-87).

The story begins by setting Machig apart from all ordinary women. Her birth is the culmination of many lifetimes of striving for nirvana—both as a man and as a woman. Her transmigrating soul has been initiated by a yogini and is therefore prepared for the highest levels of sexual mysticism. This goal is announced when the mature Machig, in a state of erotic trance, encounters a dakini who assigns Topabhadra as her "dharma consort." When he says she is so advanced he has nothing to teach her, the testimony of a recognized sage is employed to verify the excellence of her spiritual state. But there is a deeper meaning to Topabhadra's words. He has nothing to teach because emptiness cannot be taught. Machig agrees. Any teaching will do, because emptiness is beyond all teaching.

Dharma is a multifaceted term in Buddhism. It refers to the cosmic law that supports the world and ourselves, the teaching of the Buddha, ethical norms ("the ways of dharma"), and the sublime "suchness" that makes every being the wondrous entity it is. The dharma-body of the Buddha stands for his eternal essence that lies beyond all representation. In this sense, a "dharma connection" between a male Buddha and a female Buddha would be a sublime union of complementary principles. The two would be uniting in their "suchness," a state beyond subject and object. The folkloric nature of the story, however, conceals the experience of the two participants. We have to depend for our information upon an outside observer, just as in the story of Nangsa Obam's union with Lama Gyaltsen.

Machig's attainment of emptiness in her ritual embrace of Topabhadra is suggested by that roomful of light that is nearly devoid of form. As she stammers before this mystery, the story-teller provides red and white spheres of light. We are face-to-face with a mystery more sublime than the union of wrathful dakinis reported by the soldiers in Nangsa's story. Our only witness is so affected that she becomes afraid and falls into a deep sleep. We are reminded of the fearful anxiety the Jewish prophets experienced in the presence of God, or the disciples of Jesus when he was transfigured bright as snow on the mountain top.[47] The landlady loses consciousness because the metaphysical event before her belongs to the realm of dreamless sleep, and she cannot resist its pull. Like those who listen to the tale, she has not developed the yogic lucidity that would allow her to remain conscious in the face of emptiness. There is nothing there to see.

SAMADHI

The emptiness of dreamless sleep suggests samadhi, the highest state of yogic consciousness, which Nishitani cites as an analogue of emptiness.

> The mode of being of things in their selfness [emptiness] consists of the fact that things take up a position grounded in themselves and settle themselves on that position. They center in on themselves and do not get scattered. From ancient times, the word *samadhi* ("settling") has been used to designate the state of mind in which a man gathers his own mind together and focuses it on a central point, thereby taking a step beyond the sphere of ordinary consciousness and self-conscious mind and, in that sense, forgetting his ego. . . . The form of things as they are on their own home-ground is similar to the appearance of things in *samadhi* (Nishitani, 1982: 128).

Nishitani does not mean that emptiness is achieved only in and through samadhi, but rather that the state of awareness beyond subject and object which describes samadhi gives us a paradigmatic instance of emptiness. Samadhi is often described as a "state of ecstatic union

---

47 "And after six days Jesus took with him Peter and James and John, and led them up a high mountain apart by themselves; and he was transfigured before them, and his garments became glistening, intensely white, as no fuller on earth could bleach them" (Mk 2: 1-3).

with the object of contemplation" or as "enstasy" (Feuerstein, 1989: 11)—not a flight *from* oneself but a sinking deeper in toward one's "original face."

The journey to samadhi involves three stages.[48] The first of these is dharana (concentration). In this state, the diffuseness of ordinary consciousness—the many trains of thought, distractions, and concerns that tumble all over one another—is brought to a halt; and the yogin focuses on a single object, such as the breathing process. The in-and-out of one's breath becomes the constant against which diffuse images, thoughts, and sensations "float" like motes in a sunbeam. In the next stage, dhyana (meditation proper), the yogin attains "a unified current of thought." One no longer has the experience of breathing but of "being breathed." My breathing is no longer something that "I do"; rather my breath is a river of process, an impersonal "being done" more fundamental that the "I" who observes it. Thoughts—"Isn't this marvelous! "I've finally done it!" or "Of course, why didn't I notice it sooner"—are interruptions in the flow, a return to the citadel of the self.

"The mandala constructing itself before you . . . the mantra flowing like a river" (Odier, 1997: 28), describes dhyana. In addition, it is universally claimed that the yogin "penetrates" the object of meditation and "assimilates" it (Eliade, 1969: 72). I perceive a condition of "no difference" between me, my breathing, and the universe at large. The expanding, contracting cosmos is breathing; and the breathing that breathes me is but the center of a universal process of in and out. I am not different from that. At this point, the "meditation" of dhyana fades into the "enstasy" of samadhi, where "mental activity ceases" in a "total absorption in the object of meditation" (Fischer-Schreiber, *et. al.*, 1989). It is a "perfect forgetting of the state of meditation which precedes it" (Feuerstein, 1990). Consciousness is aware only of itself.

The process from "one-pointed concentration" through "river of thought" to "I am That," recapitulates the development of erotic trance. Entrance onto a subtle plane where everything overflows with erotic significance amounts to an involuntary slide into the concentration of dharana. The wet spot in the bed is no longer a disgusting mess but a sanctifying substance. Nothing has meaning apart from eros, which is the background and depth dimension of all that appears. We are not distracted by cramps or the stickiness of skin upon skin. Nothing *is* for us but the world of eros. The tubular palace meditation vividly describes a form of dhyana, a river of thought moving up and down the central channel of the subtle body, unifying physiology, emotion, and imagination in a total world of process. The mandala of copulating deities that assembles itself before the third eye is also dhyana, and so is the condensed drop of bliss. But once that bliss is imprinted on the nectar so that there is no longer a difference

---

48 These three steps are collectively referred to as *samyama* ("constraint," Nishitani's "settling" and "centering") (Eliade, 1969: 69-70).

between the bliss of Indra's Heaven and the bliss that transubstantiates our subtle body, we begin to slide over into samadhi.

When we ride the divine-impressed drop of nectar up and down the central staircase of the subtle body, our "enstasy" is still dependent on the form of an object. To step beyond that, to forget the subtle body and its contents, is to enter "formless" samadhi[49] and simply, spontaneously to *be* blissfully. Here, Indra's Heaven has been emptied of all content. We have transcended imagination and myth and entered the field of emptiness.

The image of Machig's landlady falling into a great fear and losing consciousness altogether suggests a less than blissful aspect to emptiness. The discovery that the everyday world of mountains, trees, and rivers is an arbitrary social construction, and that the citadel self is nothing but a comforting illusion: these disturbing revelations imply that we are self-deluding ghosts inhabiting a ghostly world floating above an abyss of nothingness. The replacement of that ghostly world by a mythic mandala of shining beings that convinces us with involuntary belief brings with it a sense of meaning, fulfillment, and ultimacy. We know we have "ascended" from profane consciousness, re-enchanted our lives, discovered something immeasurably "more" that had long lurked unnoticed in our body-and-mind. But when body-and-mind fall away and the world of myth dissolves as surely as our ghostly web of concepts, we find ourselves faced with nothing at all.

THE CRISIS OF NOTHINGNESS

If emptiness is sublime, nothingness is an existential crisis. Nothingness, we might say, is the "shadow side" of emptiness. Nishitani calls it the "Great Doubt," "when self-existence, together with the being of all things turns into a single doubt" (Nishitani, 1981: 18). Surely this doubt is inextricably tangled with my own "no-self" and the "no-self" of every object I encounter. Everything, myself included, is lost. "Death and nihility" constitute "the final frontier of [our] self-existence" (Nishitani, 16). When this happens, the frequently cited words of the Brihadaranyaka Upanishad, "*neti, neti*" ("not this, not this"), strike terror in our hearts. The Upanishad wants to direct our attention away from this empirical world of illusion to the ultimate brahman. But if the emptiness doctrine is correct and brahman, too, is empty, we are faced with the loss of all possibility of security. The "Great Doubt" which might have led to enlightenment leaves us on the brink of a "cosmic" abyss.

---

49 There are two forms of *samadhi*: *savikalpa-samadhi* (enstasy supported by the *form* of a meditation object) and *nirvikalpa-samadhi* (formless enstasy). *Vikalpa* can be translated as "form"; *sa* means "with"; *nir* means "without" (Feuerstein, 1990).

The fact that this line of thought is no Western-entrenched distortion of Eastern mystical practice is brought home to us by a story told by a female "Vimalananda" whom we meet in a book written by Daniel Odier, *Tantric Quest: An Encounter with Absolute Love* (1997). Having been introduced to Hinduism at home in France through a much older woman, a painter on whom he had had an immense crush when he was only sixteen, Odier managed to get himself to India in 1968 at the age of twenty-three to take photographs for a book on Tibetan painting. No sooner had he completed his commission, however, then his cameras and all his film were stolen in a train station in New Delhi. After an extended panicky search and consultation with the police, he decided to forget about the publication project and to go in search of a spiritual teacher. Just over the border in Tibet, Kalou Rinpoche took him on as a disciple in the Mahamudra tradition and gave him the dharma name Karma Sonam Tcheupel ("One who is blessed by karma and who can seize the way") to honor the fact that his spiritual adventures had been occasioned by the "karma" of the theft in New Delhi. By the end of a year of practice, he had arrived at a very high level of mandala meditation[50]:

> that state in which one desires only one thing: to remain in meditation for hours, unmoving as if fixed in the center of space; full of warmth, energy, openness; breathing deeply, regularly, and silently—the mandala, constructing itself before you as if projected, each detail intensely present, the mantra flowing like a river, the phases of absorption following one another smoothly until the final void (Odier, 1997: 28).

It was not until 1993, however, at the age of forty-eight, that Odier finally met the Bhairavi who structured his final initiation on the Tantric path. He knew this woman only as "Devi," and reports her teachings and stories very much in the style of Svoboda's much lengthier and more exhaustive accounts of Vimalananda. As regards the disciple's potentially devastating first encounter with nothingness, Devi tells him a story from an earlier portion of her life when she was living as a kind of anchorite:

> After leaving my master, I decided to go meditate in a cave, alone. Certain spots in the mountains, many days or even many weeks by foot from any village, have been known to ascetics for thousands of years, and often one becomes only one more occupant of a cave where dozens of sages have lived. Sometimes, one finds Buddhist sutras engraved in the stone, sometimes Sanskrit letters or mantras. The caves are often found in a place in the mountains that resembles a hive, and it happens sometimes that many dozen ascetics are living within the range of each other's voices. There you find Tibetans, Hindus, tantrikas—sometimes even Chinese and monks of the Small Vehicle with their saffron robes. I've even seen Japanese

---

50 Note that this is a rather different impression of the discipline than Stephen Beyer's (1973) account, cited in our previous chapter, of the monk's strenuous effort deliberately to compose the mandala before his mind's eye.

93

monks with their straw hats and black gowns. Sometimes one of the hermits goes down to look for food. Sometimes they speak to each other as they draw water from the spring; they laugh and they dance, though the people in the village can't imagine it. Sometimes a hermit dies, and they burn him or bury him or leave him to the vultures.[51] Sometimes a hermit gets sick or is taken by what we call "the immense fear." All hermits know this or will know it one day. It is the ultimate crack in the Self, the doorway of the divine (Odier, 1997: 87-8).

Devi says no more about this "immense fear" that is "the ultimate crack in the self." She leaves us with the image of hermits innocently happy in the pursuit of their separate mystic paths until one day an existential crisis opens up a paralyzing void beneath not only the world but one's very self. The path itself is part of the comforting delusion. We are reminded of the words of the great German mystic, Meister Eckhart (c. 1260-1327), "Whoever is seeking God by ways is finding ways and losing God" (Colledge & McGinn, 1981: 183).

Devi's hermits very likely include some of the most earnest and devoted spiritual practitioners to be found. Their ability to laugh and dance, their tolerance of one another's separate doctrines and cultural assumptions, and the care they show one another all tell us that these are not rigid fundamentalists. In their great respect for the multiplicity of their separate paths, however, lurks the recognition that no path is "ultimate." The "immense fear" and the fact that they "all know this or will know it one day" means that they are consciously and deliberately skating on thin ice. Apparently each of them knows—or will one day learn—that the holy ladder of the path will eventually crumble and that they have no alternative but to climb it in all sincerity knowing they are in for a fall. They are courting that fall, even as they live in terror of it.

In the chapters of Odier's book that follow upon this story, Devi contrives exercises for her disciple designed to open up that "crack in the self." He has to meditate alone in the forest for three days and nights, then stand naked, meditating on the edge of a cliff for another seventy-two hours; finally he is abandoned in a community of lepers. Each time he constructs for himself comforting mystical illusions much more profound and simple than his reader is apt to be capable of inventing. Each time his ladder collapses.

If the truth of human existence be known, we have no need to seek the cliffs and trees outside a remote Indian village to know this nothingness, this fall into an existential void. It can happen to us at any moment, as William James knew very well:

---

51 Presumably the disposition of the body is chosen according to the religious tradition in which the dead hermit lived. Parsees, for example, expose the corpses of the dead on towers to be devoured by vultures. Vultures embody the spiritualizing potential of death for Zoroastrians, ancient Egyptians, and a large number of American Indian cultures.

Whilst in this state of philosophic pessimism and general depression of spirits about my prospects, I went one evening into a dressing-room in the twilight to procure some article that was there; when suddenly there fell upon me without any warning, just as if it came out of the darkness, a horrible fear of my own existence. Simultaneously there arose in my mind the image of an epileptic patient whom I had seen in the asylum, a black-haired youth with greenish skin, entirely idiotic, who used to sit all day on one of the benches, or rather shelves against the wall, with his knees drawn up against his chin, and the coarse gray undershirt, which was his only garment, drawn over them enclosing his entire figure. He sat there like a sort of sculptured Egyptian cat or Peruvian mummy, moving nothing but his black eyes and looking absolutely non-human. This image and my fear entered into a species of combination with each other. *That shape am I*, I felt, potentially. Nothing that I possess can defend me against that fate, if the hour for it should strike for me as it struck for him. There was such a horror of him, and such a perception of my own merely momentary discrepancy from him, that it was as if something hitherto solid within my breast gave way entirely, and I became a mass of quivering fear. After this the universe was changed for me altogether. I awoke morning after morning with a horrible dread at the pit of my stomach, and with a sense of the insecurity of life that I never knew before, and that I have never felt since. It was like a revelation; and though the immediate feelings passed away, the experience has made me sympathetic with the morbid feelings of others ever since. It gradually faded, but for months I was unable to go out into the dark alone.

In general I dreaded to be left alone. I remember wondering how other people could live, how I myself had ever lived, so unconscious of that pit of insecurity beneath the surface of life (Novak, 1970: 59-60).[52]

Such an existential crisis marks the end of a certain delusional way of life and opens up the possibility of emptiness as a "field of consciousness" that may be called nirvana. But we may still fall short of this mystic goal, as William James did. Although he died more than three decades before the publication of Sartre's *Being and Nothingness*,[53] James' solution to his immense fear has much in common with that of the French existentialist. James chooses to "believe in my individual reality and creative power": "Life shall [be built in] doing and suffering and creating" (Novak, 61). The American psychologist makes the heroic choice to construct a bridge of moment-to-moment decisions over the emptiness of the void.[54] Buddhism,

---

52 Quoting *The Writings of William James*, ed. John J. McDermott (New York: Random House, 1967), p. 6. This story also appears in James' *Varieties of Religious Experience*, where it is attributed to a "Frenchman." However, in a letter to the French translator of *Varieties*, James admits that it is his own experience.

53 James died in 1910. Sartre's *L'être et le néant* was published in 1943.

54 This, at any rate, has been the standard interpretation of James' experience. In fact the dating of these passages is unclear, and it may well be that James" experience of nothingness followed upon

in contrast, would have us plumb that void to the very bottom. Nishitani says, "The reality that appears from the bottom of the Great Doubt and overturns it is none other than our "original countenance" (Nishitani, 1982: 21). The terror of nothingness, therefore, is the beginning of the wisdom of emptiness. Instead of building a bridge of fog over the abyss of nothingness through willful choosing, Nishitani invites us to sit in the void and realize that our immense fear is but the shock of recognition that our loss of world and self is a dis-illusionment. We have cherished the old illusions so dearly that "the world of primary fact" scares us. To get beyond that dread is to see all things new, and at the same time as old as the hills.

THINGS NEITHER EXIST NOR DO NOT EXIST; THEY ARE EMPTY

We have looked at three approaches to emptiness and arrived at what seems to be three different places: the world of primary fact, the sublime objectless state of samadhi, and the crisis of nothingness. What holds them together and saves us from despair is that Zen story about mountains, trees, and rivers. The world our story-teller knew before beginning his study of Zen had undoubtedly been seen from the citadel of the self. By the second stage, when he no longer saw mountains, trees, and rivers, he must have done a great deal of work. He fails to tells us whether he was trembling in "immense fear" upon seeing the world dissolve into nothingness or whether he had learned formless samadhi. All we know is that he experienced some sort of "crack in the self" and the world as he had always known it had disappeared. Finally, when he had mastered Zen and again saw mountains, trees, and rivers, we have to think that he had arrived at the world of primary fact and his own original countenance.

This seemingly speculative and impressionistic synthesis is actually well founded in the history of Buddhist doctrine and shows some striking parallels with Western scientific discoveries.

The basic scriptures of Buddhism are traditionally referred to as the "three baskets" (*tripitaka*): (1) the origins of the Buddhist community (sangha) and its rules of discipline, (2) the discourses supposedly spoken by the Buddha himself, and (3) the Abhidharma ("supreme dharma") writings (third century, B.C.E., to third century, C.E.). These last are comprised of philosophical and psychological arguments designed to enable the practitioner to deconstruct the profane world and attain spiritual insight or "wisdom" (prajna). It is here that mountains, trees, and rivers are made to disappear.

---

the failure of his proto-existentialist heroics, Cf. Louis Menand, "William James and the Case of the Epileptic Patient." *New York Review of Books XLV*(20) (December 17, 1998): 81-93.

The goal of the Abhidharma literature is to teach us to analyze all our ways of knowing so as to eliminate the false assumptions that maintain the profane world (Streng, 1967: 31). Its highest aim is to reach a point where, "There is no knowledge as such, no *bodhisattva*,[55] no path of attainment, or no being who *has* knowledge, or who *is* the *bodhisattva*, or who *proceeds* on the path" (Streng, 34). All of these things—knowledge, bodhisattva, and path—are falsely conceived as entities that really exist through the ignorance of the citadel self, which the Abhidharma seeks to undermine through the doctrine of "dependent co-origination" (*pratitya-samutpada*). None of the things we take to be entities possessing a "self" is anything other than a constantly changing agglomeration of dharmas (discrete manifestations of reality). A human being, for instance, is: "a changing conglomeration of material, mental, and psychic factors (*dharmas*) [which] interact to form the experienced world. . . . For the 'arising of existence' [the empirical world] to cease, the fabricating of ignorance must cease; and the quelling of ignorance requires spiritual insight (*prajna*)" (Streng , 30). In practice, this means that the meditator learns to see her own supposed "individuality" as comprised of five "heaps" (*skandhas*) of dharmas: the body, the feelings, the perceptions, the emotions, and the acts of consciousness.

> Anything a person may grasp at, or lean on, or appropriate, must fall within one of those five groups, which make up the *stuff* of "individuality." The *belief* in individuality is said to arise from the invention of a "self" over and above those five heaps. The belief expresses itself in the assumption that any of this is "mine" or that "I am" any of this, or that any of this "is myself." . . . When the individual, as constituted by the arbitrary lump taken from those five heaps, ceases to exist, the result is Nirvana—the goal of Buddhism (Conze, 1959: 14).

The Abhidharma notion of "dependent co-origination" claims that everything, oneself included, is actually a fleeting lump that has no independent existence, for the invisible dharmas that comprise it are constantly being exchanged with the rest of the fleeting lumps that make up the empirical world. By eating bread, for example, the arbitrary lump that is my body temporarily incorporates dharmas that formerly belonged to grain and before that were to be found heaped together in soil and manure. All the lumps that comprise the phenomenal world are constantly exchanging dharmas with one another according to the causal law of dependent co-origination. By enlarging our vision from minutes, hours, and years to kalpas (world cycles), we see that everything depends upon everything else and "originates" or is assembled from the disintegration products of everything else. Every lump arises from other lumps and dissipates into still others.

---

55 *Bodhisattva*: one who has renounced taking the final step into enlightenment until all sentient beings have been saved; the ideal to be attained in the Mahayana, "Great Vehicle" Buddhism, to which the Abhidharma and Madhyamika schools belong.

The closest Western analogy of dependent co-origination is the cosmic vision inspired by quantum theory. The atoms of hydrogen, oxygen, iron, and the like, that we take to be the unchangeable building blocks of our empirical world, are in fact temporary conglomerations of subatomic particles. To understand this, we have to see the universe within the vast temporal context in which supernovae are gradually formed in temperatures very close to "absolute zero," where all motion ceases. At such temperatures, the repellent forces between subatomic particles are almost non-existent so that gravity can pull vast numbers of them so closely together that they burst into life as a star. Stars "create" atoms through nuclear fusion reactions that produce heat and light; and when the stars are big enough, they eventually explode as supernovae and distribute the newly formed atoms throughout a wide neighboring region—where they can be taken up by other stars and settle out in planets. In the broad scheme of things, stars are constantly forming and dying, constituting, distributing, and destroying the entities that comprise the visible universe.[56]

The lowest temperatures of Antarctica are "hot" by the standards of outer space—nearly four hundred Fahrenheit degrees warmer than the regions in which stars are formed. In these warmer conditions on planet Earth, relatively complicated molecules have formed through the chemical bonding of atoms. But these molecules, too, are "stable" only in the sense that they preserve a relatively constant structure through the continual exchange of components with their environment that we call "equilibrium." When these processes of exchange become sufficiently complicated and diverse that they can replicate themselves (as in the case of DNA), we begin to speak of "life." In its highest forms, life manifests unmistakable signs of mentality. But even the constitution of what we think of as a human individual—passing in the blink of a cosmic eye through the myriad changes of conception, birth, growth, and death—is by no means "constant" in its components. We eat, drink, breathe, and eliminate, constantly exchanging molecules with our environment.[57]

The doctrine of dependent co-origination, had it arisen in the twentieth century, would no doubt have seized upon these scientific facts to support its view that what we take to be entities-with-a-self are, in fact, nothing but temporary conglomerates behind which nothing permanent, "no self," can be found. All is change. The entities we naively take for "reality" are constantly arising and disintegrating. Wisdom resides in attending to the flux. Ignorance alone satisfies itself with "real entities."

---

56 I cannot recommend a more comprehensive or lucid description than Lee Smolin's *The Life of the Cosmos* (1997).

57 A very readable and full presentation of these processes may be found in Fritjof Capra, *The Web of Life* (1996).

The centrality of flux, however, is not unique to Abhidharma Buddhism and quantum mechanics. From Heraclitus in ancient Greece to A. N. Whitehead in the twentieth century, the priority of process and change over substance has been a minor theme in the philosophy of the West. In the twelfth century in the Middle East, Ibn al-'Arabi argued for impermanence and the "self-empty" nature of phenomenal entities, saying that God creates the world anew in every instant: "The ultimate reason why the world is Imagination and, like dreams, demands a hermeneutics, is to be sought in the recurrent creation, imperceptible to the senses" (Corbin, 1969: 208). A modern Sufi puts this in experiential terms: "In the constant flow of inhalation and exhalation, *and especially in the almost imperceptible pause between the two*, a vibrating model of the two worlds in which we live presents itself to us" (Sviri, 1997: 179).

The high-point of the Abhidharma school's teachings is the "wisdom" literature known as Prajnaparamita (the "Wisdom that Reaches the Other Shore," a reference to the image of Buddhism as a "raft" to us take across the "river" from samsara to nirvana). This wisdom literature, which includes the well-known *Diamond Sutra* and *Heart Sutra*, takes the doctrine of emptiness a step further. It is not only the lumps that are empty of real existence, but the dharmas that comprise them also are empty. The only thing that exists is the causal process of dependent co-origination.

This more radical standpoint of the Prajnaparamita also finds an analogy in quantum theory: namely in the Heisenberg Uncertainty Principle which states that we can know either the momentum or the location of an electron but not both. Our experiments determine what we find. The observer interferes with the observed in the act of observing it. This implies that the subject/object dichotomy we take for granted in the common-sense world is not justified by scientific experiment. Subject and object are mutually implicated, and there is something wrong with our common-sense assumption. It opens the possibility that Buddhism may be right. Perhaps neither the subject nor the object has a "self."

THREADS IN THE CLOTH

Even more radically, we cannot determine whether the electron is matter (a particle) or energy (an unimaginable flux). In most general terms, the electron of a particular atom is described as a "cloud of probabilities" which only "collapses" into behaving like an entity (matter) when we perform an experiment that requires it to respond as a particle. Otherwise, it is pure energy, pure "vibration" (flux).[58] These facts of scientific experimentation suggest that

---

58 This view is presented in nearly every book on the "new physics." A very accessible one is Fred Alan Wolf, *Taking the Quantum Leap* (1989).

the universe might be pure energy and that our sensory faculties simply require it to appear as a collection of entities with substance. If so, we are presented with the sort of cosmic vision Muktananda reports from a moment when subject and object were transcended in samadhi. Corresponding to the physicists' vibrating energy-continuum, Muktananda sees "pure consciousness" (chiti):

> The Light pervaded everywhere in the form of the universe. I saw the earth being born and expanding from the Light of Consciousness, just as one can see smoke arising from a fire. I could actually see the world within this conscious Light, and the Light within the world, like threads in a piece of cloth, and the cloth in the threads. Just as a seed becomes a tree, with branches, leaves, flowers, and fruit, so within Her own being Chiti becomes animals, birds, germs, insects, gods, demons, men, and women. I could see this radiance of Consciousness, resplendent and utterly beautiful, silently pulsing as supreme ecstasy within me, outside me, above me, below me. . . . In this condition the phenomenal world vanished and I saw only pure radiance" (Muktananda, 1978: 183).

The analogy between quantum mechanics and dependent co-origination has two parts. The particle-physicists' project to isolate the fundamental building blocks of matter parallels the early Abhidharma's effort to analyze all entities into their component dharmas. The further experimental discovery, however, that the particles themselves represent unique occurrences when an observer (or some other phenomenal "lump") has caused an energy cloud of probabilities to collapse, corresponds to the Prajnaparamita position that the dharmas themselves are empty.

> "Wisdom" in both the *Abhidharma* and the *Prajnaparamita* writings meant "looking at things as they are." However, whereas the *Abhidharma* had tried to see the nonsubstantiality of things by seeing the factors that composed them, the *Prajnaparamita* maintained that the factors themselves were empty of independent reality, and that the notions of "path," "*dharma*," or "Buddha" were meaningless if they designated entities with particular and unique characteristics (Streng, 1967: 84).

Buddhist philosophy, therefore, progressed from the original insight that I, the observer, am empty of a self to the view that both I and the object I observe are empty because we are all comprised of invisible dharmas locked in a causal process of dependent co-origination. Then the dharmas were declared to be empty, and there was nothing left but the causal process. The logical next step was taken by the great Buddhist systematizer, Nagarjuna, who declared dependent co-origination itself to be empty. There is no causal link between the "things that appear." Rather dependent co-origination "becomes the form for expressing the phenomenal 'becoming' as the lack of any self-sufficient, independent reality" (Streng, 1967: 63).[59] "Emptiness simply becomes; it is not the end of a 'becoming process'" (Streng, 65).

Nagarjuna,[60] who lived in the second and third centuries of the common era, founded the Madhyamika school of Buddhism. *Madhyamika* means "middle teaching" and can be summarized in three statements that comprise the paradox of emptiness. *It is not true that things exist*: with this statement, Nagarjuna undermines naive empirical consciousness. *It is not true that things do not exist*: with this he rejects naive nihilism.[61] *What is true is that all things are empty*: this is the "middle" position between empiricism and nihilism. Emptiness is not a symbol or word used to signify the ultimate (Streng, 1967: 142). All names, including "dependent co-origination," and all entities, including the dharmas, are empty. Even a word like nirvana, although useful to indicate complete spiritual release, does not point to anything that can be "grasped" (Streng, 69). Indeed, Nagarjuna is famous for his declaration that nirvana and samsara are the same. We cannot build a raft to take us across the "river" from the everyday world of samsara and enter the sublime world of nirvana. That river does not exist. Nirvana is precisely the world of samsara, but lived in a different manner (Streng, 145). "Emptiness" represents a shift in attitude that brings about spiritual release. "The difference between *nirvana* and *samsara* applies only to the conventional norms for truth, for ultimately both of them are empty (*sunya*)" (Streng, 75).

When Nagarjuna claims that all things are empty, he does not mean that they do not exist in the world of everyday consciousness or that the true state of reality is some sort of blank. "Rather there is only one state of existence: that things rise and dissipate through dependent co-origination" (Streng, 146-7). By analogy, it might be argued that when Ibn al-'Arabi claims that God recreates the world in every moment, he means that what we see as a constant field of objects is actually the rapid arising and dissipating of an entire world under the control of a Creator. The Abhidharma eliminated the Creator and left us with invisible dharmas assembling and dissipating according to dependent co-origination. The Prajnaparamita, however,

---

59 This philosophical development strangely parallels (albeit in a more radical manner) the development in English philosophy from Locke through Berkeley to Hume. After Locke had said all we can know is the mind, the series of thoughts that flow through it, and the causal connections between them, Berkeley eliminated the mind and Hume the causal connections, leaving us only with a flow of ideas connected by temporal contiguity.

60 The legend of Nagarjuna's origins is suggested by his name: one who was born under a certain tree (*arjuna*) and taught by serpents (*naga*). *Arjuna*, meaning "white," is also the name of the hero of the *Bhagavad Gita*, which consists in the teachings given to him by his guru and charioteer, Krishna (Fischer-Schreiber, *et. al.*, 1989). Another Nagarjuna is a legendary figure in Indian alchemy (D. G. White, 1996). These two Nagarjunas are often confused and presented as a single sage.

61 As well as dualistic Vedanta whereby the empirical world is merely an illusion.

saw things more along the lines of A. N. Whitehead: the "actual entities" which constitute the world are not substances but rather momentary "durations" within a continual but hierarchically arranged process (Whitehead, 1969). Nagarjuna's radical move of calling that cosmic process itself empty takes us beyond the world of quantum mechanics as well as that of Whitehead. However, to push the quantum physics analogy to the very end, we might paraphrase Nargarjuna as follows. *Things neither exist* (as sub-atomic particles) *nor do not exist* (as an energy continuum); *they are empty*, that is, they satisfy all our profane requirements but block our way to spontaneity, freedom, and enlightenment. This means that to experience them as "empty" is to experience them in spontaneity, freedom, and enlightenment. This is what Nishitani calls the "field of emptiness," where we live in the world of primary fact.

NEITHER EMPIRICAL PROOF NOR MYTHIC BELIEF BUT PRIMARY FACT

In profane consciousness, when we look out at the world from the citadel of the self, we see mountains, trees, and rivers—all the beings that make up the Many that constitutes the empirical world. If the question of the One occurs to us at all, we think that perhaps there may be a Creator, undivided in himself, who made this multiplicity; or we may prefer to think that the world itself is one, Gaia, the living organism whose vitality is expressed in mountains, trees, and rivers. If we leave the profane sphere, however, and enter sacred consciousness, the reality of mountains, trees, and rivers is apt to suffer. We may think that these Many are finite and temporal, merely the boards of that passing stage upon which we are to work out our eternal salvation so that our soul may be rewarded in an eternal bliss-filled Indra's Heaven. Alternatively, we may think, along with the Upanishads, that those mountains, trees, and rivers are illusory, the play of Maya, who fascinates us with her dance and keeps us in a state of ignorance (avidya). According to this perspective, the only thing that is real is the eternal brahman (or shakti), invisible to profane eyes but apparent to the eyes of mysticism. All these possibilities confirm the words of Nishitani: "We usually take the world as an extended environment that envelopes us and serves as our field of behavior. And from there, as it happens, we go on to think up another, invisible world behind this first one."

Muktananda's vision of chiti, the light-filled goddess of consciousness, however, is a good deal more subtle than any of these possibilities. For him, both the One and the Many are real. Furthermore, they are not opposed to one another but two expressions of the same reality which is simultaneously unitary and multiple: "I could actually see the world within this conscious Light and the Light within the world, like threads in a piece of cloth and the cloth in the threads." Because there is no cloth without thread and no thread not woven into cloth, the

One and the Many are not separate; and neither is more "real" than the other. Such a perspective is essential to Tantrism, where access to the One is based upon that privileged member of the Many which is my own body. Tantrism, therefore, opposes Hindu "non-dualism," which says only the One is real, while the Many are an illusion.

Since Nagarjuna, however, Buddhism has declared the One and the Many to be neither in existence nor not in existence, but empty. Thus, although a Buddhist Tantrika may well be capable of a vision resembling Muktananda's and would perhaps be inclined to identify the "light of consciousness" as an imaginal impression of dependent co-origination, neither the One nor the Many is fixed in "ultimacy." To attribute ultimacy to the cosmic light of chiti would amount to asserting the existence of the invisible world we "think up" as lying behind and lending reality to the extended environment of the Many. It would be just another thing to "grasp"—albeit a large and numinous thing. It would maintain our illusory security in the citadel of the self, and block our access to the world of primary fact.

Dropping body-and-mind and entering the world of primary fact, does not preclude a unifying vision of oneness. It simply means that in that "middle position" between subject and object that we occupy in the world of primary fact there is no "object" that is privileged as the One. Rather oneness is a quality that constantly comes to presence whenever we live the field of emptiness. Jung perceived this, for example, as he gazed upon the world "for the first time" and became its "creator." The streaming herds, nodding in their timeless suchness, brought an entire world into being—earth and sky, grass and breeze, the eternal flow of life and death—and precisely not as something exceptional but in its day-in-and-day-out naturalness as primary fact.

> Only absolute emptiness is the true no-ground (*Ungrund*). Here all things—from a flower or a stone to stellar nebulae and galactic systems, and even life and death themselves—become present as bottomless realities. They disclose their bottomless suchness. True freedom lies in this no-ground (Nishitani, 1982: 34).

When a thing becomes present as a "bottomless reality," it is no longer an object known, defined, and categorized by a subjective "self." In the "no-self" which comes to presence when the citadel self is abandoned, our human existence interpenetrates with and belongs to the same primal factuality as each thing encountered. And that thing, too, is not cut off from any other thing. Each zebra brings the zebra herd to presence; the zebra herd reveals the valley floor and its waving grasses as well as the sky and the lion lurking in a clump of trees. The whole is present in each individual thing, as the worldhood of the world becomes so evident that Jung struggles to find adequate language for it—finally coming up with that paradoxical notion that he is its "creator."

MOSES AND THE BURNING BUSH

Nishitani links this sort of experience to Christian imagery, "The Christian must be able to pick up a single pebble or blade of grass and see the same consuming fire of God and the same pillar of fire, hear the same thunderous roar, and feel the same 'fear and trembling' that Moses experienced" (Nishitani, 39). The Christian or Jew will find something peculiar in this passage. For the fact that demolished Moses' citadel self and reduced him to "fear and trembling" was the nature of that fire that took possession of the bush. The bush was on fire, but it was *not* consumed. All "empirical" expectations belonging to the citadel self were overturned. Furthermore, there was nothing "mythic" in that event—in the sense of some ancient and privileged narrative referring to an ultimate and invisible world lying behind this one. The fire that did not consume brought the bush itself to presence in such a primal fashion that Moses was moved to step out of his sandals. The world itself was manifest in its sacredness as primary fact. Again and again the Bible articulates the epiphany of primary fact in terms of shining and burning, as a brightness that excludes all conceptualization. Primary fact breaks through and burns away our concepts without burning up the facts themselves. It enables them to appear for the first time, as though the world were "creating itself" in its multiplicity and oneness before our eyes. Nishitani says, "[W]hen a thing *is*, the world *worlds*" (Nishitani, 159).

Within the sphere of Christian thought, Meister Eckhart seems to have come the closest to articulating a doctrine of emptiness, for he says that we must "turn away from ourselves" ("no-self") and no longer be "content with" Father, Son, and Holy Ghost (those mythic conceptions). Rather, we must penetrate all the way to the "ground of God" which is also the "ground of the soul" (Colledge & McGinn, 1981: 198). That this amounts to an attainment of the world of primary fact, where each thing reveals everything else, is implied in several passages. "Only that heart is pure which has annihilated everything that is created" (Nishitani, 56), because to hold onto the Creator and his creation is to remain in the conceptual world of the citadel self. When we give up that limited standpoint, everything reveals everything else: "Whoever knew but one creature would not need to ponder any sermon, for every creature is full of God and is a book" (McGinn, *et. al.*, 1986: 259).

> An empty spirit is one that is confused by nothing, attached to nothing, has not attached its best to any fixed way of acting, and has no concern whatever in anything for its own gain, for it is all sunk deep down into God's dearest will and has forsaken its own (McGinn, 248).

Whereas the citadel self always encloses itself in a small sphere separate from everything else, the "no-self" of primal experience is not enclosed but finds its center everywhere—in every tree, every mountain, every river, every porpoise, and every zebra. Jung alludes to this primal reality when he says of the "self" of his psychology—as opposed to the ego—that its center is everywhere and its circumference nowhere (e.g., *CW 6:* ¶791; *CW 11:* ¶229). Nishitani applies the same ancient paradox both to the individual's "no self" and to each thing that appears. In the world of primary fact, nothing is "enclosed"; everything, including ourselves, interpenetrates everything else without bounds or limits. When every being is the center, no circumference can be located.

> On the field of *sunyata, the center is everywhere*. Each thing in its own selfness shows the mode of being of the center of all things. Each and every thing becomes the center of all beings and, in that sense, becomes an absolute center. This is the absolute uniqueness of things, their reality (Nishitani, 1982: 146).

This interpenetration of everything in everything else is, furthermore, not restricted to spatial relations. It is not merely the valley floor and the sky that are brought to presence by the streaming herds. "Silently eating, giving birth, dying, heads nodding through hundreds of millions of years," they also gather up the vastness of history in a single moment. "On the field of emptiness, all time enters into each moment of passing time from one moment to the next" (Nishitani, 1982: 161).

Nishitani introduces this idea with quotations from the *Avatamsaka Sutra*,[62] which illustrate the field of emptiness with the image of a magician who conjures up in a single "fleeting instant" a series of worlds, each of which may seem to last hours, weeks, or hundreds of years. Each time, everything is there: "cities and hamlets, wells, rivers, and seas, sun and moon, clouds and rain, palaces and houses." In that single "now," highly detailed worlds, together with their elapsing time, are simultaneously present.

> What this passage says is that in a fleeting instant, in the twinkling of an eye, the temporal span of a whole day or a hundred years appears phantasmally, and this phantasm is the day or the hundred years in actuality. At the same time, since the phantasmal span is revealed here in its suchness, this actual instant does not cease to be this actual instant. . . . [B]ecause in the field of sunyata each time is bottomlessly in time, all times enter into each time (Nishitani, 160-61).

With this example Nishitani makes explicit a theme that has been lurking unacknowledged in all the instances of primary fact that we have considered. A *magician* makes worlds appear in which hundreds of years are simultaneously present in a single "now" and every one of those worlds is centered in a single zebra, porpoise, or tree. Who is this magician, if

---

62 *Avatamsaka Sutra*: literally, the *Sutra of the Garland of Buddhas*, which teaches that buddha, mind, and all sentient beings are one and the same." The oldest extant text is a Chinese translation dating from the fifth century, C.E. (Fischer-Schreiber, *et. al.*, 1989).

not our own imaginal capacity? When the body-and-mind of our citadel self falls away, we lose the conceptual structure of our subject/object dichotomizing and no longer rely upon our theological presuppositions whereby an invisible world is "thought up" to give traditional meaning to what lies before us. But more than our eyes and ears is involved. If the world of the first day of creation is brought to presence in this "now" as well as the hundreds of millions of years of nodding heads, giving birth, and dying, imagination has spontaneously leapt in to fill the gap. If a bush bursts into flame but is not consumed, the evidence of our sensory eyes is being filled out by something more subtle.

EMPTINESS AND THE GROUND OF IMAGINATION

What a strange paradox. The Buddhist doctrine that began by emptying out both the profane world and Indra's Heaven in a grand "surpassing," ends by restoring them—albeit not as distinct worlds that have been "thought up" but rather as inseparable dimensions of primary fact. When the lucidity of what appears burns away all our citadel concepts so as to be manifest in its suchness, an entire world and all of time comes to presence in every pebble and every blade of grass. Furthermore, when we relinquish our grasp upon brahman, shakti, Father, Son, and Holy Ghost, the suchness of primary fact gleams with the bottomless ground that inspired the stories of those mythic beings. Meister Eckhart agrees, "The 'now' in which God made the world is as near to this time as the 'now' in which I am presently speaking, and the last day is as near to this 'now' as the day that was yesterday" (Colledge & McGinn, 1981: 256).

The myth of God's making the world and giving it a destiny to be realized on the "last day" enters into every moment and reveals it as "just what it is." While theology and myth "think up" a Supreme Being and tell us a story designed to explain our extended environment, the field of emptiness reveals the ground of that story in every primary fact. If the story of God's jealous rulership has been "thought up" to structure our ethical norms, emptiness shows us every being and every act luminously gathering within itself the bottomless harmony presupposed by those norms. Emptiness turns us away from spinning out stories to account for things and directs our attention to the primary suchness that originally inspired them. In every moment, the "arising" of creation and the "dissolution" of the last day is evident in the depth of what appears.

Modern physics, in its struggle with the paradoxical results of its experiments, has also been struck by the fact that each thing may be the center of everything. Some have proposed that the universe be understood on the model of a hologram; for in a holographic image each part contains the whole. For example, that holographic eagle in flight that adorns every VISA card: if we were able to cut off the very tip of the largest feather on its left wing and had an apparatus for magnifying it, we would be able see the whole bird and the background sector of sky in that tiny speck.[63] The principle of "non-locality" in quantum mechanics implies that every subatomic particle contains the entire universal order. The world is not the sum of its parts. Rather each part sums up the All, but not in the form of a static whole like the image on a credit card. It is not frozen like a snapshot but dynamic, a "holomovement." Since every subatomic particle reflects the whole of the universe, it also contains all of time—from the Big Bang down through the present moment and on into the future.[64]

As an invisible "folded-up" or "implicate" order lying behind the "explicate" world of profane consciousness, holomovement alludes to the mystery of the world of primary fact, but has none of its immediacy. In this regard, it resembles Indra's Heaven. Only when it can shed its "thought up" quality as the invisible world of ultimacy and come to presence spontaneously when the citadel self has been abandoned, will it appear as primary fact. Emptiness occurs only when pretense and the drive for precision have been abandoned. Free of dogma and concept jealously gathered and refined by the citadel self, the world of primary fact is at once sensory and imaginal but above all spontaneous, arising and dissipating in each unpremeditated moment.

---

63 Unfortunately, the smaller the fragment of the original hologram, the less defined the image it bears.

64 The main advocate of this view is David Bohm in *Wholeness and the Implicate Order* (1983). A very readable popularization may be found in Talbot (1992).

5

THE PULSE OF THE COSMOS

Every school of mysticism incorporates three elements: the direct experience of gnosis, a path leading to that goal, and a metaphysics which describes reality so that the path and the goal are intelligible. Since only the liberated truly know what liberation is, the central fact of every mystical school is the liberating gnosis experienced by its founder and a recognized chain of initiates, some of whom may have revised the tradition. No master is able to initiate disciples without a set of graded exercises, the rungs of the ladder that leads to the goal. These methods inevitably involve a description of the essential structure of "reality," designed to overturn profane consciousness and make gnosis possible. In this sense, metaphysics is the "handmaiden" of gnosis and not the starting point.[65] Even if it masquerades as the dogmatic foundation of a school, metaphysics is actually the most derivative element of all. For it is simply a description of how reality must be configured if the indubitable fact of liberated awareness is to be made intelligible and if the path is to take us there.

The doctrine of emptiness describes the metaphysics of Buddhism. We considered it at length—not with any intention of asserting some sort of pre-eminence for Buddhism—but rather to expose the nature of mystical metaphysics. Indeed, Nagarjuna's claim that things neither exist nor do not exist is so foreign to our Western way of thought that it might be described as an "anti-metaphysics." Its very strangeness, however, is what helps us to grasp its intentions as a doctrine designed to remove obstacles from the path of the aspiring mystic. Other schools of mysticism may not seem so radical in the way they frustrate our habits of thought. But in some way or other, they all incorporate a three-stage process leading from profane consciousness through "beginner's mind" and on to enlightened or liberated awareness. The Zen story of mountains, trees, and rivers may be taken as a model for every path to gnosis.

For example, Gopi Krishna found the "mountains, trees, and rivers" of the world of kundalini to constitute a monumental defeat. The serpent energy was so out of balance in him that he believed the traditional representation of a wrathful, blood-thirsty, and sexually aroused

---

65 Just as in the Christian Middle Ages philosophy was called the "handmaiden" of theology.

goddess dancing with utter abandon on the supine body of a naked male had to have been painted by someone who had been as much crushed and humiliated by the arousal of kundalini as he had. As extraordinary as his plight seems to have been, he had not shaken off much of his profane consciousness.

Our study of the subtle body, however, has taught us that an encounter with a wrathful goddess can be transformed if we turn our attention away from her punishing dance and focus on what the shattering encounter is doing to *us*. The tubular palace meditation acquaints us with the dragon of our soul's energy, as we distill our overwhelming emotion into its components. The rise and fall of the serpent of light within the central channel of our imaginal construct occupies our whole attention, and we no longer see mountains, trees, and rivers. The common-sense world has been replaced by the indubitable reality that makes Spontaneous Great Bliss possible. At this middle point in our journey, we have exchanged profane consciousness for the tubular citadel of erotic trance and have yet to "return."

If the tubular palace meditation is practiced with a fleshly partner, we join Spontaneous Great Bliss with emptiness when we relinquish all the preliminaries associated with metaphysics and the stages of the path, drop body-and-mind, and redirect our attention to our partner. That incomparable being now centers a world without circumference, gathering all things in an absolute present that incorporates the first day of creation and the dissolution of the universe. Our union pulses and gleams whiter than snow. In the no-self of the field of emptiness, we vibrate back and forth, exchanging places as still, introverted Shiva and boundlessly expansive Shakti. Having left the citadel of our respective selves, neither of us is subject and neither is object. Our union oscillates like the figure and ground in a gestalt drawing that appears alternately as two faces in profile and then fleetingly as a vase before again dissolving into faces. Our pulsing union gathers the vibrating cosmos into itself and becomes the center of all that is, like threads in the cloth and cloth in the threads. Our oscillating consciousness participates in and contains the light of consciousness that is the universe, both One and Many, flux and substance, arising and dissolving.

SPANDA: THE DOCTRINE OF VIBRATION

It is precisely this sort of liberating gnosis that led Abhinavagupta, the principal figure in the doctrine of vibration (spanda) in eleventh century Kashmir, to react with scorn for that feces-smeared antinomian hero, Trighantika, with his distorted features and lust-inspired hangers-on. Trighantika is not without attainments. He has learned the nature of lust and gone beyond good and evil. But he is stuck there in the awareness of his achievement. This is why he exalts. He is grasping the heroic rung of the diamond ladder, justly proud of having overcome the obstacle of scandal. But his grasping locks him up in the citadel of his accomplished self and bars his way back to the world of primary fact.

Trighantika knows kundalini only as an autonomous surging forth of an energy that faces down the disturbing dragon of his appetites. In his exaltation he identifies with it as "mine" and thereby becomes a hero (vira). But he never acquaints himself with kundalini in her multifaceted wonder as the power of consciousness that raises him into the subtle sphere of the heart chakra or makes available the nectar of his crown chakra. Therefore, he never knows Spontaneous Great Bliss. In all probability his exaltation bespeaks his discovery of the essential self that appears when the manipura chakra opens in the region of the solar plexus, where the danger exists that we will identify with the powerful emotions that characterize this achievement. Trighantika's critics, the associates and followers of Abhinavagupta, have ascended beyond the stage of the antinomian hero. They have become familiar with the sublime experience of their airiness at the heart chakra (anahata), the ether of the throat center, and the identification in oneness with the cosmos through the opening of the sahasrara.

They have come to know the nature of kundalini as the form of awareness that describes both their own consciousness and the woven nature of the cosmos as vibrating light. They conceptualize it as "the ultimate," the intercourse of Shiva and Shakti, where Shiva is the introverted and motionless knowing dimension of consciousness and Shakti its ever-moving, extraverted "content." They describe a vision very similar to that of Muktananda: the light of consciousness becoming the world like threads in cloth, becoming "animals, birds, germs, insects, gods, demons, men, and women . . . silently pulsing as supreme ecstasy within me, outside me, above me, below me." Abhinavagupta's follower, Maheshvarananda, describes this pulsation (spanda) as the oscillation of figure and ground, as though "a picture of a bull and an elephant [were] drawn together in such a way that we see either one or the other depending on the way in which we view it" (Dyczkowski, 1987: 101). Perhaps a more accurate metaphor would picture a transparent cube drawn on paper. When we see its front face pointing downward and to the right, the universe is "manifest"; when the rear face jumps to the front, pointing upward and to the left, the universe has become "immanent" (see Figure 2). It never ceases to be the one reality it is, although its aspects oscillate.

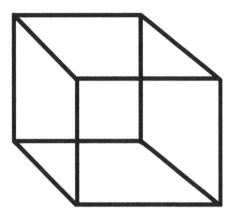

Figure 2

The Oscillation of Figure and Ground Within a Single Unity

According to this doctrine of vibration (spanda), Shiva dissolves into Shakti when her light expands into and becomes the manifest cosmos ("Thou art That"). Then Shakti is absorbed back into the single point of awareness that is Shiva, and the universe withdraws into immanence ("That is Thou"). In a state of samadhi, the yogin not only witnesses this pulsating rhythm of expansion and contraction but *is* that absolute oscillation. The practitioner is at one with the orgasmic vibration of god and goddess. One who has attained this state is *both* Shiva and Shakti and yet again is *neither* of them. It is similar to that analogous point reached in carezza where we no longer know which of us has the penis and which the vagina, and our gender seems to pulse.

The full mystical significance of this pulsating experience is realized in that definitive "now" when we are one with the universe. Indeed, it is the function of the ladder rungs of longing, scandal, and the subtle body to explore the intermediate stage where mountains, trees, and rivers are no longer seen, and thereby to prepare our return to the world of primary fact. A great deal of inner work has to be done before our ingrained habit of locking ourselves in the citadel of the self can be overcome. Only when the subject and object have dissolved into a pulsating oneness have we managed to rediscover the world of primary fact. This is the "ultimate experience" of mysticism, which Dyczkowski describes in the imagery of Kashmir's spanda doctrine, employing two passages from the *Tantraloka* (Dyczkowski, 101):

The couple (*yamala*) is consciousness itself, the unifying emission and the stable abode. It is the absolute, the noble cosmic bliss consisting of both [Siva and Sakti]. It is the supreme secret of Kula [the ultimate reality]; neither quiescent nor emergent, it is the flowing font of both quiescence and emergence (29: 116-7a).

"These two aspects, passive (*santa*) and active (*udita*)," explains Abhinava, "arise at the same time in the power and its possessor. The active passes from one domain to the other, the passive is confined within the Self [the essential nature of both]. But even so, in reality, each of them form a couple (*yamala*). Hence the emergent is the quiescent" (29: 119-20).

Shiva, the "quiescent" Self, and Shakti, the "emergent" cosmos, together as a "couple" represent the whole of reality. To know this "within, outside, above, and below" is "the absolute, the noble cosmic bliss." It is both quiescent and emergent, and it is neither. It transcends rational description in the form of a paradox, a union of opposites.

In classical Hinduism, the world "arises" into manifestation when Brahma,[66] the creator, awakes; and it "dissolves" when Brahma sleeps. A "day" in the life of Brahma is a "world cycle" (kalpa), which is said to last 4.32 billion human years. In Shaivism, this same process of cosmic manifestation and withdrawal has been configured in a metaphysics that ascribes the pulsation to Shiva and Shakti in their eternal love-play. Vimalananda says that the original Shakti (Adya-Shakti), who appears as Nature, "feels incomplete on her own and wants to reunite with her source," which is Shiva. "When she does the universe dissolves (*pralaya*)." This same event occurs at the level of the microcosm when our own kundalini-shakti reunites with our "personal Lord Shiva" (Svoboda, 1997: 146).

The Kashmiri spanda doctrine, however, also says that the pulsation of reality corresponds to the opening and closing of *Shiva's* eyes (Dcyzkowski, 1987: 30). Abhinavagupta, the eleventh century Kashmiri Shaivist, sees this entire process of arising and dissolving in a single "now," in which all of time—from the moment Shiva opens his eyes in the morning of a cosmic cycle to the moment when he closes them at night—is simultaneously present. He reveals the emptiness of the entire process, from which it becomes clear that the standard notion of 4.32 billion years is but an exoteric doctrine whose esoteric significance may be seen in gnosis by those who have left the citadel of the self. Although, as a Hindu, Abhinavagupta does not follow the paradoxical anti-metaphysics of Nagarjuna in any strict sense and even names the "ultimate reality" as "Kula," it is clear that he lives on the field of emptiness. He encounters the cosmos as primary fact. An experience of gnosis that appears in all respects to be the same as that found in Buddhism is articulated through a contrasting metaphysics.

---

66 Brahma (masculine) the creator god, not to be confused with *brahman* (neuter) the invisible reality that underlies and pervades everything that appears.

VIBRATION AND EMPTINESS

Abhinavagupta synthesized all the Shiva doctrines of his day as *Trika*-Shaivism ("Three-Principled Shiva-Oriented Tantrism") (Dcyzkowski, 1987: 10). The three principles are: (1) the world originates from the desire of Shiva; (2) only Shiva's grace enables one to realize atman; and (3) one who has realized this is qualified to lead others (Fischer-Schreiber, *et. al.*, 1989). Abhinavagupta's influence stems not only from his status as "without a doubt, the most brilliant of Kashmiri Saiva teachers and one of the greatest intellectual giants India has produced" (Dyczkowski, 1987: 10) but also from the strategic position of Kashmir—a region in India's extreme northwest, about the size and shape of Ohio, whose valley floors are about 5000 feet above sea level, and which shares borders with Pakistan, Afghanistan, Tibet, and China. The official codification of the Buddhist Tripitaka ("Three Baskets of Scriptures") in the first century, C.E., occurred at a Buddhist council in Kashmir, whence Buddhism spread to Central Asia, including Tibet (Dyczkowski, 1987: 2-3). From about 500, C.E., Kashmir was one of the most important centers of both Hindu and Buddhist Tantra. It was conquered by Islam in the thirteenth century, some 200 years after Abhinavagupta's death. The "Lotus Born" founder of Tibetan Tantra who took Yeshe Tsogyel as his favorite dharma consort, Padmasambhava, was born in Kashmir about a century before Abhinavagupta (Fischer-Schreiber, *et. al.*, 1989).

Mutual influences between Hinduism, Buddhism, and Tantra, therefore, were nowhere stronger than in Kashmir. Indeed, the emptiness doctrine of gnosis in Tibet is very similar to that of Abhinavagupta's spanda. In the Vajrayana ("Diamond Vehicle") of Tibet, the vajra, or lightening bolt (called dorje in Tibet) is the central image of gnosis.

> The *dorje* is the symbol of the clear, immutable essence of reality that is the basis of everything. Its immaculate transparency, which nevertheless gives rise to a profusion of manifestations [i.e., the phenomenal world], corresponds to the concept of *shunyata* stressed by Nagarjuna. . . . Padmasambhava [writes]:
>
>> The secret mind of all the buddhas,
>>
>> Omniscient wisdom
>>
>> Transmitted by the symbol of eternal strength and firmness
>>
>> Clarity and emptiness, the *dorje* essence
>>
>> Like heavenly space—
>>
>> It is wonderful to see the true face of reality!
>>> (Fischer-Schreiber, *et. al.*, 1989).

It is easy to hear echoes of this formulation in Kashmiri Shaivism, which declares that the universe, light, and the self are one (Dyczkowski, 1987: 63), the "eternal becoming and dynamic flux of *spanda*" (Dyczkowski, 52). The absolute is the light of consciousness (*prakasa*):

> because it makes all things manifest by shining in its universal form. The phenomena that appear in the field of consciousness are experienced directly in this way at the initial instant of perception when they are still at one with the perceiving subject. The light of consciousness is itself this direct experience made before thought-constructs interpose themselves between subject and object, thus degrading the latter to the level of objectivity, which obscures the light of the subject's immediate perception (Dcyzkowski, 1987: 69).

Furthermore, the three stages leading to the gnosis of emptiness are paralleled in the philosophy of spanda. When mountains, trees, and rivers are sundered from the citadel self through "interposed thought-constructs," we negate our true nature and identify with body-and-mind. This dichotomy is overcome in the "direct experience" of attending to consciousness itself, i.e., a withdrawal from mountains, trees, and rivers. Finally, the world of primary fact is discovered when "subject and object are held together and different objects related to one another in a single field of consciousness." The cosmic import of this realization occurs when "individual subject and object, together with all diversity, merge in the reflective awareness [which] the light of consciousness has by its nature as the universal subject" (Dcyzkowski, 1987: 74). Even Nagarjuna's view that nothing arises and nothing dissolves is embraced by spanda:

> In reality nothing arises and nothing falls away. It is the vibrating power of consciousness which, though free of change, becomes manifest in this or that form and thus appears to be arising and falling away (Dcyzkowski, 83).

> Reality cannot be discovered if we think of it as a "something" of which we are ignorant but may come to know through practice. Reality is an experience—the experience of the fully enlightened (Dcyzkowski, 110).

The primary difference between Abhinavagupta's spanda and Nagarjuna's emptiness lies in the fact that the emptiness of dependent co-origination is *personified* in the metaphysics of Kashmiri Shaivism, even as it is declared empty:

> Sakti represents the all-encompassing fullness (*purnata*) of the absolute, the ever-shifting power of awareness actively manifesting as the Circle of Totality (*visvacakra*). Siva is the Void (*sunyata*) of absolute nature. Integral and free, Siva, the abode of the Void, dissolves everything into Himself and brings all things into being. Fullness pours into emptiness and emptiness pervades fullness (Dcyzkowski, 119).

The pulsation of spanda is precisely this oscillation between fullness and emptiness, where everything both is and is empty, where everything *seems* to arise and fall away but does not. There is only undivided consciousness, the world of primary fact. What seems to be an object is but the "appearing" or "content" dimension of consciousness. What seems to be a subject is but the "realizing" or "immanent" dimension of consciousness.[67] These two dimensions are one and united in the pulsing flow of the intercourse between Shiva and Shakti.

MAITHUNA

Ritual sexual intercourse (maithuna) is not possible for those who have not familiarized themselves with the experience of the vibrating absolute and cannot enter the field of emptiness at will. Indeed, the French scholar of Kashmiri Shaivism, Lilian Silburn, places it in the first stage of her schematic account of maithuna. She warns us in the introduction to her book on kundalini, that raising the serpent energy is a dangerous business and must not be undertaken without the guidance of an initiated master, who alone has a comprehensive view of the esoteric mysteries involved. She endeavors to impart the deeper symbolic meanings of the doctrines and practices without revealing too much: "I have left enough unclarified so as not to incur the wrath of the ancient masters" (Silburn, 1988: xiv). For my part, not only do I not pretend to know those esoteric secrets, I am inclined to agree with Jung that the secrets themselves are secret because *nobody* knows them.

> The yoga way or the yoga philosophy has always been a secret, but not because people have *kept* it a secret. For as soon as you *keep* a secret it is already an open secret; you know about it and other people know about it, and then it is no longer a secret. The real secrets are secrets because nobody understands them. One cannot even talk about them, and of such a kind are the experiences of the Kundalini yoga. That tendency to keep secrets is merely a natural consequence when the experience is of such a peculiar kind that you had better not talk about it, for then you expose yourself to the greatest misunderstanding and misinterpretation (Jung, 1996: 28).

Therefore, the secrets, such as they are, will of necessity be discovered by each individual sadhaka in the course of acquiring the experiences that make the pulsating flow of emptiness and fullness the personal achievement and impersonal absolute it has always been. If we are

---

67 Thus Dyczkowski's articulation of spanda's view of consciousness bears strong similarities with Husserl's distinction between *noema* and *noesis*. It is significant that what Husserl places in "brackets" to avoid the subject/object dichotomy describes what Buddhism calls the non-reality of the citadel self (Husserl, 1962).

not going to find an initiated master to direct our course, we will have to be satisfied with schematic accounts, the rungs of a ladder which neither exists nor does not exist for those who have entered upon the field of emptiness.

With this cautionary apology firmly in mind, we can summarize Silburn's schematic account of maithuna in four stages (Silburn, 1988: 169-70).

(1) The couple unites sexually, and then both partners go into samadhi.

(2) Each partner acts separately for herself, but without a single moment's loss of contact, either physically or spiritually, with the other. This is the time that kundalini is rising through the chakras.

(3) The real conjunction of the partners occurs with their simultaneous opening of the crown chakra, when they realize the universality of atman together.

(4) Finally they realize the ultimate cosmic reality, *kaula*—what Abhinavagupta calls *kula*. "The couple, freed from the sense of ego, lost in wonder, perceive in the emerging act appeased immobility. They have reached what is called the 'inner' emergence, universal Consciousness, energy at its height. When unified quiescence and emergence are integrated and then transcended, *kaula* manifests in all its glory as cosmic beatitude."

The sketchiness of this account can be appreciated in the first step alone. They unite sexually and then go into samadhi. Putting aside entirely the difficulty of achieving samadhi, and the fact that numerous scholars have observed that many yogins work all their lives without reaching that summit, imagine being able to do so while sufficiently aroused as to be able to "unite sexually." Sexual arousal is one of the most "disturbing" experiences the average human being knows. Arousal is so exciting that it diverts our attention from everything else. Furthermore, we can hardly overlook the reality that when some performance of a contrasting sort is demanded of us at the same time, we are likely to be incapable of being aroused. The fact that both of these demands are made at the same time implies an entirely new meaning for Eliade's term "deautonomization." When the Sahajiya mystics bathe, oil, and dress their dancing girls while striving to keep their erections under control, they are aiming for a deautonomization that would render maithuna impossible. Ritual intercourse requires an entirely different sort of detachment from the autonomic process of sexual arousal. It has to occur—not fail to occur—and to do so without disturbing or being disturbed by the one-pointed focus of our attention.

This development reveals for the first time the full meaning of Vimalananda's vajroli contest. Only those whose training has rendered them so free, spontaneous, and utterly familiar with every detail of sexual arousal that nothing catches them unawares—nothing pushes them over the top and nothing lessens the physiological surge—will be sufficiently detached from the autonomous response to allow it to take its course unhindered and unhindering. Our sexual arousal has to flow with the natural grace of a porpoise, unthinkingly plunging, becoming nothing other than that pulsating, porpoising glide, while the "whalewatch" ship of our consciousness is guided by its own gyroscope, steady and undisturbed. Two parallel courses. Not fortuitous, but in the spontaneous, blissful harmony of heads nodding through hundreds of millions of years. Absolute control but without concern. Total freedom without exaltation. No longer breathing but breathed. If there is a secret to this, it lies beyond all telling. Thirty years of practice lie behind us, when mountains, trees, and rivers had been banished. They return only on the field of emptiness, where the citadel self and its obsessive control has been disengaged. Where arousal surges and the world *worlds*.

All this is but the context within which other realities come to presence. The porpoise surges without thought of sea or air, but never loses sight of the salty realm's silvery ceiling or the light domain's blue-green floor. Nor does this pulsating vision of the world's interface distract attention from the obtrusive, mechanical sight of the ship on its rectilinear course. Or the man standing at its rail. While the surging and the "worlding" take care of themselves, the partners move on to the second stage, doing what needs to be done to enhance and distill the rise of kundalini and at the same time attending to all the harmonies and discordant notes in their physical and spiritual relationship with one another. Here, again, what has been learned in the vigorous play of the vajroli contest has familiarized them with their separate physiological, emotional, and imaginal states. He feels her arousal within himself. She contains his body and spirit within her own. Their chakras open in a spontaneous, porpoising flow; and they register those distinctive states of unity that occur at the navel, solar plexus, heart, and throat. Their brows open, and they are god and goddess for one another.

None of these things is possible if it has not already passed beyond the guilt, terror, and grandiosity that re-establish the citadel self at the rung of scandal. The partners will be unaware of the nuances of their emotional connection if they have not learned to distill kundalini's energies in the tubular palace of their separate subtle bodies. But they have to have reached a stage of "deautonomization" where they can let go of these preliminary exercises and concerns. There is no calculation or counting time when body-and-mind have been dropped. The world and their bodies lose none of their rich, multifaceted, and undeniable reality. But they are no longer "objects" to be measured or discussed in our internal monologues. We flow with all the things that come to presence, centered in our union. We change our course and speed without thought like the undulating porpoise. While the world of our intercourse throbs and oscillates, we live within it. Without past to remember. Without future to anticipate. We become ourselves in our suchness, partnering our couplehood. Every time is the first time and the last time. An eternal now.

The dropping of body-and-mind clearly plays a dual role in this experience. On the one hand it clears away the conceptual citadel that shuts us off from the world of primary fact and makes the spanda vision of the pulsating light of consciousness possible. On the other hand, by letting things be in their suchness, it gives free rein to autonomous arousal and the rising of kundalini. These natural facts of our body's physiology proceed as unhindered as streaming herds and swimming porpoises, and just as incontrovertibly constitute the world in which we find our Being. Thus to join emptiness with Spontaneous Great Bliss is to enter a specific sort of primal world, one which is energized and illuminated by kundalini. An arousal that has been mastered and become as familiar as a well-tended garden provides a boost to the world of primary fact; and the cultivation of emptiness enables us to enter that energy-charged world without the clutter of our profane mind's chatter and without the protecting and distorting concepts that wall it off.

> The yogi can take pleasure in sense objects; indeed he is specifically instructed to do so, if he maintains an awakened, mindful attitude (*prabuddhabhava*) and does not just blindly follow his natural inclinations as does an animal with a bare minimum of self-awareness. The pleasure we derive from physical objects is, in reality, the repose we enjoy when the activity of the mind is momentarily arrested and delights one-pointedly in the source of pleasure. All pleasure, in other words, is essentially spiritual. It is a state the subject experiences and not a property of the object. . . . This yogi is no hedonist. He is free of the false notion that the body is the Self and so does not crave for the pleasures of the senses, although he does make use of them as springboards to project him beyond the realms of physical, transitory objectivity into the eternal sphere of consciousness (Dcyzkowski, 1987: 147).

A DISTURBING BRUSH WITH SAMADHI

Because the cosmic oneness of maithuna is based upon the physiology, emotionality, and imaginal capacity all humans share, it sometimes happens that a person who is completely unprepared for its gnosis stumbles upon it by accident. Georg Feuerstein, the historian of yoga occasionally quoted in these pages, gives several examples of this sort of experience breaking through into the lives of some of our American contemporaries. The most arresting of these anecdotes is told by his wife, Trisha, and concerns an experience she had several years before meeting Feuerstein, when she was only twenty-five years old (Feuerstein, 1993: 35-37). She recounts the story as "my mystical experience," seventeen years after the event. She had fallen in love with a man she had held on a pedestal for about two years before becoming sexually involved with him, and describes him as "one of the most mentally and emotionally uninhibited individuals I had met." She remembers nothing specific about their love-making, only that it was "totally uninhibited, frequent, and never enough!"

Her extended mystical episode, which appears to resemble samadhi, followed a night of love-making with this man. She got up in the morning, feeling as though she had spent the night and continued in a condition of being "constantly awake on some higher plane." In this regard her experience resembles that of the yogins who spend their nights in samadhi, alternately dozing and waking but without losing the lucidity of being beyond subject and object. Trisha says she was "*totally* and *perfectly* relaxed" and found herself standing outside of time for a period of about three weeks in which she had no "edges." She found that her self had no circumference to separate her from the world. "There was no me. The thought arose, and these are the exact words, 'This is what I AM in truth.'" Though she apparently saw pretty much the same things we all see, she had the conviction that there was "no difference between anything whatsoever." "Everything material seemed superfluous. It was all spontaneously and playfully arising from one great source, and it could just as well cease to arise at any moment." Consciousness was the only thing that mattered. She thought that she could lose her body and not care. She had times when she was "drowning in bliss, overwhelmed with love and compassion . . . for every being and thing I looked at." She felt she was "the source of all creation."

The three weeks of bliss ended one day when she felt that "the molecules of my body were flying apart and that if I allowed the process to continue I would simply fly apart and disappear. . . . I would leave this realm for good." Simultaneously, "knowing that I was not ready to do this," inspired an immense fear. Her citadel self "grabbed hold," divided reality conveniently into subject and object; "and suddenly I had edges again. I felt separate, complicated, neurotic, and unhappy again—all in an instant." She suffered a depression, considered suicide, and then spent years urgently trying to understand what had happened to her. Since the return of her citadel self, she has known only isolated moments of having no "edges."

Trisha's repetition of the word *uninhibited*, applying it both to her lover and to the style of love-making he introduced her to, inclines us to think it describes both the means (spontaneous sexual expression) and the trustworthy context (the man on the pedestal) by and in which she could let go of her citadel self and enter into that mystical participation which Berman describes as one of the only two situations left to us in the modern West for transcending subject and object (anxiety and lust). That she engaged in this activity frequently, eagerly, and with the sense that she could never get enough, implies that she repeatedly left the citadel of the self and came to know this condition of no-self in an unreflective way as a place of joy, simplicity, relaxation, freedom, and completeness. She was not struggling for anything and had no concept of a ladder of mystical ascent. Rather it appears that her larger being rejoiced in this experience and came to know, all unconsciously, that it did not have to identify with her body-and-mind. This seems to have introduced her to the world of primary fact as a realm of bliss and satisfaction. She had no idea how she got there, and fails to tell us whether she renewed her mystical state through repeated sexual participation with her lover during the crucial three weeks. Possibly sex itself was no longer important to her, since she had already arrived at the condition it was unconsciously designed to facilitate. She says only that after her "devastating" return to the impoverished world of ordinary consciousness the relationship with her lover "slowly deteriorated." We are left to wonder why. Was he unappreciative of what had happened to her? Or was she afraid of encountering again that "crack in the self" that had inspired her terror?

The sense that she might fly apart like whizzing molecules and "leave this realm for good" reminds us of the mad saints. We can hardly accept her terrifying image literally—that her physical body would dissolve into a mist. More likely it was her mind that was at risk. In this regard her terror was very likely realistic, for she lacked the accepting social container of Bengali mystical aspirations. There was no way for her to recognize in such a threat of insanity the possibility that it might become a divine madness (divyonmada), the gift of a frenzied, naked goddess wearing a necklace of skulls. In the context of our society, she would simply be insane; and there would be no hope of having that insanity respected and supported until the day that her psyche found a way to reorganize itself so as to contain that divine energy. She seems to have been transported—not to Indra's Heaven—but to the rung of longing where the dragon of her soul's energy frightened her so thoroughly that her ego had to reassert itself autonomously. She was left in a peculiar ambivalence, consciously longing to drop body-and-mind but unconsciously terrified at the prospect of re-encountering that crack in her self.

Her experience makes abundantly clear the need for the wise guidance of a master who knows the techniques and dangers of the path as well as for the hard work and years of discipline that the diamond ladder of sexual ascent describes. Although she has had an indelible experience of enlightenment and does not have to struggle to remember it as do most of her contemporaries, she has not familiarized herself with the dragon of her soul's energy and has no notion of how to begin to do so. Kundalini has surged forth bringing both bliss and terror, but Trisha has no means for sorting out these two dimensions of the serpent energy. Having been transported directly from the profane world to the world of primary fact and back again, she knows nothing of a world without mountains, trees, and rivers. She has not struggled with the scandalous issue of good and evil and knows nothing of transcending them. She knows kundalini—not by name—but only as the bringer of overwhelming bliss and devastating terror. She has not learned to distill these chaotic emotions with the tubular palace of her subtle body.

Trisha's incredible good luck and precipitous fall reveal the importance of the mysterious second stage in the Zen story of mountains, trees, and rivers. Those who swim like porpoises in the world of primary fact while staying sexually aroused and facilitating the rise of kundalini without losing contact with their partners do not arrive at this stage by accident. There are very good reasons the Zen story-teller spent thirty years without seeing mountains, trees, and rivers. The integration of kundalini represents a life's work. Indeed, if we take seriously the folktale of Machig Lapdron, it takes *many* lifetimes of single-minded endeavor. This is the reason Vimalananda and virtually all the experts tell us that there is nothing that *has* to be done. If we are not ready to take a wanton goddess for our Bhairavi in this life, we can face the challenges of our present life in all earnestness, courage, and humility so that perhaps we will be better prepared next time. The many-lifetimes explanation is, of course, a metaphysical doctrine designed to account for the extraordinary nature of gnosis. We may very well fail to achieve it despite our best intentions and unremitting efforts, while others may arrive at gnosis effortlessly. Nevertheless a single fleeting brush with gnosis only whets our appetites. Gnosis as a fortuitous event represents great good fortune, but gnosis as a way of life involves much more.

GNOSIS AND LIBERATION

The terms *enlightenment* and *liberation* are used almost interchangeably. To be "enlightened" means to see reality as it is, to have the gnosis whereby delusional appearances no longer confine us within the unreal world of secondary concepts and neurotic distortions. To be "liberated" means to live spontaneously and without confinement or distortion. Thus, truly to see reality as it is must be inseparable from living the life that gnosis illuminates. At bottom gnosis is a way of life, and not merely a momentary vision obtained by climbing to the top rung of a ladder. The cosmic vision of pulsating light occurs in an ecstatic (or "enstatic") moment. Even if it last three weeks, it is bound to pass. Because Abhinavagupta's vision of spanda occurs as a revelation of the ultimate nature of the cosmos and human consciousness, it may be called the foundation of gnosis in Kashmiri Shaivism. Although, in being "empty," it transcends the vision of Indra's Heaven which transformed the life of Nanda, the Buddha's half-brother, the encounter with the pulsating cosmos of light plays a similar role in the life of the Tantrika. It liberates by undermining all less-than-ultimate visions. Once one has returned to the world of mountains, trees, and rivers, gnosis manifests itself in the degree of freedom the Tantrika has day-in and day-out. Those who are lost, depressed, and nostalgic for their cosmic vision have no gnosis. By clinging to their memories of ecstasy, they keep themselves bound. Daniel Odier's guru, Devi, describes liberation as "relaxed, without goals and constraints—

free, opened, and light." One does what one is moved to do—meditation, work, maithuna, a forest walk along a mountain stream—and in the "now" when one is so moved:

> It's the continuous experience of freedom that constitutes the tantrika's asceticism, not any constraint on the spirit. When ecstasy comes, take it. When it leaves, don't worry. If you let the divine come and go as it pleases, it becomes familiar. If you force it to stay within you or pursue it, it can become terrifying. Let yourself be. Be your own master. Stop all searching, and you will find yourself in the truth (Odier, 1997: 166-7).

The divine comes when it will for those who inhabit the field of emptiness. Sexuality helps us to arrive at this gnostic freedom by joining Spontaneous Great Bliss with emptiness. There are other paths. The left-hand path of Tantra distinguishes itself only by seizing upon bodily pleasure as the fastest—albeit most dangerous—path for overturning the obstacles that stand in the way of liberation. Nothing is more fascinating and disturbing of our serenity than sexual arousal. Sexual arousal, however, is but the physiological manifestation of eros and appears as kundalini. It is consciousness in its most intense and all-encompassing form; and it presents itself readily. With no help from us, sexual arousal moves us directly onto the subtle plane and reveals the arbitrary nature of profane consciousness. Only our neurotic defenses and the internal monologues we have adopted from the persona field prevent us from recognizing this everyday fact. The roots of enlightenment lurk in the most despised of our daily inclinations. The Tantric path toward gnosis begins by having us open our eyes and see the reality of sexual arousal for what it really is. To see things as they really are—that is as primary facts—is to enter the field of emptiness. Sexual arousal has a unique capacity to boost us into that field, but only when we have learned to stop grasping, controlling, and wanting what we do not have. Because it is fascinating, disturbing, and compelling, it constitutes the most efficacious means of reaching emptiness when we can learn to know it as it is and not cling to it or try to shape it according to the predilections of our citadel self.

Maithuna is the ultimate stage on the sexual path to gnosis. It provides the most potent boost of energy, while at the same time requiring the most complex exercise in "letting go," or detachment. The participants have to let go of their separate states of sexual arousal, allowing their physiology to take its course like nodding herds. They have to let kundalini surge like a porpoise. But even as they have let go, they have to stand firm. They are not simply passive but actively engaged in the stillness of the no-self. Heidegger's analogy that human existence—*Dasein* (Being-here)—is the "shepherd of Being" suggests this role of a guide who also "lets be." At the same time that they are shepherding kundalini and sexual arousal, however, the partners never lose touch with one another. They shepherd their mutuality as well as their separate internal processes. A whole world of activity is allowed to be as primary fact and at the same time lived through a mystical participation as "creator" (Jung) or "source"

(Trisha Feuerstein). They *are* that surging Being and at the same time are its shepherds. Their consciousness pulsates, being in one split second all that is and in the next they are right "here" without circumference as its well-grounded center. Letting be and Being oscillate as figure and ground.

The cosmic vision of a universe of pulsating threads of light reveals the arising and dissipating of the phenomenal world. It is the larger meaning of the partners' couplehood. Cosmic meaning emerges out of the consciousness which is neither subject nor object but the primary fact of union. Spanda philosophy claims that we may begin with any fact at all; for when we penetrate all the way into it, we find pulsating at its center the cosmic consciousness/light/bliss.[68] Here is the ultimate experience of each primary fact becoming the circumferenceless center that gathers a whole world into itself. We have already seen that modern physics seems to be stumbling toward a similar vision. But modern physics does not stand on the field of emptiness. Rather quantum mechanics presents us with a complex conceptual structure explicated in mathematical equations—a structure built up by the citadel self. On the field of emptiness, by contrast, the vision of cloth in the threads and threads in the cloth appears spontaneously and without calculation. The fullness of physiology, emotion, and imagination coalesce on the field of emptiness through the energetic boost of maithuna, and the primary fact of union between partners reveals the larger primary fact of cosmic emptiness.

PULSING COSMOS OF LIGHT

In the gnosis central to Tantrism, the cosmic vision of the pulsating light of consciousness has recurred again and again over the last 1500 years. It has been painted in countless variations on a few standard themes in the form of the yantra, a mandala comprised of geometric figures. Such paintings simultaneously represent (a) the cosmos, (b) the human body-and-psyche, and (c) coupled male and female principles as lines of energy, all emanating from a single point at the center, the bindu. Most frequently yantras employ intersecting triangles, some with their points upward which are said to represent the phallus of Shiva, and some with their points downward, evoking Shakti's vulva. Others are composed of intersecting swastikas and have a heritage that dates at least to intaglio seals unearthed from the Harappan civiliza-

---

68 "Each aesthetic experience, had with mindfulness and a disciplined attention directed toward heightening our general level of aesthetic sensitivity brings us a little closer to the sustained wonder of the pulsation (*spanda*) of consciousness which permeates all experience. The yogi at first practices to penetrate into this state of wonder through the medium of objects more easily pleasing and then, as he makes progress, he learns to discern that same sense of wonder in himself even when confronted with the foulest things or in times of great trouble and pain" (Dcyzkowski, 1987: 149).

tion of 3000, B.C.E. (Khanna, 1979: 10). The ancientness of this tradition suggests again that, although Tantra emerged as a defined philosophy and practice only in the first centuries of the common era, its cosmic vision is central to Indian civilization as a whole. Its provenance is very likely not limited to any single culture but belongs to all humanity. For even if we confine our attention to Kashmir between the tenth and thirteenth centuries, the moment we wonder about how the cosmos itself is constructed—apart from the pulsating way it appears in consciousness—we cannot avoid concluding that the vision of consciousness, light, and bliss in spanda must be a primary fact of human physiology and imagination.[69]

Indeed, research into the human faculty for entering ecstatic states of consciousness reveals four stages. In the first, one sees "dots, zigzags, grids, sets of parallel lines, nested curves, and meandering lines," all bright and pulsating. They "enlarge, contract, and blend one with another." At the second stage, one sees some of them momentarily assume familiar forms, such as cups and snakes. At the third stage, one is drawn or seems to be flying through a tunnel or vortex whose sides bear the geometric lines of stage one. At the other end of the tunnel, in stage four, one finds oneself in a mythic world, "like a motion picture or slide show." "The geometric percepts are still present, but chiefly peripheral" (Clottes & Lewis-Williams, 1998: 16-17). On the basis of these findings, Jean Clottes and David Lewis-Williams have interpreted the Ice Age cave paintings as visions gained in shamanic ecstasy.

Gerardo Reichel-Dolmatoff has found the same four-stage process among the Indians of the Upper Amazon, who employ psychotropic drugs in the form of yajé, a thick infusion which is drunk, and ayahuasca, a powder which is inhaled (Reichel-Dolmatoff, 1971, 1975). Reichel-Dolmatoff participated in a yajé ceremony and reports a bewildering and unintelligible sequence of lines, zigzags, and curves—technically referred to as "phosphenes." Not knowing what sense to make of this experience and wondering whether he had seen the same hallucinations as his informants, he induced them to draw what they had seen and found that their drawings very closely resembled his own. But for the natives each line and shape had a precise mythic meaning. Universal consensus among the Indians of the Upper Amazon is trained and supported by free and open discussion of all the details of yajé experience. The myth is constantly being taught and explored. "The collective ritual of yajé trance, then, is an experience from which the individual emerges with the firm conviction of the truthfulness of the traditional origins of his culture, and of the guiding moral principles of the Creation story" (Reichel-Dolmatoff, 1975: 181).

When we apply these findings to the Indian version of the cosmos of conscious light—its threads in the cloth of the phenomenal world and the cloth in the threads—it is hard to avoid

---

69 Kashmiri Shaivism says as much: "In reality, succession [of one event after another] and its absence are not objective properties of an entity but only formats of perception" (Dcyzkowski, 1987: 82).

the conclusion that entry into the ecstasy of samadhi introduces the yogin to the phosphenes of the first stage of human ecstatic experience wherever it is found. That the yogin sees this vision as a coherent image of the cosmos arising and dissolving over and over in a timeless "now" is by no means surprising when we think that Indian civilization has been freely and openly discussing the metaphysics of consciousness for centuries, if not millennia. If we wonder why the yogin does not proceed onward to the fourth stage of ecstasy to encounter gods, demons, men, and women engaged in mythic narratives, the answer is to be found in the Tantric theory of the yantra.

In the widest meaning of the term, a yantra is any diagram of the real which represents the microcosm of the human being—especially the body—as homologous with the macrocosm. In this sense, the most detailed yantras are mandalic palaces of the gods; and geometric yantras represent the detailed multiplicity of that mythic world in its subtlest form (Khanna, 1981: 141). When the archetype of the sacred cosmos is resolved into a diagram, the resulting "mesocosm" (D. G. White, 1996) reveals the structural identity of microcosm and macrocosm (Khanna, 1981: 106). Icons of divinities in a celestial palace are reduced to geometric symbols, and the latter are further reduced to the bindu, which is their center-point (Khanna, 129). This whole process of simplification corresponds to the *involutional* thrust of Tantra:

> Involution is a compulsion into the spiritual. It implies moving against the current of life. In subjective terms it means thirsting for a higher state of consciousness, suppressing the "lower" by ascending the ladder of multiplicity into unity, a spiritual itinerary which takes the form of a return to the state of cosmic foetalization, the *a priori* state before experience begins. Such a return shifts the centre of the personality from a fragmented awareness of his ego-centric consciousness to cosmo-centric wholeness, and brings about the union of the individual and cosmic consciousness (Siva-Sakti). It means a death of the profane self, the perishable phenomenal ego, and a rebirth to an eternal, deathless state of being. The entire discipline of yantra-ritual and meditation is directed towards this single goal, a return to the Supreme Centre. The yantra makes the process of involution conscious to the adept (Khanna, 1981: 80).

"Moving against the current of life" has been the theme of the ladder of sexual ascent at each rung since we considered carezza. The current of life moves toward external orgasm and the spilling of seed; carezza reverses it. At the rung of longing, the natural drive to preserve the ego is reversed through embracing madness. At the rung of scandal, the natural course of upholding the values of the persona field is reversed by the hero who strives to surmount good and evil. At the rung of the subtle body, the natural tendency to be riveted by a threat or enticement that disturbs us is reversed when we pay attention to what the wrathful divinity is doing to our state of consciousness. On the field of emptiness, finally, we seek out "the *a priori* state before [citadel] experience begins." If at this point the yogin sees pulsating lines, zigzags, and nested curves, these are centered automatically and without effort in a primary fact whose gathering of the cosmos is simultaneously an act of perception and an act of imagination. The field of emptiness reverses the natural current of life whereby the phosphenes of zigzags and curves are elaborated into a "thought up" world which lies behind empirical phenomena. The yogin remains in the world of primary fact as it reveals itself in samadhi. The joining of Spontaneous Great Bliss with emptiness in maithuna attends only to consciousness itself and is not misled by the objects to which it would attach itself. The cosmos as primary fact is not an object separated from a subject. Consciousness itself is the primary fact in which subject and object participate mystically. Its pulsation reflects not only the throb of physiology, but the oscillation of figure and ground in the light by which everything that is may appear.

Mutuality

6

MUTUAL PARTICIPATION

The metaphor of a ladder of ascent, as ubiquitous as it may be, leaves much to be desired in articulating the nature of mysticism. Every ladder inevitably describes the author's own predilections and is valuable only insofar as it provides a useful set of distinctions between the various challenges and achievements required by the mystical path. The best masters, however, will be flexible with their disciples and reorder the rungs of their teaching so as to complement the natural talents and personal difficulties of each disciple.

The ladder outlined in the preceding chapters has this advantage and failing, and it may also come dangerously close to giving the impression that mystical achievement is entirely a matter of "internal work" which the individual practitioner can undertake more or less in isolation. It might be true enough, for example, that if Trighantika would only renounce his fanatical disciples, stop his exalting, and humbly take up the work of acquainting himself with kundalini through an exercise like the tubular palace meditation, he might achieve Spontaneous Great Bliss and open the way to emptiness. But would a madman like Trighantika be able to relate to a partner? The ladder metaphor will certainly have misled us if we have come to think that "internal work" is all that is required and that one's partner in maithuna is merely a necessary tool for one's own personal advancement and is never appreciated as an individual with a path of her own. Such a view appears to be supported by the male-authored texts emphasized by Eliade in which the ideal partner is described as an "untouchable," a polluted woman who gratifies the need for what is forbidden and serves only as an impersonal figure to make the *divine* relationship possible. Although she must be worshipped as a goddess, we may well wonder what this does to the woman herself. It appears from such texts that relationship and mutuality—to say nothing of ordinary human respect—play no role at all. The Sahajiya who bathes his dancing girls and Gandhi's "chastely" sleeping with female followers to test his own conquest of sexual attachment surely lead us to suspect that the female partner may have been abusively treated as an object. The same suspicion applies to the Sufi who practices the "witness game" with naked, "beardless" youths.

Recently a woman told me the story of her relationship with an avid American Sufi who practiced an unbending form of carezza. In the beginning he seemed to her a wonderful partner insofar as his refusal to ejaculate and detumesce revealed her own capacity for multiple orgasms. Sex had never been so good. She said she had had "no idea my body could do these things." But eventually a resentment began to grow as she became convinced that he could not be budged from his own private accomplishments. He was unyielding and in a deep sense untouchable. She felt she was always required to submit orgasmically to his self-satisfied superiority. He never met her half-way, never joined her in the oceanic transpersonal moment of mutual orgasm. She began to feel that she was nothing but an object to him. The whole relationship began to feel "creepy," and she found it was not difficult to break off.

A story like this reveals the shadowy dimension of the ladder of sexual ascent when it is pursued as a personal indulgence. If such a private pursuit of excellence reminds us of the self-righteous attitude of fundamentalists who appear to have lost all sense of the human dignity of those whose ways of life they reject, our suspicions may not be ill placed. It brings to our attention an issue which has been mentioned from time to time in previous chapters but never given a ladder rung of its own—namely that of mutuality, reciprocity, or interpersonal relationship. In fact, mutuality does not deserve a special place because it plays an integral role at every step. We did speak at some length, for example, of Vimalananda's eternal and spiritual love for his Bhairavi whom he left only because he had been "ordered" to begin a life of teaching. But if we down-played the role of mutuality at the rungs of scandal and the subtle body, we did so primarily in order to emphasize the great changes that have to be effected in the individual. It is, at bottom, our own awareness that needs to be changed. Whatever practices we undertake, their goal is not feats of prowess but the expansion of consciousness, freeing it from the limitations imposed by our neurotic fears and the narrowness of social conformity. Indeed, the ultimate reality in this work that takes us from the empirical world to the subtle plane and then to emptiness is consciousness itself.

But consciousness is not something locked away and isolated in our citadel self. Even if we live our entire lives without encountering the "crack in the self" and never cease to be Cartesian tourists on planet Earth, we fall under the influence of other people's consciousness every day. We may walk into a room, for example, and find the atmosphere thick with strife. If not a single contentious word is uttered, we find ourselves cautious, defensive, and on the look-out for an explanation. Perhaps we feel unwelcome as an intruder or that our sympathies are being silently demanded from all sides, even though we are unaware of the issues at stake. Similarly we can feel another person's anxious or erotic energy, sometimes without being able to pinpoint what it is about that person which stirs up anxiety or lust in ourselves. The story of the sexual therapist, Juliet Carr, who is able in a few hours to stir up enough eros in her client, Bill, that he can keep himself and his wife satisfied for weeks has given us a dramatic instance of interpersonal influence. The mystical path, whether it embraces sexual practices or not, is always founded upon the mutual influence of master and disciple or partner and partner.

The power of maithuna, indeed, is not to be sought merely in the complexity of the detachments and "shepherding" described in the previous chapter, but in the mutual inductive effect of each partner's eros upon the other. We do not need to be mystics to know that our partner's state of arousal—or disinterest—has a direct effect upon our own erotic state of consciousness. Although we may suppose that in profane consciousness many couples remain ignorant of one another's real feelings during intercourse, physiological, emotional, and imaginal influences invariably play at least an unconscious role.

In maithuna, however, each party must be clearly aware not only of her own kundalini's arousal but also of that of her partner. Maithuna always aims for *samarasa*, "a 'unity of emotion,' or more precisely, the paradoxical, inexpressible experience of the discovery of Unity" (Eliade, 1969: 260). Samarasa, however, is obtained not merely through the conscious effort of "shepherding" by which our arousal is guided into a tandem relation with that of our partner. It is obtained above all through the "letting go" of a condition of mutual influence that takes place autonomously. Such an "alignment" of two beings in maithuna resembles the way that our internal monologues are "arranged" by the semi-conscious forces of the persona field, but at a much deeper and more unconscious level. We may well describe this phenomenon in terms of a "field of atman" that arranges our emotions, imaginal experiences, and even the raising of kundalini, as though it is the *atman* of each partner which mutually influences the other. The atman field[70] may even be said to operate as a kind of third agent which brings the two partners into alignment with one another at the level of *atman* or "self."[71] Mutual influence takes place autonomously, much as the atoms of a piece of iron are "aligned" by the influence of a magnetic field. "If one of the partners fails to enjoy a permanent awakening, he or she may receive it from the other" (Silburn, 1987: 160). In this way samarasa simply comes to be in its "suchness" when intercourse takes place on the field of emptiness.

---

70 Elsewhere I have referred to this phenomenon as the "self field." In this context, however, in which we have been talking about the *citadel* self, the term "atman field" may be less confusing.

71 I have argued this point at some length in terms of the self-self relationship that obtains in psychotherapy (Haule, 1996; 1999a), in romantic love (Haule, 2010), and in shamanism (Haule, 1997).

MUTUAL HYPNOSIS

A dramatic example of this deep sort of influence is described in a series of experiments designed by Charles Tart to explore what he calls "mutual hypnosis" (Tart, 1972: 297-315). Tart started with the question of how to "deepen" the hypnotic trance and theorized that the *rapport* between hypnotist and hypnotized subject may be the deciding factor. Believing that the rapport is more powerfully felt by the subject than by the hypnotist, he expected that if the hypnotist were also in a state of hypnotic trance, both the rapport and the depth of trance would increase. To test this hypothesis, he selected two of his students who had already demonstrated moderate talent both for hypnotizing and for being hypnotized. Both were in their twenties. Tart refers to them as Bill and Anne. He had one hypnotize the other and then had them switch roles without leaving the trance state. The procedure worked. Bill hypnotized Anne and instructed her to hypnotize him. With urging from Tart, each then worked to deepen the other's state of trance, wherein they reached subjective assessments of trance depth that went beyond the agreed-upon scale. In the hypnotic state, they both learned to be far more dramatic, forceful, and imaginative practitioners of the hypnotic art.

But an unexpected development occurred when they employed hypnotic "dreams" as a means for imaginatively deepening their respective states. Bill took them both into a sloping tunnel whose depth was to parallel their mutual state of trance. In that dream it was discovered that they were in full communication, even when their eyes were closed and they were not speaking to one another. Back in ordinary consciousness, their separate reports of the adventure in the tunnel not only agreed in all respects but "possessed complete experiential reality," although it was "unworldly" and was possibly "God's house," the "heaven of the Greeks, . . . a heaven without finality" (Tart, 309). They felt they had heads and faces but often no bodies and occasionally "walked *through* each other" (Tart, 310).

> It also came out in conversations some weeks later that this passing through each other was accompanied by a sense of merging identities, of a partial blending of themselves quite beyond the degree of contact human beings expect to share with others (Tart, 310).

> This seemed like a partial fusion of identities, a partial loss of the distinction between I and Thou. This was felt to be good at first, but later the Ss perceived this as a threat to their individual autonomy (Tart, 312).

> Because of the sudden and unexpected intensity of these feelings the couples [Bill and Anne, as well as several similar cases of couples who took LSD-25 together] had a great deal of difficulty in their emotional relationships to each other for several months afterwards, all centered around feelings that they had seen too much of each other's real selves, more than their previous relationship had prepared them to handle comfortably (Tart, 314).

There were two other results of interest. The first was that in one of the sessions a third student, Carol, had entered the room unexpectedly while the mutual hypnosis experiment was in progress. Although she sat in the corner and was subjected to no induction procedure, she, too, entered into trance and found herself in the tunnel with Bill and Anne, a fact that the two principals perceived immediately. Bill ordered her out, but she tagged along guiltily and seemed to have experienced precisely the same tunnel as that traversed by Bill and Anne. Furthermore, all agreed that this was "Bill's tunnel," and had the sense that they were encountering a private dimension of Bill's psyche. Bill was extremely uncomfortable about this self-exposure and subsequently lost all interest in hypnosis, while Anne went on to explore hypnosis avidly on her own.

Although Tart's hypothesis of mutual hypnosis bears faint relation to Eastern meditation practices, and indeed Tantrism, it certainly seems that the subjects stumbled upon a degree of mutuality they found "holy" and completely outside their expectations or prior understanding of what might possibly occur between human individuals. They appear to have entered the field of atman in which the boundaries of the citadel self were completely lacking. For both of them—especially Bill—the experience seemed to come very close to discovering the "crack in the self," and provides a highly suggestive hint regarding the state of samarasa or "emotional unity" defined by Eliade.

If a similar loss of I and Thou is regularly experienced when a couple practices maithuna, the mutual effect is likely to be greatly heightened when ritual intercourse is performed by a circle of couples, as in the story told by Promode Chatterjee. In his account of an Aghora chakra ceremony, Chatterjee noted two facts which belong to the realm of mutual influence. One was that he himself—like Carol in the mutual hypnosis experiment—was brought into a profound state of erotic trance so that when the scene was illumined by a flash of lightning the imaginal eye of his brow chakra was opened and he saw "light figures of naked gods and goddesses in the midst of their divine play, surrounding a large statue of Hara and Gauri, as still and profound as the Himalayas." If the participants had this effect upon Chatterjee, an unprepared observer, how much stronger must have been the effect they had upon one another, sexual mystics who had trained their sensitivities toward the "emotional unity" of samarasa? The other piece of evidence lies in the contrast Chatterjee observes between the "play" of the couples making up the circumference of the circle and the stillness of the central couple. He even says that those on the outside acted "intoxicated and lustful," while the Bhairava and Bhairavi in the center remained "absorbed in trance." The couples on the periphery were arousing themselves to the utmost so as to effect by mutual influence a powerful energetic boost to the couple in the center, whose wedding of Spontaneous Great Bliss with emptiness might be shared by all.

This "division of labor" based upon mutual influence represents a universal principle, equally applicable to the cosmos at large, to the participating couples in the maithuna circle, and to the individual human body. For here, again, we observe the homology of macrocosm and microcosm through the enactment of a mesocosm in the form of a mandala or yantra. In a hymn by Ksemaraja, one of Abhinavagupta's disciples, this whole process is described as taking place in the heart chakra, the locus of sublime influence between individuals. Dcyzkowski summarizes it as follows:

> [Ksemaraja] portrays the goddesses of the senses as seated on the petals of the lotus of the Heart [i.e., the traditional mandalic representation of the heart chakra] arrayed around the Divine Couple, Anandabhairava and Anandabhairavi, Who are in the calix. The goddesses move restlessly hither and thither in search of the most pleasing sensations to offer in worship to the Couple in the Center (Dcyzkowski, 1987: 145).

Abhinavagupta, himself, salutes each in turn, beginning with the Bhairava and Bhairavi of bliss (ananda) in the center, and then the goddesses on each of the petals, naming what they contribute to the experience of unity. Finally, he concludes with these words:

> I venerate in this way the circle of deities eternally active (*satadodita*) in my own body, ever present in all beings and the essence of the radiant pulsation of experience (*sphuradanubhava*) (Dcyzkowski, 146).

We are familiar from "mob psychology" with the fact that the larger the group that is moved by a common emotion, the baser its actions will be, as though each mob is reduced to its "least common denominator." Less ominous examples of mutual influence can be given by anyone who has participated in a group meditation or a training workshop to develop our innate ability for intuition or entering imaginal scenes. In all such cases, our habitual ego-defenses are weakened when five, ten, or a hundred individuals participate in some exercise in non-ordinary consciousness. I have observed the same tendency when leading dream-interpretation groups or conducting group supervision sessions for psychotherapists. It seems clear that the group very readily enters a participatory space where the dream or case material gathers us together almost as though we become the several pairs of eyes and mouths of a single reflecting psyche. We are often surprised by our capacity for cooperation and by the unexpected insights that we voice.

YESHE INITIATES HER RAPISTS

When these sorts of experience are applied to the practice of ritual intercourse by groups of Tantrikas, it is easy to imagine that the group very quickly and powerfully reaches a state of mystical participation, where the energy of each couple has an effect upon the whole. If less trained and disciplined individuals were involved, we might expect that the whole procedure would degenerate by way of "mob psychology" into a chaotic orgy. The fact that it does not is based upon the Tantric principle of "involution." Ordinary mob interaction devolves toward the basest of gratifications; but by reversing this natural tendency and drawing all sensory phenomena toward the center point (bindu), disciplined Tantrikas make everything coalesce into the One at both the microcosmic and macrocosmic levels. Mutual influence draws energy from the most ordinary and even dangerous sensory activities and uses them for Spontaneous Great Bliss and emptiness.

A powerful example of this is provided in Yeshe Tsogyel's "autobiography"—which, it will be remembered, was discovered on the subtle plane some centuries after the alleged events had occurred. In the incident I refer to, Yeshe is traveling alone under orders from her guru when she is set upon by seven bandits who rob her of her possessions and then rape her. As soon as they are finished having their way with her, Yeshe sings a song to introduce them to "the four joys" of the mystical path. That song includes the following lines:

> Apprehend the very essence of lust,
> Identify it as your creative visualization of the deity,
> And that is nothing but the Yidam[72] deity himself.
> Meditate upon lustful mind as Divine Being
> (Dowman, 1984: 118-9).

No sooner does she finish her song than the "seven thieves gained simultaneous spiritual maturity and release." In the end, she has gained seven new disciples. Dowman comments on this episode:

> Tsogyel's method of making a rape a positive experience was to accept the situation and then control it. Through visualization identifying herself with Tara, the Goddess of Service, who is willing to do whatever is necessary to serve the Guru who is all sentient beings, the victim was transformed into the Saviouress (Dowman, 264).

---

72 Yidam: "Tibetan, literally 'firm mind.' In Vajrayana Buddhism, a term for a personal deity, whose nature corresponds to the individual psychological make-up of the practitioner" (Fischer-Schreiber, *et. al.*, 1989).

The most conservative reading of this story would take the encounter between Yeshe and the rapists as a dramatization of what may take place within the psyche of any accomplished Tantrika—namely that one's lust may become "the Yidam deity," that is the god corresponding to one's own psychology, the divine dimension of the individual's own being. A holy possibility, the unification of Spontaneous Great Bliss with emptiness, lurks in the shadow of our lust. A somewhat more daring interpretation—but one that is also integral to Tantra—would begin from the everyday fact that we externalize our psyche in projection by way of our internal monologue. In this case, a woman beset by rapists in profane consciousness encounters her impotence before the demon of her own lust when brutish men embody that lust in attacking her. The profane and "natural" course of action is to take the brutality of that lust as an incontrovertible fact and either to fight a losing battle with it or to reluctantly submit in a realistic admission that the seven men have overwhelming physical force on their side. The woman, then, is violated, humiliated, even destroyed.

Yeshe, however, takes a realistic stand on the subtle plane. Looking inward to the surging reality of kundalini, she knows without doubt that the brutality of lust is a human fact that harbors the sublime reality of the Yidam deity of lust-consciousness whose higher meaning is Spontaneous Great Bliss. By accepting both the lower form of lust and its higher divine meaning, she "accepts the situation and controls it." She turns her attention to the rising kundalini which begins in the lust and impotence of the navel chakra but finds its transcendent meaning in the opening of the crown chakra. In submitting to the rape, she transforms it; and in transforming it, she transmutes profane violation into mystical victory. Thus, while the woman in profane consciousness is dragged down through mutual "mob" participation to the brutal realm of her rapists' lust, Yeshe elevates them all through sublime mutual participation into the sphere of the Yidam deity. The story tells us that every human encounter is based in mutual participation. If we know the nature of lust and that it harbors a Yidam deity, we have a choice. Either we can succumb as victims, or we can "take control," accepting the situation as a mystical opportunity. If we do so, we transform the entire episode.

Seen in this light, the story of Yeshe and the seven bandits provides an illuminating commentary on our contemporary society's obsession with victimhood. Identifying ourselves as victims lends us a certain perverse righteousness and opens the door to litigation whereby the horizontal rights of our human dignity can be defended in an entirely profane manner. The mystical realization of Tantra turns this litigious struggle upside-down and asserts that the whole notion of "victims' rights" misses the involutional opportunity whereby an unacknowledged vertical reality, the Yidam deity, remains silent and denied by the persona field. Furthermore, when the potential victim has her wits about her and has realized the transformative potential of kundalini in her own life, she turns the brutal challenge into mystical opportunity and thereby becomes the "saviouress" of brutes whose consciousness has hitherto known only the base realities of "perpetrators."

SHAKTIPAT

To be a savior and win disciples rather than perpetrators is founded upon the reality of mutual participation. Sanskrit has a word for the mutual influence which elevates: *shaktipat*. *Shakti-pata* means "descent of power" and refers to the "transmission of psychospiritual energy (*shakti*) from the adept to the disciple" (Feuerstein, 1990). Shaktipat may be conferred by a touch, the bestowal of an article of clothing, a word, a glance, or even a thought. Often it is used in the phrase *shaktipat diksha*, "initiation (*diksha*) by the descent of power." Yeshe initiated the seven rapists through the act of intercourse they believed they were forcing upon her when the energy of her raised kundalini elevated their lust and opened their higher chakras through the inductive force of shaktipat.

> [In *shaktipat diksha*] the master directly transmits his energy to the student to remove the final obstacle, awakening the sleeping serpent and leading her upward. One who is functioning on a higher level may sometimes unconsciously influence those around him in the same way that a magnet influences metal objects in its proximity. . . . As a magnet influences a particular metal, such a teacher influences those who are prepared. . . . In shaktipat the influence is conscious and extremely intense. Through a look, touch, or thought the master transmits his own power to the aspirant, who is suddenly transported into a realm of blissful divine consciousness (Rama, 1990: 39).

Generally the transmission of shaktipat is understood to take place through the heart chakra of master and disciple, for the anahata is above all the locus of sublime unity between individuals. The transmission inspires expansion, love, and the sense that one stands above "the surface of the earth." It is a "spiritual" transferal, but it takes place "from body to body" (Silburn, 1987: 87). It "enhallows" (Feuerstein, 1989: 27) the disciple along the three dimensions of mystical experience we have emphasized: physiology, emotion, and imagination. Sometimes the recipient enters directly into dhyana or samadhi and remains there for an extended period of time. "After shaktipat, meditation becomes natural, and takes place without strain or striving" (Desai, 1990: 75). It is often described as a "divine" transmission, for it is based in the guru's capacity for becoming one with the cosmos, "the infinite realm of illumination" (Silburn, 1987: 87). The disciple experiences the master "as a spiritual reality rather than as a human personality" (Feuerstein, 1989: 26).

As might be expected, Vimalananda has a number of provocative things to say about shak-tipat, and many of them suggest a reciprocity between master and disciple not emphasized elsewhere. Indeed, he implies that shaktipat is but a spiritual and elevating form of the mutual influence which obtains between all individuals, even in profane consciousness. True shak-tipat requires genuine connection with and solid experience of impersonal, divine realities. Because the guru will be an expert in this field, the burden of converting mutual influence into an elevating transmutation of the disciple lies with the master. For example: "A guru al-ways wants to make his disciple into his own guru. The Self, the Absolute Reality, is the true guru" (Svoboda, 1994: 279). This implies not only that the guru has to be able to see beyond appearances and is not fooled by the disciple's personal and neurotic limitations. The disciple, too, is an embodiment of the divine—analogous, perhaps, to the saying of Jesus, "As you did it to the least of my brethren, you did it to me" (Mt 25:40). Elsewhere Vimalananda suggests that the mutual influence which elevates the disciple can also diminish the saint's spiritual power. This claim, too, is reminiscent of words ascribed to Jesus when a woman afflicted with a hemorrhage was healed upon touching the hem of his garment: "And Jesus, perceiving in himself that power had gone forth from him, immediately turned about in the crowd, and said, 'Who touched my garments?'" (Mk 5: 30). Vimalananda's statement is more sobering:

A true saint is the embodiment of his deity and the energy emanating from him is the energy of that deity. By touching a saint's feet you collect a little of that energy, which purifies your own consciousness and makes it more subtle. The saint loses some of his own peace of mind by this which is uncomfortable for the saint; this is how many saints go bad (Svoboda, 1997: 262).

Because mutual influence works both ways, the one who is elevated may diminish the more spiritually advanced. On a more ordinary level, I have encountered this phenomenon in some of my patients who are "energy healers" and massage therapists. They often find themselves depleted or made ill by patients who seem to leave their offices in an improved state of bodily and mental health. I have also found that the level of my own consciousness can be lowered and my habitual sense of having a coherent self temporarily fragmented by an interaction with a poorly integrated patient who clearly seems to have benefited from our exchange.

Finally, Vimalananda suggests that if we pay attention to how the presence of another person subtly changes our consciousness, we can arrive at an assessment of the other person's spiritual state. This is particularly helpful when we find ourselves before a naked Sadhu who has all the trappings of spirituality but may be a charlatan:

> Sit quietly and don't say much; listen, and try to keep your mind blank. If when you sit near him you find yourself forgetting the things of the world and becoming more peaceful, then he is a good saint; his halo is quieting your mind. If not, run away! (Svoboda, 1994: 267).

Muktananda emphasizes the sexual foundation of shaktipat when it dawns on him that the reason he had to struggle with a bewildering and humiliating manifestation of overwhelming sexual desire was to turn him into an urdhvareta,[73] one in whom the "sexual fluid" rises and becomes "the source of the power to give Shaktipat" (Muktananda, 1978: 32, 99). Sexual arousal, transmuted on the subtle plane to kundalini, makes one an initiate by transforming his own being and giving him the power to transform "other beings, indeed, the entire universe, through his limitless powers" (D. G. White, 1996: 272). D. G. White summarizes the Tantric doctrine of shaktipat as it appears in scriptures written between the tenth and fourteenth centuries. Here we encounter a magical flavor, even a literal physicality, which many later sources eschew.

> The guru, having entered the body of his disciple (whose *kundalini* has been awakened) unites with that *kundalini* within the disciple's body and subsequently raises it from the disciple's lower abdomen up to his cranial vault. The form the guru takes as he courses through his disciple's body may be that of a drop (*bindu*) of seed or speech. In many descriptions of this operation, the guru is said to exit the disciple's body through the mouth and thus return back into his own body through his own mouth (D. G. White, 312).

White makes it clear that this is fundamentally a sexual process, albeit with gender "polarities reversed": "given that it is a feminine *kundalini* which awakens, stiffens, rises, even rushes upwards towards the cranial vault, the cavity that is the place of the passive male Siva" (D. G. White, 320).

Although the Hindu doctrine of shaktipat is distinguished by the fullness of its descriptions, the reality of mutual influence is also well known in Sufism, where elevating influence is often described as "perfecting" an "imperfection" in the disciple. Probably the most common practice is that the shaikh who recognizes such an opportunity for elevating a disciple invests himself with a special article of clothing, the mantel (khirqa), and by meditation places himself in the mystical state of consciousness he wishes to induce in his disciple. Then he ceremoniously removes the khirqa from his own body and places it on the body of the disciple,

---

73 *Urdhva-retas*: "the physiological process by which the semen (*retas*) flows upward (*urdhva*), and . . . the *yogin* in whom this process is alive" (Feuerstein, 1990).

transferring the desired state at the same time (Wilson, 1993: 144). In her biography of Ibn al-'Arabi, Claude Addas cites several references from "The Greatest Shaikh" attesting to the "immediate transformation" that is produced in the disciple by means of the khirqa (Addas, 1993: 145). A passage from Ibn al-'Arabi's *Revelations at Mecca*[74] is very explicit:

> So it is when the masters of spiritual states perceive some imperfection in one of their com-panions and wish to perfect that person's state, they resort to the custom of meeting with the person alone. The master then takes the piece of clothing he is wearing in the spiritual state he is in at that particular moment, removes it and puts it on the man whom he wishes to guide to perfection. He then holds the man closely to him—and the master's state spreads to his disciple, who thereby attains to the desired perfection (Addas, 1993: 146).

Jalaluddin Rumi's practice of baring his breast when in an ecstatic state of divine love and pressing it against the chest of a disciple (Schimmel, 1978: 217) not only dispenses with the article of clothing as a necessary element but also seems implicitly to acknowledge the Hindu doctrine that mutual influence is in some sense a bodily transfer with sexual implications and that the bodily locus of mutual influence is associated with the heart chakra. Rumi speaks of the saint who knows with the heart and leads the disciple with his heart:

> [The gnosis of the heart[75]], is one of the distinguishing features of the mystical leader. He is a lion, and the thoughts of others are like a forest which he can easily enter. . . . [H]e discovers in the unpolished stone the wonderful figures which people see in the polished mirror. That is why he can show the novice the path which leads him best towards self-realization and ap-proximation to God, calling the figures out of the stone "heart" (Schimmel, 315-6).

Sufism also speaks of the intense concentration of master and disciple upon one anoth-er [tawajjuh] that brings about "spiritual unity, faith healing, and many other phenomena" (Schimmel, 1975: 366). By tawajjuh, the master "enters the door of the disciple's heart"; and through his "knowledge of things that exist potentially in God's eternal knowledge, he is able to realize certain of these possibilities on the worldly plane" (Schimmel, 237). From the side of the disciple, it is said that he "passes away" or that his ego-personality has been "annihilated" in the master (*fana' fi'sh-shaikh*), who, in his turn has already been annihilated in the Prophet Muhammad. By this means, the shaikh "becomes the Perfect Man and thus leads his disciples with a guidance granted directly by God" (Schimmel, 237). This doctrine of the passing away (fana') of one's ego so as to discover one's greater self (baqa') through the

---

74 Citing *Futuhat*, I: 187.

75 The technical term employed, *ferasat*, is rendered as *cardiognosy* by Schimmel, evidently derived from *kardia* (heart) and *gnosis*.

relationship with one's shaikh, directly parallels the Hindu notion of shaktipat, whereby ego gives way to atman through the transforming influence of the guru.[76]

THE RECIPIENT OF SHAKTIPAT

Ibn al-'Arabi gives us a hint as to how such an elevating influence feels to the disciple when he is transformed. In the following passage, he describes what happened to him early in his mystical career while he sat face-to-face in tawajjuh with Abu Ya'qub al-Kumi. He reports two effects, a conscious experience of trembling and a revelation from his dream that the shaikh's power emanated from the brightness of his heart chakra:

> I saw him in a dream on one occasion and his breast seemed to be cleft asunder and a light like that of the sun shone out from it. . . . When I would sit before him or before others of my Shaikhs, I would tremble like a leaf in the wind, my voice would become weak and my limbs would shake (Ibn al-'Arabi, 1971: 70).

The American initiate of Tibetan Buddhism, Tsultrim Allione, describes even more vividly the effect upon herself when, in her first interview with Chogyam Trungpa Rinpoche, they sat face-to-face in silence for forty-five minutes. At first she waited in puzzlement for him to speak. Then it began to dawn on her that something of quite a different order was occurring. It was only much later that she grasped what it was:

> Now I realize that what happened was some kind of mind-to-mind transmission, but at the time I only knew that I had experienced something that was completely beyond words and form. . . . It was an experience of space[77] that extended outward without any reference back. This space was luminous and bliss-provoking, a release, similar to, but beyond, sexual orgasm (Allione: 1986: xvii-xviii).

The German initiate of Tibetan Buddhism, Lama Govinda Anagarika, describes his own experience of receiving shaktipat through a light touch from the hand of his guru. Govinda perceived "a stream of bliss" traversing his whole being which he felt vividly in his body, "so that all that one had intended to say or ask, vanished from one's mind like smoke into blue air" (Govinda, 1988: 33). Some years later he experienced an analogous elevating influence

---

76 I have explicated the doctrine of fana' as it applies to romantic love at some length in *Divine Madness* (Haule, 2010).

77 "Space (*dbymgs*) is not the interval between objects and it is not spatiality; it is better conceived as an all-pervasive, all-penetrating, sub-atomic plenum" (Dowman, 1984: 241).

from the Great Hermit at Gomchen, who had refused to meet him. He was told to wait overnight at some distance from the hermitage in a "horribly cold and draughty wooden rest-house":

> But before I could fall asleep a strange thing happened. I had the sensation that somebody took possession of my consciousness, my will-power, and my body—that I no more had control over my thoughts, but that somebody else was thinking them—and that slowly, but surely, I was losing my own identity. And then I realized that it could be none other than the hermit . . . due to the power of his concentration and my own lack of resistance in the moment when I was hovering between the waking and the sleeping state (Govinda, 101).

The eighteen-year-old Narendra, who became Ramakrishna's favorite disciple, was frightened and repelled at his first meeting with the forty-five year-old saint. Ramakrishna raved and wept in "anxious desire" and claimed that Narendra was the reincarnation of the ancient sage Narayana. Narendra concluded that Ramakrishna was a "monomaniac." In his second meeting, however, Narendra received shaktipat:

> As I was thinking [Ramakrishna was about to create another embarrassing scene], he quickly approached me and placed his own right foot on my body, and immediately I had an unprecedented experience at his touch. As I looked, I began to see that all the things in the room, with the walls themselves, were spinning wildly and dissolving into somewhere. . . .terrible fear . . .this itself was at the threshold of death. . . . [Finally Ramakrishna relented] and said, "Then enough now, the work doesn't have to be done all at once. It will come about in good time" (Kripal, 1995: 211).

An American student of yoga, D. R. Butler, describes his own first experience of shaktipat, which took place in Upstate New York in 1973 when Butler was in his mid-twenties and had already been studying yoga for five years. At a week-long yoga retreat, Yogi Amrit Desai, who until that moment had been completely unknown to the group, led them in a meditation.

> The first thing I noticed was a wave of euphoria softly permeating my being. I felt intensely happy. I didn't know the reason for the wonderful feeling but I determined to relax and enjoy it.
>
> Suddenly surges of energy—like electrical charges—streaked up my spine. These gradually evolved into a steady current of hot energy flowing from the tip of my spine to the top of my head. . . .
>
> Brilliant colors swirled inside my head; I thought I would burst with happiness. Nothing had ever felt so good! Suddenly a scream burst from the back of the room, then another. In a few moments the place was a madhouse (Butler, 1990: 185).

Only after an extended outbreak of pandemonium did Desai halt the demonstration and explain to the uninitiated students that what they had felt was shaktipat. Those who wished could leave the room. About half did so. Then Desai resumed his transmission with even greater intensity.

> My body was filled with a brilliant white light and I allowed myself to be absorbed in it. I felt that my life as I previously had known it literally came to an end. My ego identity became meaningless; there was no time; past and future did not exist. All that existed was pure light and pure bliss. I was content to remain in this state forever.
>
> When I opened my eyes again I noticed that my body had bent forward; my forehead was touching the floor (Butler, 187).

Muktananda's reception of shaktipat from his guru, Nityananda, is described in too much detail to be summarized (Muktananda, 1978: 64-71). Suffice it to say that it included all the elements we have seen, including the transferal of a cloak and pair of sandals from the guru's own body. Muktananda describes with greater economy several instances in which he conferred shaktipat on someone else. There is an intriguingly inadvertent element in each of them. In one case an airline officer begs to be allowed to clean Muktananda's bathroom. His request having been granted, the officer had hardly begun when he fell into a stillness and sat in meditation for four hours. Subsequently, the officer reported, people who entered his own meditation room would enter immediately into unexpectedly deep states of meditation (Muktananda, 144).

Nityananda intended to initiate Muktananda; Amrit Desai deliberately created chaos among unprepared students; and Ramakrishna, despite his tendency to spend extended periods of time completely out of his mind in divyonmada, knew exactly what he was doing in conferring shaktipat on the ambivalent young Narendra. Nevertheless, it is clear that not a few instances of elevating influence occur autonomously, quite to the surprise and amazement of the individual through whom the conferral takes place. In the following example Swami Rama makes it clear that, in his experience, a genuine shaktipat initiation originates from an impersonal source over which he himself has no control.

> One day [my master] told me that a swami would come the next morning and that I was to touch him on the forehead, thereby initiating him in shaktipat diksha. I protested, saying that I had no such power to arouse the kundalini in another person. But he said to me, "Don't you know, it is not you acting. You are just the instrument of a higher power. Let the power work through you."

. . . Suddenly I found my arm being raised. It was not at all under my control. I touched the swami and he remained in samadhi for several hours. . . . There may be someone to whom I wish to impart this experience, but nevertheless I cannot. Yet with a few rare individuals I feel such a strong impulse that I cannot resist (Rama, 1990: 41).

Guy Claxton, an English disciple of Irina Tweedie (whose spiritual autobiography will be discussed shortly), inadvertently conferred shaktipat on a neighbor who had been hounding him for instruction in the techniques of meditation. Claxton refused him six times before deciding the man was serious. However, he got no further than the initial instructions for relaxing the body when:

I felt a rush of psychophysical energy seemingly enter my body from beneath and explode out toward him. My speech became slurred and my eyelids got heavy, but I kept my eyes focused on him. As the wave of energy hit him, he visibly jerked back, looking at me fearfully. Then a second wave passed through me, and again he startled. By the time a third rush of energy reached him, he was in deep meditation. I felt a force field connecting our bodies, and while I stayed in meditation, he too remained meditating (Feuerstein, 1991: 133).[78]

THE END OF THE LADDER

The ladder of mystical ascent, which the novice sees as a set of exercises and objective steps, one lesson after another—like arithmetic, algebra, and trigonometry as the precursors of calculus—and which later becomes an internal ladder identical with the subtle body, finally collapses with the experience of emptiness. For emptiness reveals that all the exercises and metaphysical explanations belong to the intermediate phase, when the world no longer appears as mountains, trees, and rivers. They constitute a necessary withdrawal from the socially sanctioned world of the citadel self in order to pave the way back, where trees, mountains, and rivers can be encountered as primary facts.

Shaktipat, the reality of mutual influence, which we largely ignored while defining the steps of the ladder, may now be seen to play a crucial role in mystical ascent. On the one hand, it seems to confirm the discrete steps of the ladder insofar as it is employed to lift us from the ignorance of the ladder rung of our most recent accomplishment to the insight of the next stage through a kind of borrowed illumination. For example, one who has guessed that there is more to sex than the physiological release of profane orgasm, may be transported

---

78 Citing Guy Claxton, *Wholly Human: Western and Eastern Visions of the Self and Its Perfection*. London: Routledge & Kegan Paul, 1981.

to erotic trance through an encounter with an American Bhairavi like Juliet Carr. A certain shaktipat, inadequate but useful, has lifted her client Bill into a more satisfying relationship with his wife. Those whom overwhelming eros has led to an unconscious state of divyonmada might be lifted to the realization that the soul has its own dragon which will bring them beyond the socially sanctioned dichotomy of good and evil. At that stage, the disciple has been guided through the turmoil of the navel chakra to the solid realization of "essential being" in the manipura of the solar plexus. Further conferrals of shaktipat may open the sublimity of the heart chakra or even induce the samadhi which is characteristic of the crown chakra.

In this manner, shaktipat confirms the structure of the ladder. It may even be the ultimate "secret" of mystical ascent that may not be spoken. Mentioning it, however, or even describing it in a general way as we have done, accomplishes little for the disciple. One has either been initiated by shaktipat or one has not. We have either been lucky enough to have encountered a master with the ability to transport us past our personal obstacles, or we continue to struggle with our exercises. It is often said that for the soul that is prepared, anything can occasion enlightenment. Swami Rama says he cannot confer shaktipat to whomever he wishes, but only when ordained by a power that transcends his own personal consciousness. Imponderable considerations—above all "grace" in the sense of a fortuitous transcendental factor—are involved.

We hardly dare say there is no progress without shaktipat or some form of "divine intervention," yet the alternative seems unlikely. Mystics may spend years in isolation, but we know of none for whom interpersonal influence has not played a crucial role. Since this is the case, it appears that the ladder of ascent is a useful conceit, a teaching device that establishes valuable distinctions only after the fact. Only those who have gnosis are in a position to describe the obstacles they have overcome. Our future course remains shrouded in "secrets" which no one is "keeping." It is never a matter of information being withheld but of an experience that has not yet been had. Possibly for each of us a master resides somewhere in the world who is uniquely suited to advance us through mutual influence. Possibly that individual has never even heard of a ladder of ascent, despite possessing the key to our own personal lock. Surely those who have conferred shaktipat without ever having heard of it—Muktananda's airline officer, for example—are unwitting masters. But whether we will have the good luck to meet this unknown master resides in the imponderable secret of our "fate."

IRINA TWEEDIE

Notions of fate, destiny, and grace—mysterious words, impossible to specify—seem to play so crucial a role on the mystical path that a well-developed understanding of the ladder of ascent may serve more as a distraction than a help. Such appears to be the theme of Irina Tweedie's 800-page mystical diary, *Daughter of Fire* (1986). Tweedie was born in Russia a decade before the Bolshevik Revolution, was educated in Vienna and Paris, and married a British military officer after the second World War. Widowed in 1954, Tweedie began a search for religious meaning and was working for the Theosophical Society in London in 1959 when a friend insisted that she had to meet a certain guru in India. She was fifty-five years old and considered herself an old woman when she met the man she calls Bhai Sahib ("Elder Brother"). He was some thirteen years older than she and an initiated master in the Naqshbandiyya Order of Sufis.

Founded in the fourteenth century by Baha'uddin Naqshband, who traced his own initiatory tradition back another two centuries, the Naqshbandiyya has many adherents in Central Asia, including Pakistan and India. Judging from the form it takes in Bhai Sahib's teaching, it may incorporate a large number of Hindu words, concepts, and practices. Bhai Sahib says Sufism is not a religion but a way of life that is compatible with any religion.[79] The Naqshbandiyya pursues a sober path based upon the silent repetition of the divine Name (dhikr in Arabic; japa in Sanskrit) in the heart, intimate spiritual conversation between master and disciple (suhbat) and the shaktipat-like concentration in spiritual unity (tawajjuh) which aims for the experiential "certitude" of divine/human unity. Its main teaching is the "education of the heart" by which the disciple is "spiritually purified" (Schimmel, 1975: 363-73).

Bhai Sahib informed Tweedie that there are two paths: the slower and less painful way of *dhyana* (meditation),[80] and the faster "Path of Fire" which requires no effort but great suffering. One does not choose the Path of Fire; one finds oneself chosen and can either accept the path or refuse. There appears never to have been any doubt in either disciple or master that Tweedie had been destined for the Path of Fire and that she would not refuse.[81] It is evident from her diary that the Path of Fire is based in shaktipat, mutual influence from heart chakra to heart chakra, and that the suffering has to do with learning to accommodate oneself to powerful unanticipated changes in physiology, emotion, and imagination. "I was broken

---

79 In this regard, Bhai Sahib's understanding of the Naqshbandiyya differs quite radically from what the tradition has become in this century, as presented in Buehler's historical overview (Buehler, 1998). According to Buehler the tradition has become a rather superficial means of declaring one's identity as a Muslim. Evidently Bhai Sahib's practice represents an earlier form of the Naqshbandiyya in which the shaikh is an instructor in esoteric disciplines.

80 "To put somebody in Dhayna—it can be done—but it would only show that my will is stronger than yours" (Tweedie, 1986: 21). "If I give the order, anybody can put anyone in Dhyana" (Schimmel, 500).

81 The Shishya [disciple] has every right to test the Guide; but once he is satisfied and accepts the Guide . . . then the Guide can take over, and the disciple has no free will for a while (Tweedie, 21).

down in every sense till I had to come to terms with that in me which I kept rejecting all my life" (Tweedie, 1986: x).

Tweedie's journal begins with her first meeting with Bhai Sahib on October 2, 1961, and ends March 9, 1967, about six and a half months after her master's death. Regarding that first meeting, when she was exhausted and rumpled from her long journey, she describes a powerful experience of mutual influence: "I caught my breath. . . . wild cartwheels were turning inside my brain and then my mind went completely blank. And then it was—it was as if *something in me* stood to attention and saluted . . . I was in the presence of a Great Man" (Tweedie, 6). Thereafter, every time she meets with him, and even if she only enters his room, she finds herself in dhyana, her thoughts slowed down, "Thoughts come and go, lazily, slowly, just a few, and far in between" (Tweedie, 12). When he talks, she fails to understand at the conscious level but gives answers that amaze her. Evidently he is speaking to her unconscious mind which answers without the participation of her ego. This is why she needs a guru, she says, "Because by yourself alone you can never go beyond the Mind" (Tweedie, 20).

Bhai Sahib explains that it all has to do with the awakening of kundalini, a power that includes sex but is more comprehensive. It is the way things are done in the Naqsbandiyya: "We awaken the King, the Heart Chakra, and leave it to the King to activate all the other Chakras" (Tweedie, 36). She has visions of his face as "sheer energy" and is "plagued by constant vibrations in her whole body" (Tweedie, 37-8). "It is just like the beginning of falling in love. Falling in love with what??" (Tweedie, 93). On December 1, 1961, the last day of her second month's association with her guru, she marvels at her ability to pray, "My mind is still, transparent, as though paralyzed, and my heart flies away like trembling bird" (Tweedie, 75). He is in every one of her dreams at night (Tweedie, 77). A month later he begins pointedly to ignore her, and she is hurt and angry (Tweedie, 92-4). Still, she finds that when she prays, she prays to him and sees his face clearly before her (Tweedie, 102). By the middle of the fourth month, she is plagued with sexual vibrations in the muladhara (base of the spine) which hisses, tickles, flutters, and spins. She is flooded with sexual desire and "an uncontrollable fear—primitive, animal fear" that goes on for hours (Tweedie, 108-9). "Hideous beings, leering, obscene, all coupled in sexual intercourse, elemental creatures, animal-like, performing wild sexual orgies" create "cold terror" in her and fill her with shame (Tweedie, 110-1). Her whole being is filled with uncontrollable energy. She can remember everything he says and does but absolutely nothing else that happens from day to day (Tweedie, 123).

By February 8, 1962, four months after meeting him, the grotesque horrors of the svadhisthana chakra in the lower abdomen begin to give way to symptoms associated with the anahata: "I can actually HEAR the Heart Chakra spin round and round at a terrific speed; the physical heart responds by beating madly, missing out beats, and behaving as if trying to jump out of the thorax" (Tweedie, 125). She has visions of "luminous blood" coursing through her subtle body and sees that it extends outside her physical body and belongs to the "Web of the Universe" (Tweedie, 127). More and more she is plagued by his neglect of her and his solicitude for his other followers who "ask the most irrelevant questions"(Tweedie, 135). He explains that keeping her constantly between emotional ups and downs is essential to his method, "to cause suffering which will defeat the Mind" (Tweedie, 187). A voice in a dream tells her, "Only the one who is loved is tortured" (Tweedie, 194). By May of 1962 she is withdrawing all of her money from her extensive world-wide investments and giving him huge sums which he immediately turns over to needy charities. She is "fascinated" by the process (Tweedie, 200).

She is told she has to give up all her beliefs, especially those she has learned from Theosophy. "Everything in me cried out in despair." Then suddenly, "It felt like a click, a snap, and then stillness. . . . A bell-like thought floated into my mind: a belief which is taken up can be given up" (Tweedie, 279). Later, this sort of "click" brings about "a ceaseless streaming . . . absolute glory," which she finds she can just "sink into." It is "a tremendous pull, a wave of love" (Tweedie, 283). But now, eleven months after her first meeting, she begins to provoke huge fights with him, based on her morose feelings of neglect; and he fights back. They read like lovers' quarrels (Tweedie, 288-93). Two months later, he tells her he is speeding up the process so that her training will be complete by the time of his death. She is going to have to leave him for a while, because those who remain with him all the time do not make progress. (Tweedie, 325). At the end of fifteen months, she asks if he effects these changes in her deliberately with his eyes. He answers that the process is not deliberate, but admits that sometimes the disciple does see "streams of light flashing from the eyes" of the guru (Tweedie, 430). Her kundalini vibrations are now never felt below the waistline (Tweedie, 432). She concludes that this relationship is so difficult because: "It is not a human relationship at all. It belongs to 'the other part of me'" (Tweedie, 445).

On April 30, 1963, she reluctantly follows orders and returns to England, where she remains for two and a half years, meditating, teaching, and writing him letters two or three times a week, often filled with bitter recriminations for rejecting her. He never replies. When she returns in January of 1966, his first lessons concern the disciple's "passing away" (fana') into the guru who has "passed away" into God. Eventually she, too, will have to learn to "pass away" into God—"the most difficult" stage of all (Tweedie, 515-7). More outbursts of anger. He does not condemn her: "It is beyond the power of the human being to control anger. But after the anger, look at it: from where it came, why and how it came, and what it did to you. You will learn many things" (Tweedie, 637-8). She finds that his method of teaching is to fall silent so as to let her "intuition speak" (Tweedie, 664). She walks the streets "as though drunk" and wearing blinders—something that happens all the time in India but never in London (Tweedie, 719-20).

On July 25, 1966, the eve of his death, which she does not consciously suspect, she is worried but inwardly still and at peace. He gives her the look "of a divine lover." "My heart stood still as though pierced by a sword. . . . I was so profoundly disturbed that I literally ran away" (Tweedie, 744). She remains in his town for two weeks after his death and then goes to a retreat in the Himalayas, repeating the Divine Name "all the time." Her consciousness is changing, but she does not understand it (Tweedie, 774-5). Six weeks later it dawns on her that his whole work was to make her "pregnant with God" and that her mistake was to think that she had to "get God" from him (Tweedie, 793). "Something intangible very slowly became a permanent reality. . . . My heart is incessantly humming its song to Him [God]" (Tweedie, 797). After four months, this realization has become well established: "Deep, deep within there is this love and that is the ONLY REALITY—this love that digs deep into the heart, its blazing abyss, this love that enwraps and exalts my whole being and the whole of creation as one" (Tweedie, 804). "All I know is that the goal will be always receding, 'For the Beloved can never be known'" (Tweedie, 814).

From Tweedie's extensive diary—written and published only because Bhai Sahib insisted—we can detect the entire process of the diamond ladder, but undertaken without any of the corresponding concepts and without any "left-hand" practices. Kundalini is aroused and feels disturbingly sexual. Tweedie is amazed at such bodily sexual sensations and fantasies in an "old woman" like herself. She enters an erotic relationship that has all the characteristic jealousies and attachments we know from our own experiences of romantic love. We can appreciate the effects of kundalini's arousal in the physiological, emotional, and imaginal experiences Tweedie reports. It begins in the muladhara, leads to torment and terror in the svadhisthana, and the sublime sensations of the anahata. At times her ajna's third eye is opened. The central problem and source of suffering takes the form of her longing for union, intimacy, and exclusivity with her guru and his resolute insistence on frustrating this literal-minded and limited desire. She can come to know God only through personal love directed toward a specific friend and then has to lose that personal friend in order to find the Absolute Friend who hides within each personal attachment.

Her guru relentlessly spurns her attachment to his own person by ignoring her and sending her back to England, where she has to rely upon her own experience exclusively. But only when his death removes him finally from the scene does she realize that his role was not to "give" her God, but to make her "pregnant" with God. Shaktipat brings about substantial changes, by-passes the ego, introduces her to erotic trance and meditative states. But in the end she has to realize that those changes belong naturally to her own body and consciousness. Shaktipat begins in dependency, like divyonmada, but ends only when a "self" has been created and she comes to realize that God dwells there naturally and not merely in the guru to whom she was attached. Shaktipat takes her through the rungs of longing, scandal, and the subtle body and succeeds when she realizes the primary fact that life is a love affair with a divinity who is not different from the cosmos—or, indeed, her own heart.

The theme of Tweedie's diary—that shaktipat is the ultimate secret in mystical ascent—parallels certain more ordinary interpersonal relations. For example, psychotherapy patients whose ego has proven inadequate to their daily lives often display the slowness of thought Tweedie had every time she entered her guru's vicinity. A powerful erotic bond establishes itself between analyst and analysand. Sometimes it enters consciousness disturbingly, but often it works silently below the surface of their exchanges. When this happens, the patient may find himself filled with a new power. It comes and goes. Perhaps he carries the analyst around with him through the week, discussing his life with that imaginal partner. His focus narrows while his horizons expand. He gets a clearer sense of what is real. One patient claimed she was successful in her daily activities only when my soul had entered her and she found that it did the work instead of she.

This describes the sort of shaktipat connection that Heinz Kohut (1977, 1984) calls a "self-object" relationship. The patient experiences the analyst functioning within her, taking the place of her missing "self," and supplying the coherence and resolution she is incapable of mustering on her own. A patient so strengthened by a "self" borrowed from the analyst may begin to master some of her daily tasks and family relationships. Her internal monologue begins to change, and she shows more self-confidence. But she has not finished her transformation until she can separate from the analyst—convinced that she, too, has a self. Such patients enter analysis in a far more "obstructed" state than Tweedie was when she met her guru. And they are not apt to visit the upper rungs of the diamond ladder. But they are elevated to a higher order of functioning, and the mechanism for this change is shaktipat conferred and overcome.

THE FEMININE PRINCIPLE

It has often been observed by historians of religion—and this is particularly true of the mystical traditions—that the preponderance of texts have been written by men and have a masculine bias giving our constructions of mystical ascent a regrettably patriarchal tone. Certainly Evola's dogmatic assertions of masculine superiority render aspects of his account of mysticism questionable. Eliade's emphasis on the "polluted" nature of the ideal female partner appears to contribute to this bias until we reflect that overturning the caste system of purity and pollution belongs to an essentially antinomian stance. The taken-for-granted dictates of the persona field must be overcome before we can explore the realities of the field of atman. Once we recall this context, we are not surprised to learn that most of the women mystics whose stories are told by Johnsen (1994) and Allione (1986) have taken consorts from a social stratum lower than their own, have left the husbands forced upon them by their families, or have transformed those husbands by initiating them.

Our overwhelming patriarchal bias is based in the historical fact that all of the major religious traditions in the world today arose during a long period of male dominance which includes the patriarchs and prophets of Judaism as well as the Aryan superimposition of male sky-gods over the prehistoric goddess religions of India. It seems that somewhere around 1500, B.C.E., a major shift occurred in the Middle East and in the Indian sphere of civilization. Thus, the rise of Tantra in the early centuries of the common era can be seen as a fortunate recovery. The predominance of the goddess suggests that the feminine principle has reappeared as a sort of "unconscious compensation" along the lines of Jung's thought.

Jung argues that because men have consciously identified with their masculinity and its logos-orientation (the predominance of *word* and logical connection), their unconscious psyche bears a feminine face, the "anima" which represents everything that is not conscious, including the man's unconscious femininity. The anima operates according to the feminine principle of eros where the issue of relationship and the realm of feeling-connection predominate. If Jung is right about this, it is not surprising that male mystics have emphasized and idealized the role of the goddess, for she would be the unknown, fascinating, and disturbing aspect of divinity which is missing from their masculine consciousness. The psychological compensation theory, however, would expect that a women's mystical path would be more logos-oriented—based on her need to come into contact with her unconscious "animus," which contains the masculine principle lacking to her conscious identity.[82] That women, too, are drawn to the goddess may well have to do with their need to revalue their own conscious selves within a patriarchal culture which gives all the power to men.

Such a perspective may well account for Yeshe Tsogyel's vision of a red, naked woman who presses her vagina against Yeshe's mouth and from which she drinks a copious flow of menstrual blood, filling her "entire being with health and well-being." Allione interprets this scene as making the statement that "primal lust binds the universe together" (Allione, 1986:

---

82 Jung's theory has won both praise and vituperation from feminists. The fact that it seems to be supported by the mystical traditions lends it weight, but one never forgets that Jung was born in 1875 in the most conservative country in Europe, where universal feminine suffrage can today be counted in years rather than decades. In Jung's writings, the anima is presented much more positively than the animus.

34). "Primal lust" would be the eros-principle experienced in its most passionate form, a reality that is also presented in the Tantric image of the goddess as naked and frenzied, with flying, unbound hair, and brandishing weapons and skulls. She is the enemy of the citadel self with all its isolating defenses, ordering the universe as an assemblage of "objects" linked by concepts and ultimately dead. Yeshe is nourished with the most "polluting" and feminine of substances, affirming the superiority of her woman's nature and giving her a thoroughly antinomian position *vis-a-vis* the exoteric patriarchal tradition. Eros binds and gives life. Logos separates and kills.

This makes a good deal of psychological sense—particularly for us Westerners, whose embarrassingly simplistic characterization of gender differences gives all the power and prestige to men. Shaw's summary of this Western attitude is surely not wrong: we understand men to be active agents and women passive victims; men are praised for their sexual prowess and exploitative power in business, while women are condemned for sexual promiscuity and seen to be powerless and easily exploited; men are taken to be intellectual and spiritual, while women are said to be unconscious, emotional, and biological (Shaw, 1994: 9).

The Tantric tradition, however, does not place the superiority of the feminine principle only in the transcendental realm of theology and divine iconography. Universally, it claims that women are by their very nature more apt for mysticism in all respects: physiologically, emotionally, and imaginally. What takes a male practitioner a year to accomplish, can be obtained by a woman in a single day (Silburn, 1988: 190). Wile's historical overview of the Chinese literature on sexuality and mysticism comes to the same conclusion, "Woman is superior to man in the same way that water is superior to fire" (Wile, 1992: 11). Wile notes that the Chinese texts agree that "the energetic essence pursued by men in their female partners" may be obtained by women in solo meditation. Women have the raw material of mystical transformation in abundance and by their very nature, whereas men require involvement with female partners in order to get it. D. G. White finds a very similar argument in the *Rasarnava*, "the greatest work of Tantric alchemy":

> The lineage nectar of the alchemical lineage (*sampradaya*) is, like that of other Tantric sects, transmitted through female sexual emissions. [The author of the *Rasarnava*] also prescribes sexual intercourse and erotico-mystical worship as means to alchemical transformation. . . . Elsewhere a female "laboratory assistant" (and, especially, her sexual and menstrual fluids) is crucial to the alchemist's practice (D. G. White, 1996: 172-3).

There is no way forward without the feminine principle—here understood very literally to reside in female sexual fluids. Women, like men, produce sexual fluids when aroused. The text seems to imply that the woman's fluids are essential, whereas those of the man are not.

For a woman's arousal is sufficient in itself, while a man's arousal must be joined with that of a woman to have mystical effect. This same perspective is implied in the depiction of kundalini as a goddess.

Irina Tweedie's guru also claims that the difference between men and woman resides in a "substance," but for him that substance is a metaphysical principle, *prakriti*, the feminine principle, sometimes translated as "nature" or "matter," and used to describe the phenomenal world.[83] In the philosophy of yoga (sankhya) the ultimate is realized when the ever-moving, ever-manifesting prakriti is joined with the stillness of the spiritual, male principle, purusha. Bhai Sahib says:

> Men have a substance in them and women have not. It makes men absorb the very essence of the Master. But men have to learn to control *prakriti* in themselves, and for this purpose practices are given to them. Women, because they are nearer to *prakriti*, are fertilized by the Divine Energy which they retain in their *Chakras* and because of this, very few practices are needed. Women are taken up through the path of love, for love is a feminine mystery. Woman is the cup waiting to be filled, offering herself up in her longing, which is her very being (Tweedie, 1986: 400).

No doubt this principle goes a long way to explaining why the vast majority of our texts have been written by men. Men are into words and concepts. These are the things that make up texts. Women are into eros. The eros that can be named is not eros. Eros is the secret that cannot be named. Sometimes men have named it shaktipat.

Two pages later, Bhai Sahib implicitly links this perspective with shaktipat—the erotic connection with the master which elevates the disciple by devotion and longing and then has to be overcome.

> For ladies, perseverance is difficult for them. It is difficult for men too; very few achieve it. Ladies have *Bhakti* (devotion) and if they get it, they get it in an instant. Otherwise it takes time. . . . In our System we make no difference—hearts are hearts. But in our System no lady was sufficiently interested to go on to the highest level. . . . One has to leave the love behind . . . nothing remains (Tweedie, 402-3).

---

83 In this regard it plays a role parallel to *hylé* ("nature," "physical matter") in neoplatonism and the various hermetic philosophies of the West, including alchemy. The central myth of alchemy is the engulfment of spirit in *hylé*, which corresponds to the Indian doctrine whereby *prakriti* plays the role of Maya and deludes us into thinking that what is physical is ultimate. The wise, in both Western alchemy and in India, are not deceived by appearances and see that spirit resides in matter and longs to be freed.

This passage makes the interesting argument that beginning and progressing on the path are easier for women because of their naturally erotic nature but that this same advantage becomes a disadvantage when the woman arrives at the final stage and has to relinquish love. Presumably Bhai Sahib means that the woman progresses easily through her attached love for the guru but can only reach the "highest level" when she has overcome this attachment in shaktipat and realizes that the guru will not "give" her God but—much more wonderfully—has already "impregnated" her with God. Tweedie made this last step on her mystical journey only after her guru was finally removed through death.

FEMALE GURUS

Because of their high aptitude for shaktipat and bhakti, women are essential to the Tantric tradition. Indeed, as Shaw points out, Tantra's insistence upon the feminine principle can be documented by the fact that there were no female Buddhas in the iconography of Buddhism before the arrival of Tantra (Shaw, 1994: 27). She tells the story of the female Buddha, Laksminkara, who became the Severed Head Vajrayogini. The legend is clearly modeled on that of the Buddha himself, Shakyamuni. Laksminkara ran away from the palace of her origins, naked, with unbound hair, her body smeared with ashes, and talking incoherently, pretending to be mad. Like Shakyamuni, she gave up her riches and social status so as to live (relatively) naked in the wilderness. But unlike her male counterpart, she had to feign madness in order to be left alone. More than this, however, every female Buddha, every Vajrayogini, has inspired a legendary life-story that has much in common with the wrathful-goddess myths of India. For example, the foremost Vajrayogini is depicted blood red, her black hair flowing and loose, and carrying a cup made from a human skull that brims with ambrosia. She is beautiful, passionate, and untamed (Shaw, 28).

Dzogchen, the school of "great perfection" that was brought to Tibet by Padmasambhava in the fourteenth century, teaches that we are all fundamentally enlightened but need to have our luminous vision reawakened through contact with an empowered teacher. On the subtle plane, however, all the teachings are held, protected, and transmitted by naked dakinis. The master is but the vehicle though which these sky-traversing female beings work. The founder of Dzogchen, Garab Dorje (first century, C.E.) predicted that the majority of those who reach the ultimate level of enlightenment would be women, for women have a natural affinity for working with energy and vision (Allione, 1986: 13-4).

Because this feminine superiority is everywhere asserted in Tantra, we can hardly be surprised that women are urged to accept and identify with the goddess within themselves—an immediate and one-step process—whereas men are advised to approach divinity slowly and to begin by worshipping the woman's goddesshood (Shaw, 1994: 42). This is also the reason why it is widely claimed that every master requires initiation through a woman. Lilian Silburn finds this tradition in Kashmiri Shaivism:

> Appeased in man, the *susumnanadi* [central channel of the subtle body] is full-blown in woman. A great master, therefore, is in possession of this function through an initiated woman. Shivanandanath, the founder of the Krama school, did not impart this doctrine to a disciple but to three *yogini* who, in their turn, initiated some men (Silburn, 1988: 190).

Miranda Shaw makes a very similar point regarding the Tantrism of Tibet, citing the *Cakrasamvara-tantra*:

> My female messengers are everywhere;
> They bestow all the spiritual attainments
> By gazing, touching, kissing and embracing.
> The most excellent place for the yogis is
> Wherever all the magical powers will be attained
> By all those blissful ones
> (Shaw, 1994: 38).

Edward Dimock's research in Vaishnavite Bengal reveals the same valuation of women. His texts reveal that the guru who gives the initiatory mantra is said to embody Krishna. But: "The guru who conducts the worshipper in his search for realization is Radha. All women participate in the qualities of Radha, therefore, all women are in some sense gurus" (Dimock, 1989: 101). David Kinsley was unable to find Hindu texts that describe Tantra from a female point of view (Kinsley, 1997: 150). Nevertheless, he did find three schools in which women function as gurus. One of them, the Pashcimamnaya, claims that Shiva revealed his teachings to yoginis who have passed them down from generation to generation (Kinsley, 149). Shaw says that the eighty-four mahasiddhas or "great adepts" described in the major sources are all male, "but if we examine the biographies and iconography, about *sixty* of them had female companions" (Shaw, 1994: 38). Furthermore, many legendary biographies, like that of Yeshe Tsogyel, show male disciples assigned to female gurus and female disciples to male gurus.

That the importance of women as initiators and gurus is not limited to India and Tibet, may be gathered from the life of Ibn al-ʿArabi. According to Wilson (1988: 175) Ibn al-ʿArabi was initiated into Sufism by a woman and called sexuality the perfect form of contemplation. Claude Addas identifies that woman as the ninety-year-old Nunah Fatimah bint Ibn al-Muthana, who was also "assiduously frequented by Ibn al-ʿArabi's mother" (Addas, 1993:

25). The Greatest Shaikh himself quotes this ancient Fatimah in language that suggests the sort of devotion that obtains between master and shaktipat-initiated disciple:

> . . . Ibn al-ʿArabi is a consolation to me, for he comes to me with all of himself. When he rises up it is with all of himself, and when he sits it is with his whole self, leaving nothing of himself elsewhere. That is how it should be on the Way (Ibn al-ʿArabi, 1971: 143).

Furthermore, Ibn al-ʿArabi names fifteen disciples whom he has initiated by investing them with the khirqa. Fourteen of them are women, including one of his wives, and eight of these shaktipat-transmissions took place in dreams (Addas, 1993: 146; Wilson, 1993: 145).

Dreams were extremely significant for Ibn al-ʿArabi. We have already seen the importance he placed on the dream image of his shaikh Abu Yaʿqub al-Kumi, with his breast "cleft asunder and a light like that of the sun [shining] out from it." Dreams give us direct information from the subtle plane and reveal realities unavailable to our sensory eyes. Ibn al-ʿArabi argues that the Sufi should be so lucid in his dreams that he can "interpret" them even while they are occurring. To interpret in this sense (ta'wil) means to discover their higher meaning. When seen with the eyes of ta'wil, every physical object reveals a reality belonging to soul; every soul reality (including dreams) reveals an angelic reality; and every angel reveals its "lord," which is one of the Names of Allah, who exists beyond all concept and image (Corbin, 1969: 239-44). Thus, for a transmission of the khirqa to have taken place in a dream means that it has been effected on the subtle plane and by-passed the ego even of the shaikh. In dreams Ibn al-ʿArabi's soul invests the soul of his disciple under the direction of their respective angels. A shaktipat transmission that occurs in a dream reveals the higher significance of the teaching and guidance the shaikh gives his disciple through words and gestures in the empirical world. Psychologically, it refers to the realm of the atman field, where all lasting and transcendental influence takes place.

The persona field of the West insists that the only indisputable realities are those empirical facts which can be demonstrated by laboratory experiments that quantify the results and prove mathematically that our eyes and intuition have not deceived us. From this highly patriarchal and logos-inspired perspective, eros (and its further explication as kundalini) is a highly dubious factor. Undoubtedly it expresses itself in physiological changes which *can* be quantified. But the emotions and images eros generates are seen as too idiosyncratic to merit attention. Truth for the West is above all a collection of statistical proofs from which the consciousness of the individual has been "factored out." Mysticism takes precisely the opposite route. Consciousness is the indisputable fact and not the object of which we are conscious. To get to the underlying reality of consciousness itself, mysticism attends exclusively to eros and attributes its physiological, emotional, and imaginal products to the higher reality of the subtle plane.

Sometimes mystics indulge in the conceptual structures of metaphysics to describe the reality of the subtle plane. But metaphysics is always secondary to erotic consciousness. Gnosis precedes description and explanation, and the roots of gnosis are sunk deep into eros.

Eros, despite its being the name of a male god in ancient Greece, is a mode of human knowing and functioning that expresses itself more naturally and abundantly in women than in men. Ultimately this is the reason Tantra places such strong emphasis on the feminine principle. On the subtle plane the divine reality—from dakinis to Kali-like goddesses all the way up to the cosmos as the light of chiti, like thread in the cloth and cloth in the threads—is predominantly feminine. On the empirical plane very much the same is true. Dependable advancement in mysticism depends upon shaktipat, and women have better access to this erotic potential for transformation. The great secrets that must remain unknown because they are fundamentally unspeakable have a feminine character. Although women are more familiar with these secrets, they are no better than men in articulating them. The diamond ladder—a masculine construction *par excellence*—makes some useful distinctions revealing why some erotic achievements are superior to others; but its rungs are shaped of eros. Its secrets are hidden in eros, and eros is a feminine mystery. This is why in Tantra Bhairavis play a more important role than Bhairavas, yoginis than yogins.

Nevertheless, the literature of Tantra remains primarily the work of men; and despite the importance of women, the texts generally assume male masters and male disciples. Allione regrets this emphasis in that guidance for women mystics has been neglected. She argues that to make the Tibetan Tantric path more available for women, there ought to be specific directions for women to follow—methods of practice and guidelines for finding and working with male consorts. She believes that a masculine "daka" principle ought to be as well developed as that of the dakini (Allione, 1986: 17). The fact that eros is more natural and well-developed in women is no excuse for neglecting the equally obvious fact that the erotic principle has to be awakened and integrated—even in women. If Tantra is the foremost tradition to have recognized and developed the universally human fact that mystical union occurs through the erotic interpenetration of male and female, it would seem that a woman's progress on the path would have some differences from a man's. These differences ought to be explored and made explicit. In the end a new picture of the diamond ladder might result—perhaps a pair of ladders with different numbers of rungs and specific cross-over points based in shaktipat.

7

SEXUAL WAYFARERS

The mythic autobiography of Yeshe Tsogyel presents a tricky, headstrong, and wanton woman who created "conflict and schism within the government" (Dowman, 1996: 267) and was not above "taking life while keeping her hands clean"—when on one occasion a group of Bönpo[84] leaders committed suicide at her behest (Dowman, 268). Living at a time when Tibet was predominantly a pre-Buddhist Bön society, Yeshe had to wander the roads and trails of a mountainous country that was hostile to Buddhists. Nuns were known to be pledged to celibacy but nevertheless had a notorious reputation, deriving perhaps from rumors of a sexual antinomianism that was not understood (Dowman, 263). She called herself an "unlovable spinster rejected by Tibetan men" as well as "wanton, uninhibited, passionate, and stubborn" (Dowman, 267). "She was the Emperor's priestess, the abbess of the principal monastic academies, and the Guru of many prominent figures in government" (Dowman 268). In short, her conquest of lust by finding the Yidam deity that lives within it made her powerful and suspect. The story of her conversion of the seven rapists, while certainly hagiographic, asserts a central claim of her Buddhist tradition: the lowest forms of sensory compulsion lie open to transformation through Tantric involution—reversing the natural flow of physiology and emotion that disperses our spiritual strength, forcing it to flow upward and back to its spiritual source.

Yeshe represents the "Old School" (Nyingmapa) established by Padmasambhava in the eighth century, a synthesis of Buddhism, Tantra, and shamanistic Bön practices. It "has been damned as a Hindu Saivite school, a Tantrist school, a path of immoralists and heretics, but without doubt it contains the most potent and efficacious *yogas*, precepts, and metaphysical formulations of the entire Buddhist *dharma*" (Dowman, 1996: 235). The story of Yeshe, its primary female representative, flirts with notoriety and raises suspicions of dissolute sensualism so as to expose the effectiveness of the "clear mind" that is central to her Nyingmapa

---

84 Bönpo: the priests of the Bön religion in Tibet, which is a collection of "various religious currents" that existed in Tibet before Padmasambhava introduced Buddhism in the eighth century. In the eleventh century it organized as an independent school, strongly influenced by Buddhism but continuing to preserve the continuity of the old Bön tradition (Fischer-Schreiber, 1989).

tradition. Clear mind sees the Yidam deity in the basest of human propensities and declares on the basis of its gnosis that everything is an opportunity for spiritual ascent.

Yeshe spent most of her life on the road, vulnerable in her female body and Buddhist trappings, often traveling hundreds of miles to find a particular consort revealed on the subtle plane, generally through the words of her guru. In this regard, she may be taken as the transcendent model for all the Buddhist women who live as hermits and wandering yoginis. They have tended to avoid the monasteries, where patriarchal bias predominates (Allione, 1986: 14-5) and have therefore been marginal characters—attempting to survive and flourish spiritually through their clear mind while held in suspicion or outright hostility by the established powers of government, religion, and popular opinion. However gullible the popular imagination may be deemed to have been and despite the magical legends that abound, such wandering female anchorites have lived in a world without physical or ideological security, "wanton, uninhibited, passionate, and obstinate" in their clear mind.

More than eighty years ago, when Mme. Alexandra David-Neel wandered over vast tracts of Tibet that had never before been seen by Westerners, she put together a very human picture of the lamaseries where, "[S]ubtle philosophy, commercialism, lofty spirituality, and eager pursuit of coarse enjoyment . . . are so closely interwoven that one endeavours in vain to completely disentangle them (David-Neel, 1971: 99). Men who begin their training as mere lads emerge from this incoherent environment in rather motley fashion: "a small élite of litterati, a number of idle, dull, sleepy fellows, wanton braggarts, and a few mystics who resort to lonely hermitages and life-long meditations" (David-Neel, 99). Furthermore, despite the several well-defined schools of mysticism and the chains of initiation running from disciple to master back through the centuries, David-Neel found little evidence of orthodoxy. "Humble or lofty, as may be, the goal of each monk remains his secret, and he may endeavor to reach it by any means he chooses. No devotional services in common, nor uniform religious practices are enjoined on the monks of the lamaseries" (David-Neel, 104). A lama "may even be an utter unbeliever; this concerns himself alone" (David-Neel, 105).

WANDERING ANCHORITES

If all this is true of the monasteries, we have to imagine that the wandering anchorites, both men and women, have been no less a collection of lazy dreamers, con-men, braggarts, sorry refugees on the lam from irate spouses and occasional victims, as well as a small core of sincere and gifted mystics, some practicing celibacy and others maithuna. The women among them, we have to assume, have had very little option other than to wander in small bands insofar as they have not often been welcome in the relative safety and order of the monasteries. For centuries they must have resembled the naked Sadhus of India, constantly wandering without any fixed dwelling place and never staying more than a few days in any one spot (Hartsuiker, 1993: 72). In a cultural and geographical environment like this, wandering itself becomes the symbol and primary practical exercise of following the mystic path. The world may be filled with orthodoxies aplenty, but the anchorite is determined to pursue the truth that reveals itself within her own soul, learning from everyone she meets, from the sanest of the orthodox to the craziest of idiosyncratic gurus, learning and teaching with those who accompany her for weeks or months of her journey, seeking out the most highly reputed among the hermits and lamas whose legends are eagerly exchanged by the sincere and the gullible of those encountered along the way.

David-Neel presents a vivid picture of a wanderer who travels *without discipline*, mental training, or coherent notion of what is sought:

> Such a man sees a lake in the east, and, being thirsty, hurries away to the water. When nearing the shore, he perceives the smell of smoke. This suggests the presence of a house or a camp. It would be pleasant, he thinks, to get hot tea instead of water, and a shelter for the night. So the man leaves the lake without having actually reached its shore and proceeds to the north, the smoke coming from that direction. On his way, before he has yet discovered any houses or tent, threatening phantoms spring up before him. Terrified the wanderer turns away from the fearful beings and runs for his life towards the south. When he deems that he has gone far enough to be safe, he stops to rest. Now, other wanderers pass who tell him of some blissful land of joy and plenty that they intend to reach. Full of enthusiasm, the vagrant joins the party and goes off to the west (David-Neel, 118).

Death will take such a wanderer on the road, and he will never have clarified the purpose of his life. He will resemble the vast majority of humans, homeless or wealthy, whose lives reek of dissipation, superficiality, and spiritual blindness. In contrast, "the enlightened one" is never distracted from the goal. Seeing through "the mirages and allurements of the roadside, this man controls the forces begotten by his concentration of mind and his bodily activity." If he dies on the way, his clarity of mind will not have been without attainment; and in his next incarnation, he will take up where he left off (David-Neel, 119).

We should not read David-Neel's emphasis on the goal too concretely, as though it were a specific geographical place that is sought. Rather the wayfaring of anchorites is guided by inner realities—intuitions, and convictions obtained on the subtle plane. We have to imagine that the spiritual wayfarer lays out few plans in advance. Perhaps no more than the notion that over the next few weeks I will travel in search of such-and-such a hermit whose teachings and way of life have been continually brought to my attention by the people I have met whose level-headed sincerity has convinced me, and the dreams that have visited me by night. "A pilgrimage distinguishes itself from an ordinary journey by the fact that it does not follow a laid-out plan . . . but relying on an inner urge which operates on two planes: on the physical plane as well as the spiritual plane (Govinda, 1988: xvii).

Sometimes, we should imagine, sexual wayfarers following the example of Yeshe Tsogyel travel with companions of equally spiritual intent as well as with occasional disciples and perhaps a rag-tag band of lost souls, all living from the shaktipat effect of an enlightened being whose inner resolution and spiritual accomplishment provides a halo of security and sense of purpose—a borrowed "self-object" in an uncertain and confusing world. We can imagine them stopping from time to time to give themselves over to meditation, where again the elevating influence of those who are well-grounded in the spiritual life has a powerful effect upon the whole group—not unlike the people who visited the meditation room of Muktananda's airline officer. Perhaps maithuna would occasionally be practiced on the road, with a disciple who is ripe for the most powerful form of shaktipat or with a spiritual peer who has a unique capacity for mixing Spontaneous Great Bliss with emptiness.

In the short term a group like this, picking up and dropping off followers as it goes, will be guided by the intentions of its central figure. If she has been directed to a specific hermit some weeks down the road, she moves resolutely but without haste, knowing that the events that occur along the way are as important as any destination. Such happenings may in fact provide precisely the lessons that will prepare her for meeting that hermit. She expects no secrets will be revealed in words. She has no specific expectations for what will happen when she arrives. Perhaps he will tell her that he has nothing to teach. Perhaps he will want her to teach him. Perhaps they will simply sit in silence before one another for a few days until she moves on. Perhaps they will practice maithuna. Nothing is determined in advance. She knows only one thing. Each enlightened being is a unique embodiment of wisdom.

Just as each human being on earth makes love the same as and yet wholly different from every other, and therefore every sexual partner presents a unique opportunity to learn about love; so every spiritual master teaches and touches in a different but identical manner as every other. Each master presents us with a unique opportunity to appropriate wisdom and shaktipat. Each provides a new perspective on openness, spontaneity, and bliss. Each meeting between enlightened beings is a unique instance of spiritual union, a new and irreplaceable encounter with the pulsating light of consciousness. If each act of union recapitulates the love-play of Shiva and Shakti or the Buddha and the Vajrayogini, each is also a unique primary fact. Each time is the first and the last, each encounter completely the same and wholly different.

Anchorites are those who move between orthodoxies, nourishing themselves with one true doctrine after another, as they pass from monastery to monastery, hermit to hermit. Gathering the pollen of wisdom like bees, they cross-fertilize the mystical blooms they encounter. The wandering of sexual wayfarers continually asks the central Tantric question: What are you learning from your relationship? Those who are preoccupied with the horizontal questions of material and social security wonder whether the future holds the happily-ever-after compatibility of a monogamous marriage. They avoid the present moment in their hopes of putting a lonely past behind them and embracing a smooth and mutually supportive future. Those who are on the road, however, endeavor to cling to no past and no future. They seek to abide in a "now" with negligible horizontality but open to a boundless verticality. They may well be tried and rejected by the hermit they have expended weeks in finding. But they are not set back. What am I learning from my rejection—is just as important as—What am I learning from the cross-pollinating bliss I share with Hermit X?

MOVING ON AND STAYING PUT

Wandering like this with fierce purpose but without goal, there is also no reason to avoid monogamy if an opportunity should appear that offers just the learning I have been seeking without knowing it. In his discussion of the wandering dervishes called Qalandars, Peter Lamborn Wilson describes just such an instance of permanency in the most changeable of all rag-tag bands: "Nur Ali married a beautiful girl, Bibi Hayati, who became a dervish and wandered with him; this unusual woman also composed a divan of charming erotic/mystic poems in which her husband becomes the 'divine beloved'" (Wilson, 1993: 151). The divine beloved is always One and encountered anew in each lama and each hermit the anchorite encounters along her wayfaring path. Sometimes, however, the seeker encounters a partner through whom access to the One is inexhaustible, always spontaneous, and redolent of wisdom to be learned. Nur Ali and Bibi Hayati played this role for one another. Irina Tweedie and Robert Svoboda each settled down with a single guru whose wisdom was seen to be inexhaustible, and remained with that guru until his death. Only then did they begin their wandering.

In fourteenth century Kashmir, a female anchorite wandered naked like a Sadhu singing of her love for God. Some 200 of her songs have been written down and are popularly revered today in her homeland. Known as Lalla[85] ("Darling"), she left her marriage at twenty-four and studied with at least three male masters, distinguishing herself by her nakedness and ecstatic clarity. Without shame and without the cover of madness, she simply sang the lesson she con-

---

85 "She is also known as Lal Ded, Lal Didi, and Mai Lal Diddi, all of which mean Granny Lal, Grandmother Lalla. And in Sanskrit she is called Lalleswari, Lalla the great yogini, prophetess and practitioner of yoga" (Coleman Barks, in his "Introduction" to Lalla, 1992).

stantly learned on the path—all is One. The One is to be met in everyone and anyone. What is essential is the consciousness which both is and knows the One.

> Don't talk of different religions.
> The one reality is everywhere,
> not just in a Hindu, or a Muslim,
> or anywhere else! Realize:
> your awareness is
> the truth about God
>   (Lalla, 1992).

In the last analysis, what I am learning from my relationship determines whether I move on or stay put. Every mountain, every tree, every river reveals the One on the field of emptiness. For some, like Lalla, this realization ordains a life of wayfaring. Others like Saraha, one of the founding fathers of Tantric Buddhism in the eighth century, wandered until the moment the path led only upward. Saraha's legendary life neatly summarizes most of the themes of this book. He began his religious journey with a long course of study at Nalanda University. Thus he began like Caitanya, the Bengali ecstatic who was said to be both Krishna and Radha. He had memorized the Vedas and important scriptures of Hinduism and was committed to the rules of purity proper to his Brahmin caste. His son, Shavaripa, became a hunter and practiced the Yoga of Spontaneity (*Sahaja*), just as did the followers of Caitanya. Father and son wrote songs (*caryapada*) that distain ritual worship and academic scholarship. They exalt in an uninhibited antinomian spirit, spontaneously erupting in divine effusions. Eight centuries later Saraha was reincarnated as Drukpa Kunley (Dowman, 1988: 149, *n*. 1).

Saraha's life was changed the day he allowed "some girls"—faint shades of Bhairavis, no doubt—to convince him to drink beer in violation of his monastic vows.[86] In his drunken euphoria, a bodhisattva appeared to him and told him to seek out a mystically talented arrow-making woman whom he would find in the city. Following orders, he went to the marketplace where, among the arrow-makers, one woman was at work with such spontaneous and exacting deftness that he recognized deep meditative concentration.

> Wholly focused on her task, she never looked up or became distracted as she cut the arrow-shaft, inserted the arrowhead, affixed the feathers, and checked the arrow for straightness. Sar-

---

86 Possibly this life-changing enounter with beer suggests a karmic connection with Drukpa Kunley's love of chung.

aha tried to break the ice with a trivial question but, not one for trivialities, her first words to him were, "The Buddha's meaning can be known through symbols and actions, not through words and books." Instantly realizing that he had found a worthy teacher, Saraha put off the monastic robes and devoted himself to his yogini guru. The arrow-maker accepted Saraha as her disciple and Tantric companion. According to Taranatha, she taught him the meaning of things as they are and enabled him to see reality as it is (Shaw, 1994: 132).

The arrow-making yogini taught him "a mode of companionship that is beyond attachment." His wandering was over. He lived the rest of his life in a mountain retreat with his guru and partner, earning his living by making arrows (Shaw, 131-3). For he said, "Only now am I a truly pure Bhiksu (Buddhist monk)" (Dowman, 1988: xxvi). This story makes the essential point—that neither wandering nor settling has any value in itself. The crucial question is whether my encounters are teaching me anything. There may be an endless series of encounters between mystics on the path. Or a single meeting may suffice for a lifetime. What is essential is to learn, like Saraha, to give up our dependency on words, rules, and concepts. Leave the citadel self behind—even a theologically sophisticated citadel self like Saraha's. What is indispensable is that opening the arrow-making yogini provided. Saraha knew immediately he had no need of his robe or the orthodoxy for which it stood. The path lies outside of all established form. In her nakedness, Lalla had it right. We can only imagine the extensive wayfaring those two arrow-makers accomplished—though they never left their hermitage.

THE RETURN

In our preliminary sketch of wayfaring anchorites, we have imagined how their mystical intent never slackens. Although they wander without setting any goal—apart from temporary notions of seeking out some storied adept who resides perhaps only a few weeks' journey from where they are—their wandering itself amounts to a mystical practice. We have been concerned with the enlightened ones, those who know the experience of mixing Spontaneous Great Bliss with emptiness, and we imagine that they never exhaust the value of that bodily and psychic experience. We suppose that as teachers in their own right they continue to initiate disciples through word, through shaktipat, and above all through being the centered individuals they have become. They bring peace, conviction, and the hope of ultimate attainment to the most serious-minded of their disciples; and they continue to seek out others who have reached pinnacles of mystical attainment—cross-pollinating, enriching, and more firmly establishing their own attainment.

The unexpressed theme in this account is what happens *after* one has ascended to the top rung of the diamond ladder, mixed Spontaneous Great Bliss with emptiness, and in the process demolished the ladder itself. Although we may often think that mysticism is a never-ending climb to higher and higher realization, in fact another question lurks unasked in the background. How does life go on for the mystic who has reached the summit? Is it possible to stay there on the ultimate plane of emptiness, standing on the top rung of the ladder like Simon Stylites on his desert pillar? Does one return to the everyday world of eating, sleeping, shivering in the cold, and baking in the heat? Is mysticism about the upward journey exclusively or is there some possibility—even necessity—of returning? And what is it like to return to the empirical world, once one has seen the threads of light in its cloth? Do the threads remain a part of one's everyday perceptions; do they come and go; or is that vision a fleeting glimpse that the mystic seeks again and again to regain, with greater or lesser success?

In his retreat manual, *Journey to the Lord of Power*, Ibn al-'Arabi makes it clear that in his experience being "absorbed in God," which occurs at the summit of the ladder, is only the penultimate stage of mystical attainment. It is a greater accomplishment to return. Further-more, among those who return are two types: the mystic ('*arif*) who has learned something for himself alone and the one who is sent back as a knower ('*alim*) to guide others:

> I shall first describe (may Allah grant you success) the nature of the journey to Him, then the procedure of arriving and standing before Him, and what He says to you as you sit on the carpet of His vision. Then the nature of the return from Him to the presence (*hadra*) of His actions: with Him and to Him. And I shall describe absorption in Him, which is a station less than the station of return (Ibn al-'Arabi, 1989: 26)

> As for the returned ones, there are two types of men among them. There is one who returns to himself alone; he is the descender whom we have mentioned. This sort of man is the gnostic, '*arif*, among us. He returns to perfecting himself from other than the road which he traveled. Also among them is the one who is sent back to Creation with the language of direction and guidance. He is the inheriting knower, '*alim* (Ibn al-'Arabi, 51-2).

Ibn al-'Arabi lets us know not only that the return from mystical absorption is a very high level of achievement but also that mystical absorption by itself is not sufficient for "perfec-tion." Gnosis is a wonderful thing and well worth a lifetime of struggle, but gnosis leaves a new task before the gnostic: "perfecting himself from other than the road which he traveled." A great deal of "perfection" is required to ascend the diamond ladder to its summit. But there are other dimensions to our life; and after we have ascended and had the gnostic vision, our "imperfections" remain in the spheres we have neglected. Perhaps they manifest in our bound-less impatience when accidents or interruptions frustrate us. Perhaps we are remote from our spouse, tyrants with our children, cowards before our boss. These problems remain, though it is to be hoped the work we undertook on our journey up the ladder has done some good. The struggle with good and evil and the inversion of attention whereby we learn to see what the disturbance is doing to *us* rather than fixate on the disturbance itself: these lessons apply everywhere in life. Ultimately, this is the reason Tantra never tires of repeating the maxim that *everything* can be an opportunity for enlightenment. Tantra, in fact, *seeks out* disturbing experiences; for each harbors one's Yidam deity. The divinity who corresponds to the make-up of our personal being dwells not only in lust but in anger, terror, and every one of the frustrations and peeves that afflict every day of our lives. Every occasion for an unprintable expletive conceals the Yidam deity of our being. Until we can elevate each of them effortlessly, we remain trapped in the profane world as surely as any tethered pashu.[87]

The Persian mystical poet, Farid ad-Din 'Attar (d. ca. 1229), said that those who do not return from Annihilation in the Essence "bring back no news" (Wilson, 1988: 70). They have something to teach us, but only if they come back changed. Life ought to be different after they return. 'Attar might have said, If they come back unchanged, they bring back no news. For it is in the transformation of their being that we recognize their achievement. We would wonder about a petty, supercilious, or dishonest mystic, regardless of what she claims to have seen.

Al-Hallaj, one of the most revered early Sufi spokesmen, was famously crucified for blasphemy in the early tenth century. His crime was to claim, "I am the Truth," in a theological context where Truth is one of the Names of God. He claimed he was God—that this was the nature of his mystical absorption. He brought back news that was too threatening to hear—although his crucifixion probably did more to further the cause of his mystical claims than decades of quiet living and teaching might have accomplished. Some two and a half centuries later, Ibn al-'Arabi seems to agree about the nature of absorption in God. But he says not, "I am God," but, "God is me"—in the sense of the Yidam deity.[88] Ibn al-'Arabi performed a great service in collecting the oral traditions descended from the Sufism that went before him and systematizing them. In doing so, he was very conscious of slipping his views past the censors.[89] Very likely he handled his everyday life after absorption more effectively than the brash Al-Hallaj. But even Al-Hallaj preached the importance of the return. After the "effort" (*mujahada*) of climbing a ladder of spiritual exercises and after the "constraint' (*idtirar*) whereby effort has

---

87 *Pashu*: (Sanskrit) literally an "animal"; a human being who is as unfree and "tethered" as an animal.

88 "Whoever imagines that he sees the Reality Himself has no gnosis; he has gnosis who knows that it is his own essential self that he sees" (Ibn al-'Arabi, 1980: 77).

89 "Yet Ibn 'Arabi's words and his works created such a violent reaction in his time that the people destroyed his tomb after his death without leaving any trace of it" (Sheikh Muzaffer Ozak al-Jerrahi, "Introduction," in Ibn al-'Arabi, 1989: 10).

to be relinquished so that divine grace can take over and move us into union, the successful mystic "goes back to life and lives an ordinary life in an extraordinary way" (Sviri, 1997: 42).

The Hindu and Buddhist schools of mysticism agree with Islam on the importance of the return. Vimalananda asks: "What is the use of these spurting samadhis anyway? . . . I think it is much better to remain conscious on this plane even while you shift your main focus to other realities" (Svoboda, 1997: 157). Silburn's work with the Tantric texts of Kashmir comes to the same conclusion, "In Tantrism, indeed, unification must be achieved in the course of ordinary life experiences, whatever they may be" (Silburn, 1988: 138). Shaw outlines the work of Tibetan Buddhism in four traditional stages: the *outer*, when one pictures the deity in vivid detail; the *inner*, when one envisions one's own body as a mandala with the deities at different points; the *secret*, when one attains bliss through yogic meditation on the subtle body; and the *final* stage, when one recovers the natural state of mind, now "purified of delusion" (Shaw, 1994: 121). Even more explicitly she says, "The ultimate achievement, after all the complex visualizations, is a divine simplicity, an ability to be spontaneously and fully present to each moment of awareness in a state of pristine clarity" (Shaw, 87).

The sublime clarity of mind that describes a successful return from mystical absorption is called the "fourth state" (*turiya*, in Sanskrit). It transcends the three states of waking, dreaming, and dreamless sleep in a way of life which constantly realizes the nature of the atman as "pure, unified consciousness, unspeakable peace" (Fischer-Schreiber, *et. al.*, 1989). It is an enduring state of clear-mindedness that is not dimmed by the necessity of living in the everyday world. Whether asleep, driving on the interstate, or "processing" words, I have an abiding sense that it is not I who lives but atman lives within me. Atman (or "no-self") pulsates in the threads. The pulsating vision may be unavailable to my conscious mind, but atman lives in that world, whether "I" see it or not. Turiya is that state of mind where I know with utter and constant conviction that my ego's reality is but an epiphenomenon of atman's life.

In his synthesis of the Kashmiri doctrine of vibration (spanda), Dcyzkowski describes the return as an "abiding awareness of Turiya":

> The yogi is fully absorbed in this state of consciousness and takes possession of its power when he is able to rise from contemplation (*samadhi*) carrying with him the abiding awareness of Turiya throughout his waking, dreaming and deep sleep. When he achieves this constantly, he continues to experience those states individually, but they no longer obscure the insight (*pratibha*) he has acquired because he realizes that they are all aspects of the bliss of Turiya. . . . The yogi who manages to maintain *Turiya*-consciousness comes to experience the three states of waking, dreaming and deep sleep as the constant flow of the bliss of consciousness

in which all traces of the relative distinction between these states and their contents is eradi-cated[90] (Dcyzkowski, 1987: 214-5).

Quoting the *Digha-nikaya*, Eliade describes the aim of lucidity in Buddhism in very simi-lar terms: "Whether he is eating, drinking, chewing, reposing, or whether he is obeying the calls of nature . . . in going, standing, sitting, sleeping, watching, talking, or keeping silence, he knows what he is doing" (Eliade, 1969: 168).

Dowman's account of the return according to the Tibetan tradition that shapes Yeshe Tsogyel's autobiography can be summarized in a short phrase, "The starting point is the goal," meaning that "[E]very human experience whatsoever is cognized as primal purity":

> The good and the bad, pleasure and pain, all emotion and passion is the path itself. The greater the intensity of pain or passion the greater the potential of creative expression (*rtsal*) and pure pleasure (*bde-chen*); but although pain and passion are not to be rejected, neither are they to be cultivated. If excess is an individual's karmic destiny then the path of excess will surely lead to wisdom, not through an eventual understanding of passion's futility, or the hedonistic pleasure of indulgence, or the hiatus of exhaustion and childlike ingenuousness, or a reactive swing to puritanical expression, but through immediate, spontaneous Aware-ness. The traditional metaphor for this Awareness is a lotus redolent of compassion growing uncontaminated in a putrid swamp (Dowman, 1984: 236).

In other words, when we return we simply take what life presents. The "putrid swamp" of the empirical world is part of that givenness, but so is our own nature, or "karmic destiny." These two factors, the objective world and our subjective karma, unite in the single phenom-enon of everyday life after the return from mystical absorption. This unified world—which is neither object nor subject but their unification—describes life, day-in and day-out, on the field of emptiness: "To transit endlessly through time in search of the home-ground of the self is the true form of our karma, that is, of our being in time, our life" (Nishitani, 1982: 248).

The various biographies of Ramakrishna provide powerful hints as to how the vision of divine absorption where "everything is made of consciousness" and therefore constitutes the world as a "mansion of fun" becomes gradually known during the return. Ramakrishna's vision of "the ocean of consciousness" seems somewhat less integrated than Muktananda's "threads in the cloth and cloth in the threads," though this may be more a matter of verbal expression than a noteworthy difference in the experience itself:

> Suddenly, without warning, there is light. In such a flaming state, human beings appear as pillows bobbing up and down on the ocean of consciousness. . . . Souls are like countless

90 Citing the *Sivasutravimarsini*, p. 12.

bubbles in the water. . . . Trees appear as cosmic bouquets, perched on the head of the cosmic man (Kripal, 1995: 184).

Later we learn that this vision occurred when he meditated with his eyes closed and that when he opened them he saw that the vision of light became indistinguishable from the world itself, shot through with God: "I used to meditate with my eyes shut, but is the Lord not there when I open my eyes? When I open my eyes, I see that the Lord dwells in all creatures, in man, animals, trees, the sun and the moon, the water and the ground" (Kripal, 185). Later still, he reports a further refinement: "Long ago *Vaishnavacharan* said that when one has the vision of God in a human form one's knowledge is complete. Now I am seeing that he wanders about in each [human] form" (Kripal, 229; Kripal's brackets).

This series of developments in Ramakrishna's maturity as a mystic reveals the gradual integration of the vision of absorption with everyday life. It describes one man's successful return. His countryman, the poet Ramprasad, has come to the same conclusion. He has a visionary encounter with Yama, the Lord of Death, and realizes that death is but "the destructive nature of the world, represented by the Goddess." Here he "first confronts the fact that there is really no Goddess as a mother goddess to be seen, she is only that world with which he will finally be united at his own death. . . . [There is] no crossing to the other side" (McLean, 1998: 112-3).

> Stay on that raft floating on the world ocean,
> Float up with the flood tide and down with the ebb
> (McLean, 115).

SPONTANEITY

Spontaneity is not a quality we would associate with antinomian heroes. There is something too determined and aggressive about the adepts of the rung of scandal. Although they have broken the "leash" of the persona field's ethical maxims and gone beyond good and evil, their achievement is too single-minded, even coarse. They overcome their obstacles with the brute force of a kundalini who courses through their being like lightning bolts—dazzling the heroes, too, as she vanquishes the dragons of their appetites. Heroes like Trighantika never distill kundalini into her components, never slow her down and make her acquaintance. Indeed, *spontaneity* only entered our mystical vocabulary when we reached the rung of Spontaneous Great Bliss. Since then we have mentioned spontaneous conduct with some frequency but never paused to examine it.

As a preliminary approach to the nature of spontaneity, we might consider the accomplishment of Yeshe Tsogyel with the seven bandits. Those brutal men certainly posed a violent challenge and may have elicited a more heroic response from someone less subtle than Yeshe. She did not obliterate anyone and she stood no one down. Her response was spontaneous rather than heroic. By the time the bandits had wrestled her to the ground, she had already converted a violating confrontation into a cooperating opportunity. She greeted the rapists' lust with her own and revealed its Yidam deity. When confronted with an immanent rape, few can go beyond the perpetrator/victim dichotomy of the persona field. It is deeply ingrained in the way we collectively construe our environment. We see it played out in the survival-of-the-fittest game that describes our scientific understanding of nature; it characterizes our business deals, political positions, and our negotiation of automobile traffic in terms of win-or-lose. There may be some situations where our internal monologue insists that we win and others when the victimhood of losing seems foreordained by our fate.

Confronted with an immanent rape at the hands of seven violent men, our very life would be at stake, and the obvious fact of our coming defeat and violation would be inevitable in the win-or-lose dictum of life as "everyone" knows it. This is why the stupendous feat Yeshe performed was not the shaktipat conversion of the robbers but her ability to move freely, untethered by conventional notions, even in the face of defeat, violation, possibly death. She never "fell victim." Her spontaneity manifested in her ability to see the most disturbing of challenges in a new and original light, and to do so with such utter conviction that she did not falter. The conventional view of things appears never to have disturbed her concentration. Her attention never fixated on the disturbing threat but moved inward to the emotional reality of her consciousness where she was able to find her own lust and its Yidam deity. Her familiarity with kundalini and its origin in her own lust gained on the rung of Spontaneous Great Bliss found immediate and spontaneous opportunity in the dog-eat-dog quotidian world. She had practiced for an opportunity like this. Having found the Yidam deity of her lust through her interactions with Padmasambhava and other dharma consorts to whom he sent her, she was ready for the disturbing and unexpected irruption of lust and brute violence that was sure to occur repeatedly in the course of her wayfaring.

In this sense every disturbance we meet in the course of our life—whether on the road or at home in our kitchen—manifests itself as a vajroli contest. Every incident with a strong-minded opponent or an inanimate but uncompliant object—like a toaster that insists on burning our breakfast—is striving to raise our ire, lust, or fear to the breaking point where we will succumb in an outburst of dissipating energy. Whether we tower in rage, cower in fear, or dissolve in the ecstasy of an external orgasm, we have failed to hold the tension in a contest where both parties are striving to stir an emotional and physiological disturbance that will take the other over the top; and each is equally determined not to yield. Yeshe's conduct with the rapists was spontaneous in that it recognized the opportunity for a vajroli contest in a situation where nearly everyone else would dissolve in rage, impotence, and violation. She was as tough as a wrathful dakini. And like every dakini, she was naked of all convention, flying in the open spontaneous sky of fluid flexibility, where anything can be converted into anything else, where arousal of every sort reveals a Yidam deity.

To place all this in the fundamentally Buddhist context that Padmasambhava brought to Tibet, we might consider the Buddhist "bottom line," the Four Noble Truths which tradition ascribes to the Buddha Shakyamuni's earliest formulation of his gnosis. First, all of life is characterized by suffering—even moments of pleasure and happiness are contaminated with the painful knowledge that they will come to an end. Second, the root of suffering is desire; it is only because we crave what we think will bring us happiness and cannot relinquish this desire that we are trapped in a world of suffering. Third, to root out desire is to bring an end to suffering. Fourth, desire is to be rooted out through the eight-fold path of right views, right intentions, right speech, right conduct, right livelihood, right effort, right mindfulness, and right concentration (Conze, 1959: 43).

All the practices we have considered in ascending the diamond ladder amount to fostering the elements of the eight-fold path. In her spontaneity, Yeshe demonstrated all eight of them; and as a Tantrika she took a distinctive approach to the Third Noble Truth. For her and all of Tantra, desire is not to be rooted out by suppression, numbing, or denial, but by entering wholly into it with "right views, right intentions," and all the rest. Tantra roots out desire's attachments through a grand reversal that discovers the divine possibility lurking within it. In this sense, spontaneity means slipping the bonds that our internal monologues are constantly setting for us so as to find a flexibility that is as open and boundless as the sky.

Peter Hershock's original interpretation of Ch'an Buddhism ("Chinese Zen"), *Liberating Intimacy* (1996), interprets suffering as an "interruption of our personal narrative." This comes very close to what we have been calling any disturbance that arouses an emotional reaction in us. According to Hershock's construction, it is the personal narrative of our selectively remembered past flowing into a future whose lineaments are set by our "projections of attachment and aversion" that constitutes our ego or citadel self. The main difference between his formulation and ours is that we have not taken that life-narrative to be a single thing. Rather we operate with a number of fragmentary and partially conflicting narratives maintained by our internal monologues, among which we alternate unreflectively. One fragmentary worldview after another autonomously emerges in unconscious response to the situation confronting us in the moment, and we respond in stereotyped ways. "The only way to bring suffering—a personal narrative—to an end without making some karma which will return to the same configuration is to dissolve the source of the suffering, the 'I' who views the world through the projections of attachment and aversion" (Hershock, 1996: 98). He argues that the disturbing interruption must be spontaneously taken up as the first gesture of an improvisation which will creatively transform the incident.

> [T]he end of suffering is best construed neither as an escape nor as an attainment of unbreached control, but as the creative incorporation of what originally arises in our experience as a disruption of the order or timing of our life-narrative. A talented jazz musician will take an accidental or mistaken chord or note and improvise with and around it, creating in the process an entirely novel passage within the context of a perhaps quite familiarly ordered piece of music. And, in much the same way, the interruptions of suffering afford us the opportunity of conducting ourselves in an unprecedented and manifestly liberating fashion (Hershock, 20).

In profane consciousness, we think that our suffering is a matter of unfortunate incidents that happen to us and to which we react. We think we establish our (citadel) self in the privacy of our pure and uncontaminated subjectivity into which those painful events "intrude." We have seen how the Buddhist doctrine of emptiness turns this perspective inside out, saying that both objectivity and subjectivity are illusory. In the world of primary fact, everything centers a world; everything gathers everything else into a whole from which we are not separate. We are Being-in-the-world. The world and ourselves are not separate. Hershock takes these facts and renders them dynamic. According to him, the Buddhist lives in a world that "is irreducibly *dramatic*." This dramatic world is the stage on which we perform; and every move in the performance that is our life story displays how "our choices determine the meaning of our jointly articulating lives" (Hershock, 47). "It is our situation itself that directs us" (Hershock, 189). Because everything is a center without a circumference and nothing can be privileged as the basis of reality, "[W]hat matters is simply the manner in which things come together, their quality of interdependence" (Hershock, 132).

Enlightenment, therefore, is not something we realize privately through climbing the diamond ladder and challenging ourselves in isolation. Rather it is "a unique way of *conducting ourselves* in the narrative space of interpersonality" (Hershock, 63). Hershock means that enlightenment is never a matter of some private vision but rather is expressed only "on the way," while sojourning through the ordinary world in an extraordinary manner, that is by greeting each incident as an opportunity for improvisation. Improvisation is the spontaneous creativity that occurs only between one person and another or between people and events. There is always an established melody within which a particular note or chord surprises us. It can cause us suffering when we dwell on its departure from the rhythm or tonality of the established song. Or it can be taken as inspiration for an improvisatory riff. Enlightened beings are masters of spontaneity and improvisation. They have rooted out suffering by freeing themselves from the internal monologues whose ceaseless rigidity reacts to interruption and discord with pain. Instead, they wander through the world without goals and find opportunity for creative spontaneity everywhere.

In the improvisatory and spontaneous encounter by which enlightenment is realized, there are no pre-determined goals and the meaning results from how two individuals meet. They respond to one another like jazz players who improvise on the melody and rhythm to redeem and transform discord, finding "in it a sign of continued vitality" (Hershock, 79). "Ch'an orients us to . . . a choreo-poetic pedagogy of joint improvisation" (Hershock, 65). In this process, we relinquish our citadel selves "indirectly" through a partner "with whom we can enter into lively and mutually 'self'-effacing concourse" (Hershock, 148). Indeed, this "partner" need not be human, as we can see from Ch'an stories in which "a stone striking a stick of bamboo, the honking of a flock of geese, or the moonlight shining through a tracery of autumn branches" occasions the dropping of body-and-mind (Hershock, 222).

DHARMA COMBAT

Nevertheless, the primary teaching device in Ch'an, as in Zen, is the encounter between master and disciple in which the latter is "in a very literal sense . . . tricked into enlightenment" (Hershock, 148). This sort of training encounter is called *fa ch'an*, which Hershock translates as "dharma combat" (Hershock, 80), whereby he reveals its resemblance to Vimalananda's vajroli contest. Dharma combat seeks to undermine "everything familiar and comfortingly secure," to deliberately introduce "suffering" in the sense of a disruption of the disciple's personal narrative. But the master is as much at risk as the student; for the master, too, must "drop every pretense, every hope of security in order to awaken" (Hershock, 81). Enlightenment, clearly, is not accomplished once and for all, but only appears "in-between" individuals at ever renewed moments when suffering has been evoked as an opportunity for a crisis-resolving improvisation (Hershock, 63). That this is the paradigmatic structure of Ch'an is shown in the reverence afforded to the outrageousness of its best loved masters:

> The most loved masters of Ch'an . . . are those who display the wildest personas, whose teaching is the most iconoclastic. . . . [E]ach one of them is what we might call a "real character," a kind of spiritual maverick. Some are outright rascals, . . . ready to sprout angelic wings, ... [or] as earthy and carefree as the village idiot. . . . In Ch'an, not only are idiosyncrasy and uniqueness not leveled down with the realization of enlightenment, they seem if anything to be accentuated (Hershock, 191).

Finally, the training of a disciple is designed to force the student into one communicative crisis after another. When the disciple has exhausted one master's capacity for original and spontaneous disruptions, she is urged to travel to another who is sure to produce crises of a new sort (Hershock, 114). She becomes a wayfaring anchorite like Yeshe Tsogyel, where the events that occur along the path of the journey are no less important than the dharma combats designed by the masters holding forth at every waystation.

A story is told about the ninth century master, Lin-chi,[91] who was instructing his disciples on one of his favorite themes: "[T]he true person of no rank (*wu-wei-chen-jen*)—a person who has no fixed place from which s/he acts, no set patterns of behavior or unchanging tasks and goals." A monk in the audience interrupted, demanding to know who exactly this person of no rank is. Lin-chi leapt off the dais, "began throttling the monk and demanded that he 'Speak! Speak!' When the monk failed to respond immediately, Lin-chi thrust him away, exclaiming, 'What kind of dry shit stick is this "true person of no rank"!'" (Hershock, 193).

This dharma combat is begun by the obstreperous monk who interrupts Lin-chi's lecture. In doing so he calls into crisis Lin-chi's favorite thesis, in that the interruption comes from the "floor," from a man of lesser "rank" than Lin-chi and exposes Lin-chi's position on the dais as a potential contradiction: "Here is a man with the highest imaginable rank lecturing us on having 'no rank.'" It would be a painful moment for the average teacher, but for Lin-chi this is an opportunity. Immediately he leaps down from the dais, his place of rank, and conducts himself as a highway robber, a man of "no rank." Because he hesitates not an instant, he shows by his conduct that rank means nothing to him. He reacts with a spontaneous improvisation—completely unexpected and wholly out of character for a man of rank. In this manner he redeems the interruption and turns it into an opportunity to *enact* the thesis he has been expounding. In throttling the obstreperous monk while shouting, "Speak! Speak!" he announces that his second move in the dharma combat requires a third—as though to say, "If you're going to challenge me to dharma combat, you had better be ready to reply." He disrupts the saucy personal narrative of the irreverent monk with a humiliating crisis. Furthermore by throttling him while demanding he speak, Lin-chi assumes the shape of the dragon that is the poor fool's pride. Being in the grip of his own internal dragon, he would be speechless even without fingers tightening on his throat. He "falls victim." He has found no Yidam deity lurking in Lin-chi's violation of his dignity.

The Yidam deity the obstreperous monk might have found in his terror and humiliation was surely disguised in his victimhood. In that abject place where his ego is destroyed with shame, he might have perceived that having no ego is precisely the goal. In becoming one with his victimhood, he might have become one with the cosmos—in whose threads and

---

91 Lin-chi I-hsüan, known in Japanese as Rinzai Gigen, d. 866/7. Founder of a school named after himself which became the most influential school of Ch'an and the most vital school of Chinese Buddhism (Fischer-Schreiber, *et. al.*, 1989).

cloth shines the oneness that his opponent strives for. If he goes through a process like this in an instant, he might be composed enough to say, "A monk who is a ruffian throttles his master." This impertinent comment turns choking into victory. He points out that Lin-chi has just exchanged the rank of his dais for that of a perpetrator, merely traded one posture of power for another. And the man he is throttling is his own professed ideal, "the true person of no rank," as though he were to say, "In strangling me, you're snuffing out the one you claim to be." As in the vajroli contest, each monk strives to create the greatest possible disturbance to his partner's line of "riff." Each tries to push the other over the top, where the dragon of panic will get the better of him. Whether in a combat of sexual moves or of ripostes, we lose when we cannot spontaneously convert the crisis into an improvised variation on our partner's theme. "Truly great improvisations occur only when 'we' stop trying to *make* music and simply allow it to play through us" (Hershock, 161).

SPONTANEITY AND PLAY

Dharma combat is earnest business; but it is also play, a matter of letting go and letting be so that inspiration can show its capricious face. "Ch'an practice occurs as the virtuosity of the middle path between control and caprice, between having (*yu*) and not-having (*wu*)" (Hershock, 123). While the citadel self strives to abolish ambiguity by presenting itself as a permanent subject-entity encountering equally permanent object-entities, the earnest play of dharma combat makes fluidity possibly by embracing ambiguity. "If ambiguity and not entitative existence is held basic, morality is most naturally not an orientation toward preserving integrity but toward intensifying intimacy" (Hershock, 189). Intimacy always occurs as a boundary-dissolving encounter revealing the "no-self" of the participants.

Hinduism and Buddhism describe the rigidity of the citadel self, its having-become-what-it-is, as karma. According to karma, our construal of the world and our citadel self is an interlinked accumulation of expectations based on memories, conscious and unconscious, and setting habitual patterns of action. In its most superficial manifestation, karma reflects the work of our autonomous internal monologues; more deeply it is said to have been constructed through the habits of past lives and therefore lurks deep in our unconscious psyche where it is extremely impervious to change. According to the doctrine of karma, "[O]ur intentions constitute what-has-come-to-be, and how there is no arbitrary line demarcating what we are responsible for and what not" (Hershock, 47). But insofar as karma expresses the link between the world we construe and the citadel self we maintain, it also presents itself as an opportunity. The world we construe is "thoroughly heuristic," in that every incident is an opportunity to bind ourselves further by acting out of the habits of the illusory citadel self or to free ourselves by responding to the ambiguities we habitually gloss as familiar entities (Hershock, 49).

Nishitani is in full agreement with this formulation. He says that living in the world of primary fact is a "serious and earnest" sort of play, an "elemental earnestness" in which we "take-things-as-they-come" (Nishitani, 1982: 255). What arises from moment to moment in our wayfaring life does not have to be seen as "imposed by *fate*" but can be redeemed when it is "accepted as *vocation*" (Nishitani, 259). Every incident along the path of our journey through the ordinary world "calls" us to freedom when we are conscious enough not to "fall victim" to the karma our rigid habits create. "A wild, playful, unpredictable quality erupts when experience is released from its predetermined patterns" (Shaw, 1994: 95).

> The world of karma is a world where each individual is determined by its ties and causal kinship within an endless nexus, and yet each instance of individual-existence and behavior, as well as each moment in time, arises as something totally new, possessed of freedom and creativity (Nishitani, 1982: 245).

> Shouldering the burden [of karmic debt] takes on the sense of play, and the standpoint appears from which we go forward bearing the burden spontaneously and of our own free will. The labor imposed, without ceasing to be an imposition, is transformed into play by arising spontaneously in an elemental way (Nishitani, 254).

It is clear from this perspective that enlightenment is not something we attain once and for all through some sort of private practice. It is not something that we "possess" or that belongs to us. Enlightenment appears only in virtuosic and spontaneous practice, in the way we live our ordinary lives in an extraordinary manner. Hershock cites Hui-neng, the Sixth Patriarch of Ch'an (638-713), "It is precisely Buddhist practice that is the Buddha" (Hershock, 1996: 143), namely "to conduct ourselves . . . as initiators of enlightening partnership" (Hershock, 172). Because the karma of our citadel self stops everything that happens and reconfigures it according to habitual patterns, enlightenment is enacted only when "all things flow unimpeded" (Hershock, 129). "If a buddha-land is to appear right where we stand, 'we' must get out of the way" (Hershock, 141).

Once we realize that enlightenment is a practice, an enactment, a way of life, we obtain a new perspective on Spontaneous Great Bliss. The act of intercourse that makes Spontaneous Great Bliss possible is a virtuosic interaction between partners in which each individual's move provokes a crisis along the lines of the vajroli contest. And each response is a spontaneous improvisation which redirects attention away from my "falling victim" by reinterpreting it as a new development in the riff of the interaction by which we jointly "shepherd" kundalini's rise. The attainment of Spontaneous Great Bliss amounts to the intimate virtuosity of a dharma combat conducted as a fresh and original version of a very old tune. The intercourse practiced in pursuit of Spontaneous Great Bliss is the jousting field upon which the practitioner of Mahamudra learns the true nature of spontaneity through a series of extreme crises. In the last analysis, it is a learning experience from which the successful student will resume wayfaring better prepared to respond to any crisis with the spontaneous virtuosity of Yeshe Tsogyel. Enlightenment is practiced only on the everyday journey of our life, through the countless crises that arise. The question of whether any individual is enlightened can only be answered in terms of our day-in and day-out conduct; for "Who we really are is 'how things are going'" (Hershock, 195).

THE SERPENTINE PATH

Perhaps many of those who are wayfaring through a world that tests their training every day fail again and again in the dharma combats life arranges for them. "How things are going" for them may all too often include opportunities that escape their notice or surprise them with the dragon of their appetites so that they fail in the playful work of spontaneous improvisation. Yet they differ from the rest of us substantially. Though they may fail more often than they succeed, they are *initiated* people. They have served an apprenticeship in the art of spontaneous improvisation and therefore know in principle that crises are opportunities. With their lasting, ineffaceable Tantric conviction that every interruption conceals a Yidam deity, they live on a more subtle plane. They are acquainted with the world of primary fact; and though they may spend all too much of their time forgetting emptiness, they are not surprised when it appears. They see it more clearly than do the uninitiated—as though in slow motion. In these moments—when they perceive emptiness while viewing the world through the five senses (Gyatso, 1992: 141)—they are enlightened. All humans have moments of potential enlightenment, but they pass us by so quickly that we miss them entirely. The initiated remember those moments better than the rest of us, recognize them more readily when the occur, and work at integrating them. They are always on the way toward living in a world where every event reveals the threads in the cloth and cloth in the threads.

Psychoanalyst Sudhir Kakar, in his book exploring the sexual views and practices of ordinary Indians, observes that the uninitiated person "lives on the intersection of several stories, his own as well as those of heroes and gods" (Kakar, 1989: 2). This comment implies that the ordinary Indian lives much closer to the mythic world than the average American. But it also shows the essential quality of those who are uninitiated, wherever they may be. They float through life, linking up their citadel selves with one fragmentary narrative after another—each emerging autonomously and without self-reflection—a congeries of conflicting and partial life-narratives that keeps them in ignorance of what they are about. Lama Anagarika Govinda provides an even more mythic picture of uninitiated people. In his wayfaring through Tibet, he spent some time in the village of Poo, where he found, "Nobody thought of Padmasambhava as a figure out of the remote past, but as somebody who had just passed through this valley and might return at any moment" (Govinda, 1988: 267). He says Christian missionaries had to give up trying to convert the people of Poo because they heard all the stories of Christ as the actions of Padmasambhava (Govinda, 268). Here are people who truly live in a mythic world. No doubt they, too, "live on the intersection of several stories," though one story is especially privileged. Nevertheless, the extent to which they are looking forward to the return of Padmasambhava—a holy man who evidently lives entirely on the subtle plane—they have not perceived the essential point about enlightenment. They are not initiated. They do not know that God cannot be given them, that they can only become pregnant with God.

Some eighty years ago, Alexandra David-Neel had a disturbing encounter with an uninitiated disciple of Lama Rabjoms Gyatso. This disciple was in torment because he experienced himself as being eaten alive by ghouls and ghosts, believing that David-Neel was one of them. Rabjoms Gyatso said to David-Neel: "No doubt he is [eaten alive] . . . but he does not understand that he himself is the eater. Maybe he will learn that later on" (David-Neel, 1971: 163). Being eaten by ghouls is this man's crisis. His lama evidently hopes that the day will come when the disciple will be able to see this crisis as an opportunity and by spontaneous improvisation find its Yidam deity. If we are shocked at how "psychotic" this man's brush with divinity may be, Lama Rabjoms Gyatso wants us to see that we are not so very different from that unfortunate disciple. He tells David-Neel that she may be able to follow a path "less coarse" than he, but: "[It] must be as hard as that of my disciple. If it is easy it is the wrong one."

This disturbing scene may be placed alongside another David-Neel gives us, this time of the practice of a certain sort of initiate called *Lung-gom-pao*, a person who has mastered *Lung-gom*, a practice that combines mental concentration with breathing exercises, and has become a traveler who covers great distances in a relatively short time. While maintaining their meditative state, these adepts move along their path by means of impossible strides. David-Neel once followed a Lung-gom traveler with her binoculars:

> By the time he had nearly reached us, I could clearly see his perfectly calm impassive face and wide-open eyes with their gaze fixed on some invisible far-distant object situated somewhere high up in space. The man did not run. He seemed to lift himself from the ground, proceeding by leaps. It looked as if he had been endowed with the elasticity of a ball. . . . His right arm moved slightly at each step as if leaning on a stick, just as though the *phurba* [magic dagger

held in his right hand], whose pointed extremity was far above the ground, had touched it and were actually a support (David-Neel, 203).

David-Neel is convinced her eyes have not deceived her and that seemingly superhuman feats like this are possible:

Setting aside exaggeration, I am convinced . . . that one reaches a condition in which one does not feel the weight of one's body. A kind of anaesthesia deadens the sensations that would be produced by knocking against stones or other objects on the way, and one walks for hours at an unaccustomed speed, enjoying that kind of light agreeable dizziness well known to motorists at high speed (David-Neel, 215).

The question David-Neel does not address but might seem obvious to us is whether she herself may not have been in an altered state of consciousness when she witnessed these events. If she was, we may think that the Lung-gom-pao is indeed traveling along the wayfaring path while in a meditative state, that his movements are perhaps more economical than those of a traveler who remains in profane consciousness. His subjective experience may, indeed, be of traveling at great speed with the assistance of his phurba. But it may also be that one who sees him with the eyes of profane consciousness would see only an unusual and intent sort of walking. Others who have been initiated, like David-Neel, and are therefore familiar with the subtle plane, might be shifted into erotic trance on encountering a Lung-gom-pao. Like Promode Chatterjee at the maithuna circle or Carol, the uninvited hypnosis student who accidentally witnessed the mutual hypnosis experiment of Bill and Anne, David-Neel may have observed the subtle meaning of a mystical practice.

Whether we take the story literally or symbolically, it illustrates a fundamental principle of mystical wayfaring by initiated people. The world is here as it always was, filled with stony obstacles, each a potential stopping point. But by not being fixed in conventional attitudes, the initiated wayfarer encounters each as an opportunity for an improvisatory leap. Once we know the ambiguous state of how things *really* are, there is no going back. Consensus reality is still there, but now it serves as the mud room to a mansion. I still have to buy milk and eggs. But once I have gained a certain confidence in my powers of spontaneous improvisation, even the Pick and Pay may sometimes be shot through with glory. When we get to this stage, there is no question that life is richer and more deeply satisfying. Vimalananda makes this point in his characteristically colorful fashion:

After your graduation [as an Aghori, "when the hordes of ethereal beings find they cannot tempt you"] you are awarded your degree: clairaudience and clairvoyance. Then you go anywhere, eat anything, and you are carefree, because something is directing your every move. You become just like a Yantra. The Cosmic Shakti plays through you, and you enjoy the bliss.

But this is the final stage. You must start at the bottom and go through the grind (Svoboda, 1986: 185).

When my body is a yantra, there is no difference between the microcosmic Shakti that plays within me and directs my every move as kundalini and the macrocosmic Shakti. In profane consciousness, Shakti leads us astray with her ever-changing illusions, like Maya. But for the initiated, Maya "can also serve as the self-actualization of the divine creative impulse, as the 'measuring out' (*ma*) or manifestation of pure consciousness, which is free to bind itself if it so chooses." This is what converts the phenomenal world to "a field of play for the realized (*siddha*) individual" (D. G. White, 1996: 279).

Such a point of view is not unique to India; but as Ioan Couliano points out, it belonged to the European Middle Ages. The medieval doctrine of the soul and its phantasms claimed that every reality perceptible in the empirical world had another meaning "on an ontological level inaccessible to direct experience" but available to the soul's imaginal power (Couliano, 1986: 34). Such phantasms of the soul "allegorize" actual events as symbols revealing the "intelligential cosmos" (Couliano, 40). They seem to have arrived at a perspective very close to that of Ibn al-'Arabi who said, "[T]he greatest illumination in this domain is when the vision of God is the very vision of the world" (Addas, 1993: 138).[92] He described his own mystical path as that of "servitude" (*'ubudiyya*): "[O]nly he who greets the spiritual instant (*warid*) in the full state of an *'abd* or servant is capable of mastering it" (Addas, 195). Because God is potentially revealed in every instant of our lives, we place ourselves in service to God through our spontaneous and improvisatory obedience to life's every instant. "According to the Sufis each 'time' (*waqt*) should evoke its own appropriate response in man. Whoever ignores or disregards what is appropriate to the moment, loses what it has to offer of truth" (Ibn al-'Arabi, 1971: 89, *n.* 1).

Finding subtle esoteric meanings (*batin*) within the external facts (*zahir*) of the everyday world or even in the words of the Qu'ran can be a tricky business. I have had some conversations with Islamic scholars who have used the term *batiniyya* (esoterism) with the greatest scorn. In doing so, they are responding to reckless and irresponsible "symbolic" interpretations, ones that are tangled up with the citadel-self-serving internal monologues of misguided esoterists. Esoterism is always open to abuse by the uninitiated; and this was true 800 years ago when Ibn al-'Arabi wrote. For this reason, he insists that true interpretation (ta'wil) always interprets "upward."[93] In this sense, those who count up the years of life ascribed to the Hebrew patriarchs in order to determine the date on which God created the world are

---

92 Quoting *Futuhat* II: 507-8.

93 Ta'wil: "the process of tracing something to its origin, to its archetype" (Corbin, 1981: 5).

pseudo-esoterists. They are interpreting "downwards" from the sublime words of scripture to the events of history. Ta'wil always moves upward from empirical facts to their meaning in the world of soul, from souls to the angels that guide them, and from angels to the lords they serve. By ta'wil the obstacles I face have a meaning for the progress of my soul on the mystic path. Thus Wilson says of ta'wil, "The symbols one penetrates are the path one follows" (Wilson, 1993: 154).[94] By ta'wil, the wayfaring Sufi travels on a "magic carpet" that moves as impossibly over obstacles as the Lung-gom-pao. Lalla, the Kashmiri songstress who refused to clothe herself or her vision in either Hindu or Islamic garb, captured the meaning of ta'wil in the following verse:

> Unconscious people read the scriptures
>
> like parrots saying Ram, Ram,
>
> in their cages.
>
> It's all pretend knowledge
>
> Read rather, with me, every
>
> living moment as prophecy
>
> (Lalla, 1992: 75).

Wayfaring on the spiritual path is called *suluk* in Arabic. The wayfarer is a *salik* (pl. *salikun*). Even a sedentary Sufi is a salik in the sense that her life is a journey to God. But unlike the hermits and the prayer-leaders in the mosque, the salikun travel from master to master in search of their distinctive teachings and conferral of shaktipat (i.e., the khirqa).[95] They seek out those in intimate intercourse with God to cross-pollinate their own experience. But God is also to be found along the road. They beg the "blessings" of everyone they meet and work for the day when every moment will bring its own blessing unasked. "The Sufi Traveler is 'begging' not just for alms but for this divine bahksheesh of signs, portents, encounters, coincidences, marvels, aesthetic shocks, spiritual insights, peak experiences, adventurous (even dangerous) unveilings" (Wilson, 1993: 154). They follow the words of the Prophet, "Be in the world like a traveler, or like a passerby, and reckon yourself as of the dead" (Glassé, 1989).

Indonesian Muslims have a "suluk ceremony" for obtaining psychic and magical powers "by withstanding terrifying assaults from the spirit world during a night in which he symbolically dies" (Glassé, 1989). The ceremony appears to have an Indian flavor: one obtains

---

94 Corbin says ta'wil is phenomenology. "It is a matter of leading the observer to a point where he will allow himself to see what it is that lies hidden" (Corbin, 1981: 15).

95 In large part, the tradition of wandering salikun is defunct today.

extraordinary powers of consciousness by successfully wrestling with wrathful yoginis. It is a journey (suluk) that takes place out of this world, entirely on the subtle plane. It describes an exercise that belongs to the heroic rung of the ladder, where the subtle plane and the everyday world are still at odds with one another. They have not yet begun to pulsate as the figure and ground of cosmic oneness. The true salik, on the other hand, the Sufi who wanders through a pulsating world of oneness, is both dead to profane existence and yet alive to everything that is. Like a dead man, he rests in unobstructed intercourse with God. But he also walks on roads of dirt and begs from the humblest he meets. Every turn in the road brings a crisis of ambiguity to be handled with spontaneous improvisation.

The scriptural archetype that grounds every suluk is the story from the Qu'ran (XVIII: 61-83) that describes Moses traveling with "one of our Servants." This servant (*'abd*) is not named in the Qu'ran, but tradition holds that he is Khidr (variant spellings include Khadir and Khezr). He is sometimes described as an angel but always as one of the *'afrad*, one of the "Unique Ones who receive illumination direct from God without human mediation; they can initiate seekers who belong to no Order or who have no human guide; they rescue lost wanderers and desperate lovers in the hour of need" (Wilson, 1993: 139). Ibn al-'Arabi is famous for three meetings with Khidr in which he was invested with the khirqa through a direct intervention from the subtle plane. Ibn al-'Arabi's recommendation that we conduct ourselves as "servants" in the face of each temporal moment as a potential theophanic *kairos* reflects his discipleship under Khidr, the prototype of the servants of God.

WHERE THE TWO WORLDS MEET

In the Qu'ranic story, Moses is traveling with his own servant, not Khidr, determined to find "the point where the two rivers meet, though I march on for ages" (v. 61). Evidently in a state of unconsciousness, they find this point because, distracted by Satan (v. 64), they forget about the fish they are carrying for their breakfast, "and it took its way into the waters being free" (v. 62). This place where the two waters meet is the *barzakh*, the border region where the *Mundus Imaginalis* or subtle plane and the empirical world overlap,[96] where vision and perception interpenetrate and one who is awake, like Khidr, can simultaneously see "the archetypal realities and hidden truths 'behind' material reality" (Wilson, 1993: 139). In losing their fish,[97] which

---

96 The barzakh is "the space between, the intermediary between the sensible and the intelligible" (Corbin, 1981: 14).

97 According to Jung, the fish is any "unconscious content" that lives invisibly distant from our conscious attitude—particularly that of the self or atman (*CW 9ii*). The junction of the two worlds is

miraculously comes to life and swims away into the subtle realm, Moses and his servant reveal their profane consciousness. The fact that he knows about searching for the barzakh of simultaneity reveals Moses' condition as an initiated one. His slip into forgetting the very purpose of his journey precisely at the moment he comes upon that border region illustrates how difficult it is to remain a servant of the moment. Moses does not miss the fish until he becomes hungry for breakfast, whereupon he has a shock of recognition: "This is that which we have been seeking. So they retraced their steps again" (v. 65). No doubt a Tantrika would point out that the Yidam deity of the barzakh is recognized by Moses precisely in his bodily appetites.

Back at the meeting of the two waters, they encounter Khidr; and Moses begs to be allowed to travel with him, so as to learn "right conduct" (v. 67). Khidr is reluctant, saying that Moses will not understand what he sees. But Moses persists and is finally allowed to tag along providing he asks no questions, "till I myself mention of it unto thee" (v. 71). Three disturbing incidents follow. Khidr drills a hole in the bottom of a poor man's boat, kills a lad, and—after being refused hospitality by a certain town—repairs its crumbling wall without asking to be paid for his labor. Each time Moses demands an explanation. The third time Khidr tells Moses he has broken his promise and can no longer travel with him. But he answers the questions. He damaged the boat so that a king would not seize it to use in a military campaign. The dead youth would have gone bad; his parents will be given another son, "better in purity and nearer to mercy" (v. 82). There is a treasure under the rebuilt wall which is to be found by a pair of orphan boys when they grow up. Khidr ends by saying that he has been commanded to do what he did by a will other than his own: "And I did it not upon my own command" (v. 83).

This set piece, which comes out of nowhere in the Qu'ran, surely appears to be a folk tale that has been smuggled into the inspired word of God.[98] Its possible origins aside, however, the tale is as inspired as every other passage in the Qu'ran. Wayfaring Sufis have adopted it as a symbolic description of suluk: one is to travel like Khidr, or with Khidr, so that every empirical event is also a theophany in which Someone Else calls the shots. Moses represents the man so attuned to the values of the persona field and so stuck in the citadel of his self that the world never pulsates for him. Khidr, on the other hand, lives in the conceptually ambiguous world of primary fact. He conducts himself like an outrageous Ch'an master, transforming

---

the place where atman is either found or lost, depending on the level of our awareness.

98 According to tradition, this story and the ones preceding and following are Muhammad's answers to three questions set him by rabbis (Pickthall, [n.d.]). The Qu'ran itself gives no rationale for including them—and has no need to, as it is merely a catalogue of the things Muhammed said when he was inspired. None of his followers had the temerity to place these sayings into a biographical context—as the four Christian evangelists did with the words of Jesus.

himself in an instant from shaikh to vandal, assassin, and chump before the astonished eyes of the Hebrew prophet. Each incident is a spontaneous improvisation. Moses is the law-giver of the Jews, the traditional author of the first five books of the Bible. The God of Muhammad makes it clear that there is a higher suluk than has been dreamed of by even the saintliest of those who are confined to the conventional world.

The irony of this Qu'ranic story is that Moses himself might well have been taken as the prototype of all salikun. He led the Israelites on a journey whose geographical goal was unknown, that lasted virtually a lifetime, and in which day-to-day guidance came directly from God, who takes on the appearance of extraordinary empirical phenomena—a pillar of fire and column of smoke. Moses parted the waters at the divine command, had a mystical vision of God on the mountain top, and was given the laws for living in the ordinary world in an extraordinary manner. The Israelites were fed every morning by food which miraculously appeared from the subtle realm, penetrating into the everyday world of the desert. True enough, Moses doubted and was not allowed to enter the promised land himself. He was more human than Khidr, but he is the primary scriptural example of one who lived the wayfaring life, following a path not laid out straight as an arrow by the citadel self, but ever bending back on itself like a serpent, winding from one theophanic moment to the next. The Exodus is the journey that gathered the Israelites into the people of God and typifies the life of every Jew, Christian, and Muslim who is aware in principle—though constantly forgetting—that this ordinary life becomes extraordinary when interpenetrated by the timeless realities of the subtle plane.

The serpentine path of Khidr (and Moses) stays always on the ever-twisting border land where the two worlds meet, the barzakh that can never be known in advance but is discovered anew in every moment, the world of primary fact where the conceptual certainties of the citadel self have been dropped off and left behind.

> If you have realized the "Khezr of your being," you may travel even to that place which is doubtless another *border* or gateway between this world and the *Mundus Imaginalis*—or, to be more precise, you may travel in both worlds simultaneously, like Khezr, seeing each landmark, as in a dream, suffused with significance and hidden knowledge (Wilson, 1993: 145).

> Everyone and everything is drawn to such a joyous wayfarer, from madmen and children to local tutelary spirits, the djinns of the locus or spirits of the place. For one in this state, to see a tree in its suchness is to meet its dryad; to bathe in a spring is to meet its undine; to touch a rock is to meet its kobold or troll; and the campfire is the veritable salamander of flame (Wilson, 154).

Wilson implies, here, that those who are at odds with themselves and struggling with their ascetic exercises will always be blind to the theophanic possibilities of the moment. Every incident will be a crisis or a trial for such an unintegrated traveler. Those who follow the serpentine path of Khidr, however, go cheerfully and without a care. They are moved by the blissful force of their soul's energy. They are open to every adventure without forcing it, without relying on their own will, but with a cultivated imaginal power gained through their initiation—a playful readiness to employ spontaneous improvisation.

Ibn al-'Arabi began his wandering in three-dimensional space in the year 1194, when he was thirty. At a certain moment in the mosque at Tunis that year, he says he entered the barzakh and never left it. Referring to a passage from the Qu'ran (XXIX: 57), "You My servants who believe, My Earth is vast, therefore worship Me," Ibn al-'Arabi called this intersection of the two worlds "God's Vast Earth" (*ard Allah al-wasi'a*). He also called it the "Realm of Symbols" (*manzil al-rumuz*) and the "Earth of Reality" (*ard al-haqiqa*) (Addas, 1993: 117).

> When I entered this Dwelling-Place, while staying in Tunis, I unconsciously let out a cry; not a single person heard it without losing consciousness. The women who were on the adjoining terraces fainted; some of them fell from the terraces into the courtyard, but in spite of the height they suffered no harm. I was the first to regain consciousness; we were in the course of performing the prayer behind the imam. I saw that everyone had collapsed, thunderstruck. After a while they recovered their own spirits and I asked them: "What happened to you?" They answered: "It's for you to tell us what happened to you! You let out such a cry that you have been the cause of what you see." I said to them: "By God, I had no idea I uttered a cry!" (Addas, 119).[99]

Here again we have the theme of uninitiated believers being transported to the subtle plane through the elevating influence of another. Ibn al-'Arabi tells the story as one who is simply amazed by the events. He was transported to that intermediate realm by some power greater than his own. The cry he let out remains unconscious to him. He cannot tell us if it was a shout of joy or a scream of terror, the death-cry of his citadel self. All we know is that, unconsciously, the entire congregation recognized it. Something in them, the dragon of their soul's energy, responded. We are led to believe that anyone who had been there would have been transported by shaktipat to God's Vast Earth. But only Ibn al-'Arabi remembers what happened and stays in that Earth of Reality. Evidently only he has been prepared by the investiture of Khidr's khirqa to know what he sees and remain in that elevated state of consciousness.

---

99 Quoting *Futuhat* I: 173.

Ibn al-'Arabi says that "God's Vast Earth" is inhabited only "by those who have realized total servitude (*'ubudiyya*) with regard to God" (Addas, 118).

> The earth in question is located in the *barzakh*—the intermediary world where spirits receive a subtle body. As Ibn 'Arabi writes: "Every body in which spirits, angels and *jinns* clothe themselves and every form in which a man perceives himself while asleep is a subtle body belonging to that earth" (Addas, 118).[100]

It would be hard to find a more explicit description of the subtle plane than this: the realm where spiritual influences are discernible through the human power of imagination. Peter Lamborn Wilson says we would be ill-advised to make too rigid a distinction between that imaginal power (which he capitalizes, following the convention established by Corbin: Imagination) and the more familiar human faculty of day-dreaming. To distrust reverie is to distrust Imagination, "for even the idlest day-dream is open to the sudden irradiation of the divine (*tajalli*), provided the heart is open" (Wilson, 1993: 143). Here, again, we encounter the Tibetan doctrine of the Yidam deity that lurks within the most ordinary and despised of our unconscious desires and impulses.

C. G. Jung makes the same point in describing the sort of reverie he advocates as an adjunct to his practice of analysis. Calling disciplined reverie "active imagination," Jung urged his patients to follow his own example in coming to know the unconscious dynamics that lie beneath our day-to-day experience. The critical ego is to be consciously held in suspension, while the waking dream is observed:

> Consciousness is forever interfering, helping, correcting, and negating, never leaving the psychic process to grow in peace. It would be simple enough, if only simplicity were not the most difficult of all things. To begin with, the task consists solely in observing objectively how a fragment of fantasy develops. Nothing could be simpler, and yet right here the difficulties begin. Apparently one has no fantasy fragments—or yes, there's one, but it is too stupid! Dozens of good reasons are brought against it. One cannot concentrate on it—it is too boring—what could come of it anyway—it is "nothing but" this or that, and so on. The conscious mind raises innumerable objections, in fact it often seems bent on blotting out the spontaneous fantasy activity in spite of real insight and in spite of the firm determination to allow the psychic process to go forward without interference. Occasionally there is a veritable cramp of consciousness (Jung, *CW 13*: ¶20).

These exercises must be continued until the cramp in the conscious mind is relaxed, in other words, until one can let things happen, which is the next goal of the exercise. In this way a

---

100 Quoting *Futuhat* I: 130.

new attitude is created, an attitude that accepts the irrational and the incomprehensible simply because it is happening (Jung, *CW 13*, ¶23).

Thus Jung makes it clear that access to the imaginal powers of the unconscious requires a partial setting aside of the citadel self with its habitual judgments. Only one who begins by attending faithfully to day-dreams will have the capacity for the spontaneous improvisation by which the serpentine path can be discerned. Furthermore, in developing this "new attitude" we do not create something arbitrary; rather we gain access to events that are already "happening" but regarding which our compulsive maintenance of the citadel self leaves us blind and ignorant. An imaginal world co-exits with this one, and we can find it at any moment if only we can learn to rein in our citadel self.

The serpentine path describes a journey to be lived, not talked about. But the very possibility of such a journey, and the fact that one can gain initiation by various means to the art of spontaneous improvisation so as to be able to recognize and convert its "moments": these are exciting facts. And serious wayfarers meet people who have experienced these things—or know someone who has—; and they cannot resist swapping stories of the Way. In the last analysis, stories are the most dependable source of information for those who have not been initiated. Stories intrigue the ego and stimulate the unconscious imaginal faculty in those who have merely heard about mysticism. For those who are sufficiently serious in their intentions and fortunate enough to have found a master capable of initiating them, stories of the Way loosen their preconceptions and call up memories of forgotten moments. Crises that were bungled and led to "falling victim" are recalled as potential opportunities for spontaneous improvisation; and the journeyman mystic is better prepared to meet such challenges in the future.

If sexual stories of lust, longing, indecency, and wrathful yoginis are among the most compelling, the reason is two-fold. On the one hand, nothing drives us more insistently and at the most "inopportune" moments than sex. On the other hand, the sex drive is but the leading edge of eros with all the physiological, emotional, and imaginal changes it effects. Whether we have learned to recognize it or not, every moment of erotic stimulation presents itself as an imaginal opportunity. Every base and panting instance of lust carries within it the Yidam deity of erotic trance. In moments of sexual stimulation, we are always standing on the barzakh where the empirical world is interpenetrated by the subtle plane. The uninitiated overlook their opportunities. The initiated miss more than they recognize. Eros and its more developed relative, kundalini, constitute the playing field where every moment is charged with lustful significance and lies open to spontaneous transformation. Every erotically interesting partner is a potential Bhairava or Bhairavi capable of opening the vertical dimension of the diamond ladder the moment we take our imaginal projections seriously as a project to be lived. The sexual stories make another fact clear. To have discovered the wrathful and blissful divinity lurking in a single partner is to open up the entire world as a potential barzakh, as Rumi tells us in five potent lines:

> If the Beloved is everywhere
>
> the lover is a veil.
>
> But when living itself
>
> becomes the Friend,
>
> lovers disappear
>
> (Barks & Green, 1997: 127).

The Beloved is everywhere because there is no cloth without the threads of light that are our cosmic consciousness. The lover is a veil because as long as we are stuck in the subjectivity of our lover-hood and believe that the Beloved is an "object," Reality is veiled by our citadel self. To drop the veil is to drop body-and-mind and enter the world of primary fact. There "living itself" becomes the Friend, because every moment is a theophany. Lovers have to disappear if there is no longer to be a subject and an object to blind us to what *is*. In this sense, Miranda Shaw's story of the arrow-making yogini and Saraha epitomizes the life of sexual wayfaring. When a single partner opens up "living itself" as the barzakh, each becomes Khidr for the other. In their arrow-making, in their maithuna, in preparing their breakfast and eating it, everything they undertake occurs at the intersection of the cloth and the threads. Spontaneous Great Bliss infuses every moment. The pilgrimage to Mecca as well as the transport to Indra's Heaven can be made without ever leaving one's kitchen. Wayfaring is not about geography. Mountains, trees, and rivers are merely its training ground. Real wayfaring occurs when the heart chakra is open and the serpentine path of the barzakh resides in every "here and now."

BIBLIOGRAPHY

Addas, Claude. *Quest for the Red Sulphur: The Life of Ibn 'Arabi. Translated by Peter Kingsley. Cambridge, UK: Islamic Texts Society, 1993.*

Adler, Gerhard (Ed.). *C. G. Jung: Letters.* Translated by R. F. C. Hull. In two volumes: *Vol. I: 1906-1950; Vol. II: (1951-1961)*. Princeton, NJ: Princeton University Press: 1973 & 1975.

Adler, Janet. *Arching Backwards: The Mystical Initiation of a Contemporary Woman.* Rochester, VT: Inner Traditions, 1995.

Ahlstrom, Sydney E. *A Religious History of the American People.* New Haven, CT: Yale University Press, 1972.

Ajaya, Swami. "Kundalini and the Tantric Tradition." In J. White, 1990: 98-105.

Allione, Tsultrim. *Women of Wisdom.* Boston: Arkana, 1986.

Anand, Margo. *The Art of Sexual Ecstasy: The Path of Sacred Sexuality for Western Lovers.* New York: Putnam, 1989.

Anand, Margo. *The Art of Sexual Magic.* New York: Putnam, 1995.

Avalon, Arthur (John Woodroffe). *The Serpent Power.* New York: Dover, 1919/74.

Barks, Coleman, and Michael Green. *The Illuminated Rumi.* Translations and Commentary by Coleman Barks, Illuminations by Michael Green. New York: Broadway, 1997)

Basham, A. L. *The Wonder That Was India: A Survey of the Culture of the Indian Sub-Continent Before the Coming of the Muslims.* New York: Grove, 1959.

Bataille, Georges. *Erotism: Death and Sensuality.* Translated by Mary Dalwood. San Francisco: City Lights, 1986.

Battacharya, Brajamadhava. *Saivism and the Phallic World.* In two volumes. New Delhi: Oxford and IBH, 1975.

Battacharya, Brajamadhava. *The World of Tantra.* New Delhi: Munshiram Manoharlal, 1988.

Bentov, Itzhak. "Micromotion of the Body as a Factor in the Development of the Nervous System." In Sannella, 1992: 127-149.

Berman, Morris. *The Reenchantment of the World.* Ithaca: Cornell University Press, 1981.

Beyer, Stephen. *The Cult of Tara: Magic and Ritual in Tibet.* Berkeley: University of California Press, 1973.

Blank, Jonah. *Arrow of the Blue-Skinned God: Retracing the Ramayana Through India.* New York: Simon & Schuster, 1993.

Blofeld, John. *The Tantric Mysticism of Tibet.* Boston: Shambhala, 1987.

Bohm, David. *Wholeness and the Implicate Order.* New York: Arc, 1983,

Bramly, Serge. *Macumba: The Teachings of Maria-José, Mother of the Gods.* New York: Avon, 1979.

Bregman, Lucy. *The Rediscovery of Inner Experience.* Chicago: Nelson-Hall, 1982.

Buehler, Arthur F. *Sufi Heirs of the Prophet: The Indian Naqshbandiyya and the Rise of the Mediating Sufi Shaykh.* Columbia, SC: University of South Carolina Press, 1998.

Butler, D. B. "Instant Cosmic Consciousness?" In J. White, 1990: 184-8.

Capra, Fritjof. *The Web of Life: A New Scientific Understanding of Living Systems.* New York: Anchor/Doubleday, 1996).

Castaneda, Carlos. *Journey to Ixtlan: The Lessons of Don Juan.* New York: Simon & Schuster, 1972.

Castaneda, Margaret Runyan. *A Magical Journey with Carlos Castaneda.* Victoria, BC: Millenia Press, 1997.

Chaudhuri, Haridas. "The Psychophysiology of Kundalini." In J. White, 1990: 61-8.

Chia, Mantak & Douglas Abrams Arava. *The Multi-Orgasmic Man.* San Francisco: HarperSanFrancisco, 1996.

Clottes, Jean, and David Lewis-Williams. *The Shamans of Prehistory: Trance and Magic in the Painted Caves.* Translated by Sophie Hawkes. New York: Abrams, 1998.

Cohn, Norman. *The Pursuit of the Millennium: Revolutionary Millenarians and Mystical Anarchists of the Middle Ages.* New York: Oxford, 1957/70.

Colledge, Edmund, O.S.A., and Bernard McGinn (Eds.). *Meister Eckhart: The Essential Sermons, Commentaries, Treatises, and Defense.* New York: Paulist, 1981.

Comfort, Alex (Tr.). *The Illustrated Koka Shastra: Medieval Indian Writings on Love Based on the Kama Sutra.* Simon & Schuster, 1997.

Conze, Edward. *Buddhism: Its Essence and Development.* New York: Harper Torchbooks, 1959.

Corbin, Henry. *Creative Imagination in the Sufism of Ibn 'Arabi.* Translated by Ralph Manheim. Princeton: Bollingen, 1969.

Corbin, Henry. *The Man of Light in Iranian Sufism.* Translated by Nancy Pearson. Boulder, CO: Shambhala, 1978.

Corbin, Henry. *Avicenna and the Visionary Recital.* Translated by Willard B. Trask. Dallas: Spring, 1980.

Corbin, Henry. "The Concept of Comparative Philosophy." Translated by Peter Russell. Ipswich: England: Golgonooza Press, 1981.

Corbin, Henry. *Cyclical Time and Ismaili Gnosis.* Translated by Ralph Manheim and James W. Morris. Boston: Kegan Paul International, 1983.

Couliano, Ioan P. *Eros and Magic in the Renaissance.* Translated by M. Cook. Chicago: University of Chicago Press, 1986.

Crapanzano, Vincent. *The Hamansha: A Study in Moroccan Ethnopsychiatry.* Berkeley, CA: California University Press, 1973.

Crapanzano, Vincent, and Vivian Garrison (Eds.). *Case Studies in Spirit Possession.* New York: Wiley, 1977.

Dalai Lama, the Sixth. *Stallion on a Frozen Lake: Love Songs of the Sixth Dalai Lama.* Translated by C. Barks. Athens, GA: Maypop, 1992.

Daniélou, Alain. *Gods of Love and Ecstasy: The Traditions of Shiva and Dionysus.* Rochester, VT: Inner Traditions International, 1992.

Daniélou, Alain. *The Phallus: Sacred Symbol of Male Creative Power.* Translated by J. Graham. Rochester, VT: Inner Traditions International, 1995.

Dargay, Eva. *The Rise of Esoteric Buddhism in Tibet.* New York: Weiser, 1978.

David-Neel, Alexandra. *Magic and Mystery in Tibet.* Baltimore: Penguin, 1971.

Deren, Maya. *Divine Horsemen: The Living Gods of Haiti.* New York: McPherson, 1970.

Desai, Yogi Amrit. "Kundalini Yoga Through Skaktipat." In White (Ed.), 1990: 69-75.

Deveney, John Patrick. *Paschal Beverly Randolph: A Nineteenth-Century Black American Spiritualist, Rosicrucian, and Sex Magician.* Albany: SUNY, 1997.

Dimock, Edward C. *The Place of the Hidden Moon: Erotic Mysticism in the Vaisnava-sahajiya Cult of Bengal.* Chicago: University of Chicago Press, 1989.

Dowman, Keith. *Sky Dancer: The Secret Life and Songs of the Lady Yeshe Tsogyel.* Boston: Routledge, 1984.

Dowman, Keith & Sonam Paljor (Tranlators). *The Divine Madman: The Sublime Life and Songs of Drukpa Kunley.* Middletown, CA: Dawn Horse, 1988.

Dresser, Marianne (Ed.). *Buddhist Women on the Edge: Contemporary Perspectives from the Western Frontier.* Berkeley: North Atlantic Books, 1996.

Dyczkowski, Mark S. G. *The Doctrine of Vibration: An Analysis of the Doctrines and Practices of Kashmir Shaivism.* Albany: SUNY, 1987.

Eliade, Mircea. *Shamanism: Archaic Techniques of Ecstasy.* Translated by W. R. Trask. New York: Pantheon, 1964.

Eliade, Mircea. *Yoga: Immortality and Freedom.* Translated by W. Trask. Princeton: Princeton University Press, 1969.

Eliade, Mircea. *Patanjali and Yoga.* Translated by C. L. Markman. New York: Schocken, 1975.

Evans-Wentz, W. Y. *The Tibetan Book of the Dead.* New York: Oxford, 1960.

Evans-Wentz, W. Y. *Tibetan Yoga and Secret Doctrines.* London: Oxford University Press, 1967.

Evans-Wentz, W. Y. *Tibet's Great Yogi, Milarepa: A Biography from the Tibetan.* London: Oxford University Press, 1969.

Ellenberger, Henri. *The Discovery of the Unconscious: The History and Evolution of Dynamic Psychiatry.* New York: Basic, 1970.

Evola, Julius. *Eros and the Mysteries of Love: The Metaphysics of Sex.* Translator not specified. Rochester, VT: Inner Traditions International, 1983.

Evola, Julius. *The Yoga of Power: Tantra, Shakti, and the Secret Way.* Translated by G. Stucco. Rochester, VT: Inner Traditions International, 1992.

Evola, Julius. *The Hermetic Tradition: Symbols and Teachings of the Royal Art.* Translated by E. E. Rhemus. Rochester, VT: Inner Traditions International, 1995.

Faure, Bernard. *The Red Thread: Buddhist Approaches to Sexuality.* Princeton: Princeton University Press, 1998.

Ferguson, John. *Encyclopedia of Mysticism and the Mystery Religions.* New York: Continuum, 1977.

Feuerstein, Georg. *Yoga: The Technology of Ecstasy.* Los Angeles: Tarcher, 1989.

Feuerstein, Georg. *Encyclopedic Dictionary of Yoga.* New York: Paragon, 1990.

Feuerstein, Georg. *Holy Madness: The Shock Tactics and Radical Teachings of Crazy-Wise Adepts, Holy Fools, and Rascal Gurus.* New York: Paragon, 1991.

Feuerstein, Georg. *Sacred Sexuality: Living in the Vision of the Erotic Spirit.* Los Angeles: Tarcher, 1993.

Feuerstein, Georg, Subhash Kak, & David Frawley. *In Search of the Cradle of Civilization: New Light on Ancient India.* Wheaton, IL: Quest, 1995.

Figge, Horst H. *Geisterkult, Besessenheit und Magie in der Umbanda-Religion Brasiliens*. Munich: Alber, 1973.

Fischer-Schreiber, Ingrid, Franz-Karl Ehrhard, Kurt Friedrichs, & Michael S. Diener. *The Encyclopedia of Eastern Philosophy and Religion: Buddhism, Hinduism, Taoism, Zen*. Translated by M. H. Hohn, K. Ready, & W. Wünsche. Boston: Shambhala, 1989.

Fogarty, Robert S. (Ed.). *Special Love/Special Sex: An Oneida Community Diary*. Syracuse: Syracuse University Press, 1994.

Giffen, Lois Anita. *The Theory of Profane Love Among the Arabs: The Development of the Genre*. New York: New York University Press, 1971.

Glassé, Cyril. *The Concise Encyclopedia of Islam*. San Francisco: Harper & Row, 1989.

Goodman, Felicitas D. *Ecstasy, Ritual, and Alternate Reality: Religion in a Pluralistic World*. Bloomington: Indiana University Press, 1988.

Goodman, Felicitas D., Jeannette H. Henney, and Esther Pressel. *Trance, Healing, and Hallucination: Three Field Studies in Religious Experience*. New York: Wiley, 1974.

Govinda, Lama Anagarika. *Foundations of Tibetan Mysticism*. York Beach, ME: Samuel Weiser, 1969.

Govinda, Lama Anagarika. *The Way of the White Clouds: A Buddhist Pilgrim in Tibet*. Boston: Shambhala, 1988.

Guiley, Rosemary Ellen. *Harper's Encyclopedia of Mystical and Paranormal Experience*. San Francisco: HarperSanFrancisco, 1991.

Gyatso, Geshe Kelsang. *Clear Light of Bliss: The Practice of Mahamudra in Vajrayana Buddhism*. Second Edn. London: Tharpa, 1992.

Haich, Elisabeth. *Sexual Energy and Yoga*. Translated by D. Q. Stephenson. New York: Aurora, 1982.

Hartsuiker, Dolf. *Sadhus: India's Mystic Holy Men*. Rochester, VT: Inner Traditions International, 1993.

Harvey, Andrew. *Hidden Journey: A Spiritual Awakening*. New York: Holt, 1991.

Haule, John Ryan. "From Somnambulism to the Archetypes: The French Roots of Jung's Split with Freud." *Psychoanalytic Review* (1984) *71*(4): 95-107.

Haule, John Ryan. *Divine Madness: Archetypes of Romantic Love*. Carmel: Fisher King Press, 2010.

Haule, John Ryan. *The Love Cure: Therapy Erotic and Sexual*. Woodstock, CT: Spring, 1996

Haule, John Ryan. "Taking Direction from the Spirit in Shamanism and Psychotherapy." *Shamanic Applications Review*, #4, 1997: 3-12.

Haule, John Ryan. "Analyzing from the Self: A Phenomenology of the Third in Analysis." In Roger Brooke (Ed.). *Pathways into the Jungian World*. London: Routledge, 1999a.

Haule, John Ryan. *Perils of the Soul: Ancient Wisdom and the New Age*. York, ME: Weiser, 1999b.

Hershock, Peter D. *Liberating Intimacy: Enlightenment and Social Virtuosity in Ch'an Buddhism*. Albany: SUNY, 1996.

Hills, Christopher. *Supersensonics*. Boulder Creek, CA: University of the Trees Press, 1976.

Husserl, Edmund. *Ideas: General Introduction to Pure Phenomenology*. Translated by W. R. Boyce Gibson. London: Collier-MacMillan, 1962.

Ibn [al-] 'Arabi, [Muhyiddin]. *Sufis of Andalusia: The* Ruh al-quds *and* al-Durrat al-fahkirah *of Ibn 'Arabi*. Translated with Introduction and Notes by R. W. J. Austin. Berkeley: University of California Press, 1971.

Ibn al-'Arabi, [Muhyiddin]. *The Bezels of Wisdom*. Translated by R. W. J. Austin. New York: Paulist, 1980.

Ibn [al-] 'Arabi, Muhyiddin. *Journey to the Lord of Power: A Sufi Manual on Retreat*. Translated by Rabia Terri Harris. Rochester, VT: Inner Traditions International, 1989.

Ignatius of Loyola. *The Autobiography of St. Ignatius Loyola with Related Documents*. Translated by Joseph F. O'Callaghan. Edited by John C. Olin. New York: Harper Torchbooks, 1974.

'Iraqi, Fakhruddin. *Divine Flashes*. Translated by William C. Chittick & Peter Lamborn Wilson. New York: Paulist, 1982.

Isayeva, Natalia. *From Early Vedanta to Kashmir Shaivism: Gaudapada, Bhartrhari, and Abhinavagupta*. Albany: SUNY, 1995.

Janet, Pierre. *L'Automatisme psychologique*. Paris: Alcan, 1889. Reprinted Paris: Société Pierre Janet, 1973.

Jankowiak, William. *Romantic Passion: A Universal Experience?* New York: Columbia University Press.

Jaynes, Julian. *The Origins of Consciousness in the Breakdown of the Bicameral Mind*. Boston: Houghton Mifflin, 1976.

Jennings, Hargrave. *Ophiolatreia*. Kila, MT: Kessinger. Reprint. [n.d.].

Johnsen, Linda. *Daughters of the Goddess: The Women Saints of India*. St. Paul, MN: Yes International, 1994.

Johnson, Sandy. *The Book of Tibetan Elders*. New York: Riverhead, 1996.

Jung, C. G. [*CW 5*] *Symbols of Transformation*. 1967.*

Jung, C. G. [*CW 6*] *Psychological Types*. 1971.

Jung, C. G. [*CW 7*] *Two Essays in Analytical Psychology*. 1966.

Jung, C. G. [*CW 8*] *The Structure and Dynamics of the Psyche*. 1960.

Jung, C. G. [*CW 9i*] *The Archetypes and the Collective Unconscious*. 1968.

Jung, C. G. [*CW 9ii*] *Aion: Researches into the Phenomenology of the Self*. 1968.

Jung, C. G. [*CW 11*] *Psychology and Religion: West and East*. 1969.

Jung, C. G. [*CW 12*] *Psychology and Alchemy*. 1968.

Jung, C. G. [*CW 13*] *Alchemical Studies*. 1967.

Jung, C. G. [*CW 14*] *Mysterium Conjunctionis*. 1963.

Jung, C. G. *Memories, Dreams, Reflections*. Recorded and edited by Aniela Jaffé. Translated by Richard and Clara Winston. New York: Pantheon, 1961.

Jung, C. G. *The Psychology of Kundalini Yoga: Notes of the Seminar Given in 1932 by C. G. Jung*. Edited by Sonu Shamdasani. Princeton: Bollingen, 1996.

Kakar, Sudhir. *Intimate Relations: Exploring Indian Sexuality*. Chicago: University of Chicago Press, 1989.

Kalsched, Donald. *The Inner World of Trauma: Archetypal Defenses of the Personal Spirit*. New York: Routledge, 1996.

Karagulla, Shafica, and Dora van Gelder Kunz. *The Chakras and Human Energy Fields*. Wheaton, IL: Quest, 1989.

Kassam, Kutub. *Shimmering Light: An Anthology of Ismaili Poetry*. Trl. F. M. Hunzai. New York: I.B. Tauris, 1997.

Katz, Richard. *Boiling Energy: Community Healing Among the Kalahari Kung*. Cambridge, MA: Harvard, 1982.

Khanna, Madhu. *Yantra: The Tantric Symbol of Cosmic Unity*. Lomdon: Thames and Hudsom, 1981.

Kinsley, David. *Tantric Visions of the Divine Feminine*. Berkeley: University of California, 1997.

Kohut, Heinz. *The Restoration of the Self*. New York: International Universities, 1977.

---

* NOTE: References to the *Collected Works of C. G. Jung* are designated by volume number, as *CW 1*, *CW 2*, etc. All translated by R. F. C. Hull, all published by Princeton University Press.

Kohut, Heinz. *How Does Analysis Cure?* Edited by Arnold Goldberg with Paul Stepansky. Chicago: University of Chicago Press, 1984.

Kripal, Jeffrey J. *Kali's Child: The Mystical and the Erotic in the Life and Teachings of Ramakrishna.* Chicago: University of Chicago Press, 1995.

Krishna, Gopi. *Kundalini: The Evolutionary Energy in Man.* Berkeley: Shambhala, 1971.

Krishna, Gopi. *The Secret of Yoga.* New York: Harper and Row, 1972.

Krishna, Gopi. *Living with Kundalini: The Autobiography of Gopi Krishna.* Edited by L. Shepard. Boston: Shambhala, 1993.

Laeuchli, Samuel. *Power and Sexuality: The Emergence of Canon Law at the Synod of Elvira.* Philadelphia: Temple University Press, 1972.

Lalla. *Naked Song.* Translated by C. Barks. Athens, GA: Maypop, 1992.

Levine, Stephen & Ondrea. *Embracing the Beloved: The Relationship as a Path of Awakening.* New York: Anchor, 1995.

Lévy-Bruhl, Lucien. *Primitive Mentality.* Translated by Lilian A. Claire. Boston: Beacon: 1966.

Lewis, Bernard. *The Assassins.* New York: Basic Books, 1970.

Lincoln, Victoria. *Teresa: A Woman, A Biography of Teresa of Avila.* Albany: SUNY, 1984.

Lu K'uan Yü. *Taoist Yoga: Alchemy and Immortality.* York Beach, ME: Weiser, 1973.

Lysebeth, André van. *Tantra: The Cult of the Feminine.* Translated by A. van Lysebeth & L. Dobler. York Beach, ME: Weiser, 1995.

Mann, John & Lar Short. *The Body of Light: History and Practical Techniques for Awakening Your Subtle Body.* Boston: Charles E. Tuttle, 1990.

Masters, R. E. L., and Jean Houston. *The Varieties of Psychedelic Experience.* New York: Dell, 1966.

Mavor, James W., Jr. & Byron E. Dix. *Manitou: The Sacred Landscape of New England's Native Civilization.* Rochester, VT: Inner Traditions International, 1989.

McDaniel, June. *The Madness of the Saints: Ecstatic Religion in Bengal.* Chicago: University of Chicago Press, 1989.

McGinn, Bernard, with Frank Tobin and Elvira Borgstadt (Eds.). *Meister Eckhart: Teacher and Preacher.* New York: Paulist, 1986.

McLean, Malcolm. *Devoted to the Goddess: The Life and Work of Ramprasad.* Albany, NY: SUNY, 1998.

Meissner, W. W. *Ignatius of Loyola: The Psychology of a Saint.* New Haven: Yale, 1992.

Merkur, Dan. *Becoming Half Hidden: Shamanism and Initiation Among the Inuit*. New York: Garland, 1992.

Merwin, W. S., & J. Moussaieff Masson (Transl.). *Sanskrit Love Poetry*. New York: Columbia University Press, 1977.

Mindell, Arnold. *Dreambody: The Body's Role in Revealing the Self*. Santa Monica: Sigo, 1982.

Mipham, Lama. *Calm and Clear*. Translated by Tarthang Tulku. Berkeley, CA: Dharma, 1973.

Moacanin, Radmila. *Jung's Psychology and Tibetan Buddhism: Western and Eastern Paths to the Heart*. London: Wisdom, 1986.

Mookerjee, Ajit. *Kundalini: The Arousal of the Inner Energy*. Rochester, VT: Destiny, 1986.

Moyne, John and Coleman Barks. *Unseen Rain: Quatrains of Rumi*. Putney, VT: Threshold, 1986.

Muktananda, Swami. *Play of Consciousness*. San Francisco: Harper & Row, 1978.

Mumford, Jonn. *Ecstasy Through Tantra*. St. Paul, MN: Llewellyn, 1987.

Mundukur, Balaji. *The Cult of the Serpent: An Interdisciplinary Survey of Its Manifestations and Origins*. Albany: SUNY, 1983.

Neihardt, John G. *Black Elk Speaks: Being the Life of a Holy Man of the Oglala Sioux*. Lincoln: University of Nebraska Press, 1961.

Nikhilananda, Swami (Ed.). *The Upanishads*. New York: Harper Torchbooks, 1963.

Nishitani, Keiji. *Religion and Nothingness*. Translated by Jan Van Bragt. Berkeley: University of California Press, 1982.

Nitschke, Günter. *The Silent Orgasm: From Transpersonal to Transparent Consciousness*. Cologne and New York: Taschen, 1995.

Noel, Daniel C. *The Soul of Shamanism: Western Fantasies, Imaginal Realities*. New York: Continuum, 1997.

Nomani, Asra Q. "Naked Ambition: Tantra May Be Old But It Has Generated a Hot Modern Market. Ancient Hindu Sex Practice Gets New-Age Makeover, Competition is Fierce." *Wall Street Journal*, December 7, 1998: A1, A6.

Novak, Michael. *The Experience of Nothingness*. New York: Harper Colophon, 1970.

Noyes, George Wallingford, (Ed.). *Religious Experience of John Humphrey Noyes, Founder of the Oneida Community*. New York: Macmillan, 1923.

O'Brien, Richard P. *Catholicism*. Minneapolis: Winston, 1981.

Odier, Daniel. *Tantric Quest: An Encounter with Absolute Love.* Translated by J. Gladding. Rochester, VT: Inner Traditions, 1997.

O'Flaherty, Wendy Doniger. *Siva: The Erotic Ascetic.* Oxford: Oxford University Press, 1973.

O'Flaherty, Wendy Doniger. *The Origins of Evil in Hindu Mythology.* Berkeley: University of California Press, 1980.

Otto, Rudolf. *The Idea of the Holy.* Translated by John W. Harvey. New York: Oxford, 1958.

Parker, Robert Allerton. *A Yankee Saint: John Humphrey Noyes and the Oneida Community.* New York: G. P. Putnam's Sons, 1935.

Pelikan, Jaroslav. *The Christian Tradition: A History of the Devolpoment of Doctrine.* Vol. 2, *The Spirit of Eastern Christiandom (600-1700).* Chicago: University of Chicago Press, 1974.

Perry, John Weir. *The Far Side of Madness.* Englewood Cliffs, NJ: Prentice-Hall, 1974.

Pickthall, Mohammed Marmaduke. *The Meaning of the Glorious Koran.* New York: New American Library, [n.d.].

Pintchman, Tracy. *The Rise of the Goddess in the Hindu Tradition.* Albany, SUNY, 1994.

Prince, Morton. *Clinical and Experimental Studies in Personality.* Cambridge, MA: Sci-Art, 1929. Reprinted, Westport, CT: Greenwood, 1970.

Rama, Swami. "The Awakening of Kundalini." In J. White, 1990: 27-47.

Reichel-Dolmatoff, Gerardo. *Amazonian Cosmos: The Sexual and Religious Symbolism of the Tukano Indians.* Translated by the author. Chicago: University of Chicago Press, 1971.

Reichel-Dolmatoff, Gerardo. *The Shaman and the Jaguar: A Study of Narcotic Drugs Among the Indians of Colombia.* Philadelphia: Temple University Press, 1975.

Robinet, Isabelle. *Méditation Taoïste.* Paris: Dervy, 1979.

Rougemont, Denis de. *Love in the Western World.* Translated by M. Belgion. Princeton, NJ: Princeton University Press, 1956/72.

Rusch, Frederik L. (Ed.). *A Jean Toomer Reader: Selected Unpublished Writings.* New York, Oxford, 1993.

Samuels, Andrew, Bani Shorter, and Fred Plaut. *A Critical Dictionary of Jungian Analysis.* New York: Routledge & Kegan Paul, 1986.

Sannella, Lee. *The Kundalini Experience: Psychosis or Transcendence.* Lower Lake, CA: Integral, 1992.

Sartwell, Crispin. *Obscenity, Anarchy, Reality.* Albany: SUNY, 1996

Schimmel, Annemarie. *Mystical Dimensions of Islam.* Chapel Hill, NC: University of North Carolina Press, 1975.

Schimmel, Annemarie. *The Triumphal Sun: A Study of the Works of Jalaloddin Rumi.* London: East-West Publications, 1978

Scholem, Gershom G. *Major Trends in Jewish Mysticism.* New York: Schoken, 1969.

Serrano, Miguel. *C. G. Jung and Hermann Hesse: A Record of Two Friendships.* Translated by Frank MacShane. New York: Schocken, 1966.

Shaw, Miranda. *Passionate Enlightenment: Women in Tantric Buddhism.* Princeton: Princeton University Press, 1994.

Sheets-Johnstone, Maxine. *The Roots of Power: Animate Form and Gendered Bodies.* Chicago: Open Court, 1994.

Silburn, Lilian. *Kundalini, the Energy of the Depths: A Comprehensive Study Based on the Scriptures of Nondualistic Kasmir Saivism.* Translated by J. Gontier. Albany: SUNY, 1988.

Sinha, Indra. *The Great Book of Tantra: Translations and Images from the Classic Indian Texts with Commentary.* Rochester, VT: Destiny, 1993.

Sivananda Radha, Swami. "Kundalini: An Overview." In J. White, 1990: 48-60.

Smith, Morton. *The Secret Gospel: The Discovery and Interpretation of the Secret Gospel According to Mark.* New York, Harper & Row: 1973.

Smith, Morton. *Jesus the Magician: Charlaton or Son of God?* Berkeley, CA: Seastone: 1998.

Smolin, Lee. *The Life of the Cosmos.* New York: Oxford University Press, 1997.

Sovatsky, Stuart. *Passions of Innocence: Tantric Celibacy and the Mysteries of Eros.* Rochester, VT: Destiny, 1994.

Stevens, John. *Lust for Englightenment: Buddhism and Sex.* Boston: Shambhala, 1990.

Streng, Frederick J. *Emptiness: A Study in Religious Meaning.* Nashville: Abingdon, 1967.

Stubbs, Kenneth Ray (Ed.). *Women of the Light: The New Sacred Prostitute.* Larkspur, CA: Secret Garden, 1994.

Sviri, Sara. *The Taste of Hidden Things: Images on the Sufi Path.* Inverness, CA: Golden Sufi Center, 1997.

Svoboda, Robert E. *Aghora: At the Left Hand of God.* Albuquerque: Brotherhood of Life, 1986.

Svoboda, Robert E. *Aghora II: Kundalini.* Albuquerque: Brotherhood of Life, 1994.

Svoboda, Robert E. *Aghora III: The Law of Karma.* Albuquerque: Brotherhood of Life, 1997.

Talbot, Michael. *The Holographic Universe.* New York: HarperCollins, 1992.

Tansley, David V. *The Raiment of Light: A Study of the Human Aura.* Boston: Routledge, 1984.

Tart, Charles T. "Psychological Experiences Associated with a Novel Hypnotic Procedure, Mutual Hypnosis." In Charles T. Tart (Ed.). *Altered States of Consciousness.* Garden City, NY: Anchor, 1972: 297-315).

Taylor, Timothy. *The Prehistory of Sex: Four Million Years of Human Sexual Culture.* New York: Bantam, 1996.

Trachtenberg, Peter. *The Casanova Complex: Compulsive Lovers and Their Women.* New York: Poseidon, 1988.

Tweedie, Irina. *Daughter of Fire: A Diary of a Spiritual Training with a Sufi Master.* Grass Valley, CA: Blue Dolphin, 1986.

van der Leeuw, Gerardus. *Religion in Essence and Manifestation: A Study in Phenomenology.* In two volumes. Translated by J. E. Turner. New York: Harper Torchbooks, 1963.

Varenne, Jean. *Yoga and the Hindu Tradition.* Translated by D. Coltman. Chicago: University of Chicago Press, 1976.

Vatsyayana. *Kama Sutra: The Hindu Ritual of Love.* New York: Castle, 1963.

Vishnu Tirtha, Swami. "Signs of an Awakened Kundalini." In J. White (1990: 94-7).

Weir, Anthony & James Jerman. *Images of Lust: Sexual Carvings on Medieval Churches.* London: Batsford, 1986.

White, David Gordon. *The Alchemical Body: Siddha Traditions in Medieval India.* Chicago: University of Chicago, 1996.

White, John (Ed.). *Kundalini, Evolution and Enlightenment.* New York: Paragon House, 1990.

White, Timothy. "Understanding Psychedelic Mysticism: An Interview with Huston Smith." In *Shaman's Drum 49* (Summer 1998): 21-29.

Whitehead, Alfred North. *Process and Reality: An Essay in Cosmology.* New York: Free Press, 1969.

Wilbur, Ken. "The Pre/Trans Fallacy." *Journal of Humanistic Psychology* 22(2), 1982: 5-43.

Wilbur, Ken. "Are the Chakras Real?" In J. White, 1990: 120-31.

Wile, Douglas. *Art of the Bedchamber: The Chinese Sexual Yoga Classics Including Women's Solo Meditation Texts.* Albany: SUNY, 1992.

Wilson, Peter Lamborn. *Scandal: Essays in Islamic Heresy.* New York: Autonomedia, 1988.

Wilson, Peter Lamborn. *Sacred Drift: Essays on the Margins of Islam.* San Francisco: City Lights Books, 1993.

Wolf, Fred Alan. *Taking the Quantum Leap: The New Physics for Non-Scientists*. New York: Harper & Row, 1989.

Yogananda, Paramahamsa. *Autobiography of a Yogi*. Los Angeles: Self-Realization Fellowship, 1979.

INDEX

About the Author

John Ryan Haule holds a doctorate in religious studies from Temple University. He is a Jungian analyst trained in Zurich and is a faculty member of the C.G. Jung Institute-Boston. In addition to *Tantra and Erotic Trance I & II*, his publications include:

Divine Madness: Archetypes of Romantic Love.
Carmel, CA: Fisher King Press, 2010.

The Love Cure: Therapy Erotic and Sexual.
Woodstock, CT: Spring Publications, 1996.

Perils of the Soul: Ancient Wisdom and the New Age.
York Beach, ME: Samuel Weiser, 1999.

The Ecstasies of St. Francis: The Way of Lady Poverty.
Great Barrington, MA: Lindisfarne Books, 2004.

Jung in the 21st Century, in two volumes.
London: Routledge, 2010.
Evolution and Archetype.
Synchronicity and Science.

Other Jungian Psychology Titles

Re-Imagining Mary: A Journey Through Art to the Feminine Self
by Mariann Burke, 1ˢᵗ Ed., Trade Paperback, 180 pp., Index, Biblio., 2009
— ISBN 978-0-9810344-1-6

Threshold Experiences: The Archetype of Beginnings
by Michael Conforti, 1ˢᵗ Ed., Trade Paperback, 168 pp., Index, Biblio., 2008
— ISBN 978-0-944187-99-9

Marked By Fire: Stories of the Jungian Way
edited by Patricia Damery & Naomi Ruth Lowinsky,
1ˢᵗ Ed., Trade Paperback, 190 pp., Index, Biblio., 2012
— ISBN 978-1-926715-68-1

Farming Soul: A Tale of Initiation
by Patricia Damery, 1ˢᵗ Ed., Trade Paperback, 166 pp., Index, Biblio., 2010
— ISBN 978-1-926715-01-8

Transforming Body and Soul: Therapeutic Wisdom in the Gospel Healing Stories
by Steven Galipeau, Rev. Ed., Trade Paperback, 180 pp., Index, Biblio., 2011
— ISBN 978-1-926715-62-9

Lifting the Veil: Revealing the Other Side
by Fred Gustafson & Jane Kamerling, 1ˢᵗ Ed, Paperback, 170 pp., Biblio, 2012
— ISBN 978-1-926715-75-9

Resurrecting the Unicorn: Masculinity in the 21ˢᵗ Century
by Bud Harris, Rev. Ed., Trade Paperback, 300 pp., Index, Biblio., 2009
— ISBN 978-0-9810344-0-9

The Father Quest: Rediscovering an Elemental Force
by Bud Harris, Reprint, Trade Paperback, 180 pp., Index, Biblio., 2009
— ISBN 978-0-9810344-9-2

Like Gold Through Fire: The Transforming Power of Suffering
by Massimilla & Bud Harris, Reprint, Trade Paperback, 150 pp., Index, Biblio., 2009
— ISBN 978-0-9810344-5-4

The Art of Love: The Craft of Relationship
by Massimilla and Bud Harris, 1st Ed., Trade Paperback, 150 pp., 2010
— ISBN 978-1-926715-02-5

Divine Madness: Archetypes of Romantic Love
by John R. Haule, Rev. Ed., Trade Paperback, 282 pp., Index, Biblio., 2010
— ISBN 978-1-926715-04-9

Eros and the Shattering Gaze: Transcending Narcissism
by Ken Kimmel, 1ˢᵗ Ed., Trade Paperback, 310 pp., Index, Biblio., 2011
— ISBN 978-1-926715-49-0

The Sister From Below: When the Muse Gets Her Way
by Naomi Ruth Lowinsky, 1ˢᵗ Ed., Trade Paperback, 248 pp., Index, Biblio., 2009
— ISBN 978-0-9810344-2-3

The Motherline: Every Woman's Journey to find her Female Roots
by Naomi Ruth Lowinsky, Reprint, Trade Paperback, 252 pp., Index, Biblio., 2009
— ISBN 978-0-9810344-6-1

Jung and Ecopsychology: The Dairy Farmer's Guide to the Universe (DFGU) Volume 1
by Dennis Merritt 1ˢᵗ Ed., Trade Paperback, 250 pp., Index, Biblio., 2011
— ISBN 978-1-926715-42-1

The Cry of Merlin: Jung, the Prototypical Ecopsychologist: DFGU Volume 2
by Dennis Merritt 1ˢᵗ Ed., Trade Paperback, 204 pp., Index, Biblio., 2012
— ISBN 978-1-926715-43-8

Hermes, Ecopsychology, and Complexity Theory: DFGU Volume 3
by Dennis Merritt 1ˢᵗ Ed., Trade Paperback, 200 pp., Index, Biblio., 2012
— ISBN 978-1-926715-44-5

Land, Weather, Seasons, Insects: An Archetypal View: DFGU Volume 4
by Dennis Merritt 1ˢᵗ Ed., Trade Paperback, 200 pp., Index, Biblio., 2012
— ISBN 978-1-926715-45-2

Becoming: An Introduction to Jung's Concept of Individuation
by Deldon Anne McNeely, 1ˢᵗ Ed., Trade Paperback, 230 pp., Index, Biblio., 2010
— ISBN 978-1-926715-12-4

Animus Aeternus: Exploring the Inner Masculine
by Deldon Anne McNeely, Reprint, Trade Paperback, 196 pp., Index, Biblio, 2011
— ISBN 978-1-926715-37-7

Mercury Rising: Women, Evil, and the Trickster Gods
by Deldon Anne McNeely, Revised, Trade Paperback, 200 pp., Index, Biblio., 2011
— ISBN 978-1-926715-54-4

Four Eternal Women: Toni Wolff Revisited—A Study In Opposites
by Mary Dian Molton & Lucy Anne Sikes, 1ˢᵗ Ed, 320 pp., Index, Biblio., 2011
— ISBN 978-1-926715-31-5

Gathering the Light: A Jungian View of Meditation
by V. Walter Odajnyk, Revised. Ed., Trade Paperback, 264 pp., Index, Biblio, 2011
— ISBN 978-1-926715-55-1

The Promiscuity Papers
by Matjaz Regovec 1ˢᵗ Ed., Trade Paperback, 86 pp., Index, Biblio., 2011
— ISBN 978-1-926715-38-4

Enemy, Cripple, Beggar: Shadows in the Hero's Path
by Erel Shalit, 1ˢᵗ Ed., Trade Paperback, 248 pp., Index, Biblio., 2008
— ISBN 978-0-9776076-7-9

The Cycle of Life: Themes and Tales of the Journey
by Erel Shalit, 1ˢᵗ Ed., Trade Paperback, 210 pp., Index, Biblio., 2011
— ISBN 978-1-926715-50-6

The Hero and His Shadow: Psychopolitical Aspects of Myth and Reality in Israel
by Erel Shalit, Revised Ed., Trade Paperback, 208 pp., Index, Biblio., 2012
— ISBN 978-1-926715-69-8

The Guilt Cure
by Nancy Carter Pennington & Lawrence H. Staples
1ˢᵗ Ed., Trade Paperback, 200 pp., Index, Biblio., 2011
— ISBN 978-1-926715-53-7

Guilt with a Twist: The Promethean Way
by Lawrence Staples,1ˢᵗ Ed., Trade Paperback, 256 pp., Index, Biblio., 2008
— ISBN 978-0-9776076-4-8

The Creative Soul: Art and the Quest for Wholeness
by Lawrence Staples, 1ˢᵗ Ed., Trade Paperback, 100 pp., Index, Biblio., 2009
— ISBN 978-0-9810344-4-7

Deep Blues: Human Soundscapes for the Archetypal Journey
by Mark Winborn, 1ˢᵗ Ed., Trade Paperback, 130 pp., Index, Biblio., 2011
— ISBN 978-1-926715-52-0

Fisher King Press publishes an eclectic mix of worthy books including Jungian Psychological Perspectives, Cutting-Edge Fiction, Poetry, and a growing list of Alternative titles.

Phone Orders Welcomed — Credit Cards Accepted

In Canada & the U.S. call 1-800-228-9316

International call +1-831-238-7799

www.fisherkingpress.com